Know All Men By These Presents, That

We the undersigned have this day voluntarily

associated ourselves together for the purpose of forming

an association to be known as The Vancouver Real

Estate Board

Object of the Board

First To provide a uniform schedule of commission and

charges for conveyancing.

Second To provide a system by which accurate and prompt

communication can be had between owners of Real

Estate and all members of this Board

Third To provide a suitable office for a central office at which

all business of the board can be conducted.

Rules and Regulations

Article I The officers shall consist of a President Vice President

Secretary and Treasurer who shall be elected by the

board

Article II An executive committee shall be formed consisting

of three

REAL ESTATE BOARD
OF GREATER VANCOUVER

75

ANNIVERSARY

Real Estate Board of Greater Vancouver

Real Estate Board of Greater Vancouver

A History Of Service

1919 / 1994

Anne Broadfoot

with editorial assistance by

Alan G. Creer

Published by
Real Estate Board of
Greater Vancouver

Designed by
Praxis

Printed by
Mitchell Press

© 1995 Real Estate Board
of Greater Vancouver

Requests for reproduction
of any part of this book, shall
be directed in writing to:
Real Estate Board
of Greater Vancouver
2433 Spruce Street
Vancouver, British Columbia
V6H 4C8

ISBN 0-9699353-1-5

Printed in Canada

CONTENTS

DEDICATION

While compiling one of his many volumes of Early Vancouver papers, venerated City Archivist Major J. S. Matthews penned the following:

"In the chronicle of human endeavour there is no story more inspiring, no tale more romantic, than that of the resourceful, courageous people whose initiative and energy, peacefully and in the briefest period of time, created out of the silent emptiness of dark, primeval forest, a monumental city of beauty and of culture; an achievement in world history which must forever interest the peoples of all nations."

Interwoven throughout the saga of Vancouver's development is the energetic role played by the city's pioneer real estate practitioners.

In 1994 Real Estate Board of Greater Vancouver celebrated 75 years of continuous service to its members and the public they serve. This history was compiled to recognize the accomplishments of those past REALTORS who established the firm standards of practice still followed today, and to acknowledge the achievements of an industry which has been intimately involved with Vancouver's development since the first settlers arrived.

Matthews' words of praise for those who built our city serve as an appropriate introduction to the Board's special dedication:

"To members of the Board, past and present, and to all citizens of Vancouver, past and present, who played a vital role in the events retold on these pages".

INTRODUCTION

*Throughout mankind's history land
has played an intimate role. He has
sought it, fought and died for the ideal
of land ownership.*

Since the beginning of time, real estate has figured greatly in the fortunes of man. Probably the most universally familiar real estate transaction took place in Biblical times when the Supreme Being gave a long-term lease on an attractive parcel of land. However, Adam, the lessee, violated a condition of the tenancy and was evicted.

Throughout mankind's history land has played an intimate role. He has sought it, fought and died for the ideal of land ownership. Discovery of new land was quickly followed by an influx of adventurous settlers, and British Columbia conformed to this basic pattern.

Many historians have recorded the beginnings of British Columbia, starting with the early voyages of Captains Cook and Vancouver, which led to British sovereignty. Because it is not our intention to rewrite the saga of West Coast discovery, this brief sketch will serve only to show how land discovery leads inexorably to growth and development.

In describing the lands he saw in 1792, Captain George Vancouver wrote in his log:

"It requires only to be enriched by the industry of man with villages, mansions, cottages and other buildings to render it the most lovely country that can be imagined."

Just as a search for adventure drives man to explore, visions and dreams compel him to endure. Little more than two hundred years later, Captain Vancouver's vision has become reality and we are all the beneficiaries of the determination, industry and enduring dreams of the pioneers who went before.

Early in the 19th century, explorations by Simon Fraser of the North West Company, in search of furs for trading, led to the development of many centres such as Fort George (now

Captain George Vancouver

Fort Victoria, 1843

Prince George) and Fort Langley on the mainland. The eventual takeover of the North West Company by the Hudson's Bay Company saw Fort Victoria established in 1843 under direction of Chief Factor James Douglas. A British Crown Colony called Vancouver's Island was created in 1849 and Douglas named Governor in 1851.

In 1858 Queen Victoria proclaimed the mainland colony British Columbia, naming Fort Langley its capital at the same time gold was discovered on the Fraser River. Tens of thousands of British, American and Chinese gold seekers heeded the siren call and the rush began.

Colonel Richard Moody and a detachment of Royal Engineers were soon dispatched to help map and build Her Majesty's new territory. They chose a high point on the north shore of the Fraser River as a site for the capital of British Columbia, which the Queen named New Westminster in 1860.

To set the record straight, it was not land that attracted the first British Columbia settlers. The stands of soaring virgin timber perfect for masts and spars of sailing ships and the rich resources of furs, gold and coal were the original appeal. Still, the first real estate "boom" in British Columbia was experienced in Fort Victoria in the late 1850s because these settlers needed to be housed. Douglas raised the price of a suburban 5-acre lot near the Fort to 25 Pounds Sterling, which was then approximately $125.00 Canadian.

Recognizing the need for order, Douglas proclaimed the first Land Law for the colonies of Vancouver's Island and British Columbia in January, 1860, and instituted its first land registry system in 1861. Systematic development of this brave new land was well underway even before the two new colonies were joined under the name British Columbia in 1866.

Hudson Bay Post,
Langley, 1862

Torrens System

The "Torrens" Land Titles system was developed in South Australia in 1857 by Robert Richard Torrens when he was a government Minister in Adelaide. So much property was passing so quickly to so many new settlers in those days the old English conveyancing system couldn't cope. It was necessary to devise a simple, secure and less costly method of obtaining title to property and to remove all risks from defective deeds so the ownership of the person in the register book was conclusive. His bill for amending conveyancing laws was passed in 1858 and Torrens was named Register-General.
The Torrens land title registration system was modified and adopted in the colony of Vancouver Island when Governor Douglas established registration in 1861 through enactment of the Vancouver Island Land Registry Act. It was extended to the combined colony of British Columbia in 1870, making this province the first in Canada to employ this South Australian system. In British Columbia, with the exception of certain Crown Lands and a very small percentage of complicated titles, all lands are registered under the Torrens system. Evidence of the right to land is constituted by a registered indefeasible title which includes the name of the owner and names of any others who have interest in the property, such as mortgages, Agreements for Sale, leases, easements, rights-of-way, etc. To establish indefeasible title, documents which transfer legal ownership or create an interest in land must be filed and registered in the Land Title Office.

Registration has the effect of passing the estate or interest in land. While registration is not mandatory in British Columbia, failure to register means the estate or interest claimed by an owner cannot be enforced against a third party.

References
Land Titles Practice Manual,
Continuing Legal Education
Society of British Columbia.
Land Titles: Registration in Canada and the USA
by Richard H. Steacy.
The Canadian Torrens System
by Douglas J. Thom,
B.C., published in 1912 by
Burroughs and Company.

The first small business opened along the Inlet was a hotel and saloon at the water's edge near Stamps' (later Hastings) Mill, started in 1867 by "Gassy" Jack Deighton. The area soon became known as "Gastown", the point from which Vancouver was destined to grow to world class stature.

Gastown, 1881

CHAPTER ONE

HOW A CITY WAS BORN

The Colonial Government sold all land until the Colony joined Confederation, and it became legal for settlers to claim land not currently under native use by pre-empting it. A pre-emptor would mark off 160 acres and be issued a Crown Grant only after the pre-emption was recorded in the Government Land Survey. After two years' continuous occupation the pre-emptor paid $1.00 per acre to gain full title.

Since the Royal Engineers conducted land surveys from their New Westminster headquarters, all properties surveyed from Vancouver to Hope were recorded as part of the "New Westminster District", and so deed locations even today refer to New Westminster District.

Gold seekers were still streaming in to try their luck but many fortunes were made in wood instead of that precious metal. The first lower mainland sawmill was established on the north shore of Burrard Inlet on 480 acres of fertile rain forest just east of what is now the foot of Lonsdale Avenue. By 1865 this Moodyville Mill was loading ships with lumber bound for Australia, the early beginnings of Pacific Rim trading.

Mills were soon established on the South Side of the Inlet, one at the foot of what is now Dunlevy Street. The local natives called this spot "Luk'Luk'I", meaning "Grove of Beautiful Trees", but the settlers used the phonetic pronunciation "Luck Lucky", perhaps hoping the name would be prophetic. Because this mill eventually provided the majority of spars and masts for the world's sailing ships, it probably was.

By the time the Granville Townsite survey was completed in 1870, logging of the area was well underway. Granville, named after Earl Granville, the British Colonial Secretary, referred to the area around Gassy Jack's saloon, but then, as now, the name Gastown stuck. By 1870 there were already nine buildings grouped in a crescent along the shore between what are now Abbott and Carrall Streets and some 50 residents called it home. Historians say a land sale which took place soon after the area survey fetched lot prices of from $50 for one "just slightly above water mark" to

A condition of British Columbia's entry into Confederation in 1871 was a rail line across the country to link east and west. Years of rancour and dispute on routes, contracts and site of the final terminus of the Canadian Pacific Railway followed.

$135 for an "outsize" piece on the southwest corner of Carrall and Abbott.

A condition of British Columbia's entry into Confederation in 1871 was a rail line across the country to link east and west. Years of rancour and dispute on routes, contracts and site of the final terminus of the Canadian Pacific Railway followed. After much political manoeuvering, by the early 1880s it became apparent the western terminus would be Port Moody on Burrard Inlet, but reports indicate there was little doubt the eventual terminus would be Coal Harbour.

At the time it was a common Burrard Inlet sight to see as many as 40 ships loading or waiting to load timber for California, Mexico, South America, the Hawaiian Islands, Australia, China, South Africa, Great Britain and Europe. Seeing this activity, Sir William Van Horne, General Manager of the CPR, became aware of the advantages offered by Coal Harbour.

To extend the rail line from Port Moody to Coal Harbour, Van Horne negotiated with Premier Smithe in 1884 to grant the railway six thousand acres of land, part of which is now the downtown area, and the remainder south of False Creek stretching between Cambie and Trafalgar streets as far as 57th Avenue. The CPR was also given the unsold lots in the old Granville townsite surveyed in 1870, bounded by Carrall, Cambie, Hastings and the shore. Those living on lots in the townsite without having purchased them were allowed to buy them at $200 each. Large private landholders (like the Three Greenhorns who had pre-empted the area now known as the West End) were also required to give one third of the lots in each block they held to the CPR, and it was soon apparent that almost all the waterfront from Gore Avenue to Stanley Park would belong to the railway.

Out of the area granted to the railway the company selected sites for its Hotel Vancouver, the railway station, railway yards on Burrard Inlet and False Creek and the water frontage needed for docks for the coastal and deep-sea shipping the CPR established later.

Over the past century many have criticized Van Horne's

As the railway drew near Port Moody, town lots there were selling for up to $2,000. By November, 1885, some transport was possible on completed trackage and freight history was made. A CPR freight train reached salt water in Port Moody in time to greet a sailing tea ship. Her tea cargo was loaded on the train and shipped East the next day. There was great fanfare when it was learned the tea arrived in England three weeks earlier than if it had been transported entirely by sea, so cross-Canada freight and rail/sea shipping became an immediate success. The first transcontinental passenger train arrived in Port Moody on July 4, 1886.

negotiations with the Colonial Government as a "give away of valuable land". It seems only fair, however, to add some balance to what critics have said by reprinting the remarks of a pioneer Vancouver real estate broker, John Pethybridge Nicolls, from his reminiscences of over half a century in real estate in Vancouver, published in 1954:

"How many millions of dollars they received for the city and suburban lots they sold is not necessary for us to know. We know it was many millions, but we must not assume this was all profit, for the taxes they have paid have been equally enormous; they paid taxes on some vacant property for fifty years or more. One CPR land agent asserted that if all the money paid out in city taxes were added up, the railway company would have been better off if they had never received the gift of six thousand acres of wilderness."

In preparation for the city that was bound to rise after the railway arrived, Van Horne sent Lauchlan Hamilton, first Land Commissioner of the CPR, to survey and name streets in the CPR land grant in 1885. Hamilton reported Van Horne felt this area was destined to become a great city and that it would be named "Vancouver" if he had the ultimate decision. But as early as a year before the name of Captain George Vancouver was under general consideration for the city-to-be, and had been so named as Western terminus of the CPR in a Portland, Oregon, newspaper.

Hamilton walked to the edge of the forest which is now the south west corner of Hamilton and Hastings, and drove a stake into the earth. He looked eastward down a trail that led to Hastings townsite, and called it Hastings Street and named the perpendicular street where he stood Hamilton after himself. He also named two trails that lead off into the bush Cambie, after Henry John Cambie, a Consulting Engineer with the CPR, and Abbott after H.H. Abbott, general superintendent of the CPR in B.C.

By driving in that first spike, Hamilton set the stage for Vancouver's street grid system. He decided the north/south axis of the city would run along Carrall Street, through the site where Gassy Jack's saloon then stood and where the statue of Gassy Jack stands in Maple Tree Square today. From this point the city was counted off to run 49 blocks west and 38 blocks east, so an address like 3700 East Hastings would mean a location 37 blocks east of Maple Tree Square.

The hundred blocks run south from the same axis for 93 blocks to the 9300 hundred block, but since First Avenue is

not located in Gastown but is 16 blocks further south on the False Creek waterfront (the streets between had been given names by Hamilton), we determine the Avenue cross by subtracting 16 from the hundred block. Location of an address at 8400 Oak Street is found by taking 16 away from 84 to pinpoint its position between 68th and 69th Avenues.

Granville was growing fast. In January, 1886, as the CPR tracks advanced down the coast from Port Moody, 432 residents of Granville signed a petition to the provincial Legislature asking that the City of Vancouver be incorporated. In February of that year land agent Hamilton recorded the existence of some 100 habitable dwellings in the town, and on February 12, 1886, the Crown Grant was issued for the lands Van Horne had obtained for the railway company.

Clearing land in the CPR Townsite and selling it to newcomers was an essential force in the march towards city incorporation. In February, 1886, logger Alex Russell felled a giant tree on the south side of Georgia Street, and where it lay covered the distance between Seymour and Granville. Lauchlan Hamilton measured it at 310 feet long and its diameter at the stump was eleven feet, eight inches. Sections of this massive Douglas Fir amazed viewers when exhibited at the Colonial Exhibition in London in 1887, and also in Eastern Canada, fueling the curiosity and prompting the speedy arrival of those who wanted to see the land that grew such gigantic trees.

Speculators, merchants, settlers and their families had been arriving in large numbers, and the first "real estate boom" was on. By mid-May at least 600 buildings could be counted. Lots that were sold for less than $300 in March were changing hands for $1,000 by May. Because of the strong building activity, lumber was at a premium and nails cost $4.50 a keg. Retail trade was expanding to serve the growing population. Flour was selling at $6.00 a barrel, rice at $2.00 a sack, porterhouse steak at 15-cents a pound, and rib roasts fetched 12 1/2-cents a pound.

Royal assent to city incorporation was received April 6, 1886, and so Granville Townsite became Vancouver, extend-

Real Estate broker J.W. Horne saw the opportunity for advertising his local services and set up this now famous Vancouver Archives photo, taken at the site where the Hudson's Bay Co. store stands today. Horne is seen in the front row, third figure from the right, pointing at a map. Some unidentified citizens and visitors from Portland are in the picture, along with Edwin Saunders, seated at far left, who later became a city Alderman, and Mr. Hemming, the U.S. Consul, standing at the far right.

ing from Burrard Inlet on the north to 16th Avenue on the south, from Heatly Avenue on the east to Trafalgar Street on the west.

First task of the residents was to form a city government. Voting regulations they established reflected the value those first Vancouverites placed on real property ownership. To participate in a civic election as a mayoral candidate, one had to own property worth $2,000. A person seeking a position as city councillor had to own property valued at $1,000 and to exercise the privilege of voting, one must be either the owner or tenant of property worth at least $300.

Inaugural meeting of Vancouver's first Council was on May 10, 1886, where Councillors announced their plan to lay the foundation for growth and prosperity. Street paving, bridge building, provision of pure water, electricity and other modern amenities were identified as top priorities to encourage growth, trade and industry. An expanding population would ensure a growing tax base, so early Councils borrowed heavily to accomplish the upgrading needed and to open up new land for development. Concessions were granted to utility and waterwork companies to locate in and service the citizens of Vancouver.

Several pioneer real estate practitioners were involved in the city's early development. Malcolm A. MacLean, owner-operator of M.A. MacLean & Co. Real Estate, was elected the first Mayor of the City of Vancouver. Two years later MacLean was a charter signatory in the formation of the city's first Real Estate Board.

Remarkable foresight was shown in the first resolution of that first City Council. It involved the Mayor sending a petition to the Dominion Government asking that the whole of Coal Harbour Peninsula known as the Government Reserve, be conveyed to the City of Vancouver for Public Park. Considering that at that time much of what we now know as Vancouver was dense forest and the population small and concentrated in a very limited area near the original Gastown, there was no pressing need to preserve such a vast green space. Thanks to approval to this request, granted by Order-in-Council on June 8, 1887, future generations were ensured a perpetual playground free of the threat of development. The park was officially opened on September 27, 1888, by Lord Stanley, Governor-General of Canada, who also gave it his name.

F.C. Innes had opened his first real estate office on Cordova Street in 1885, but moved to Powell Street after the City was chartered. In his collected papers preserved at Vancouver City Archives, there is sales information on many of his early transactions, like the sale of Lot ll, Block 5, on March 5, 1886, which sold for $450 with $150 down, and payments of $100 due on June 5, September 5 and December 5, with interest at 8% per annum.

City Council as well as local businessmen were advertising Vancouver's potential far and wide, and Innes received requests for information from all parts of Canada, the U.S., England and Ireland. A sample of the handwritten requests shows the interest those ads generated.

Henry T. Ceperley was a partner in Ross & Ceperley Real Estate, and also an investor-promoter in the first street and house electrification, switched on in Vancouver in September, 1886. In March of 1888 Henry Ceperley was named Treasurer of the city's first Real Estate Board, and continued his involvement in the city's development. In 1889 a horse-drawn street railway system was started and converted to electric in May of 1890, also under the investment and promotional guidance of Ceperley.

Another person present at that first Council Meeting was John Boultbee, the city's first magistrate, who had drawn the petition to incorporate the City of Vancouver. While not connected to real estate brokerage at that time, he contributed to the industry by founding a line of well known real estate practitioners who will be recognized later on these pages.

The real estate boom accelerated with the birth of Vancouver. Incorporated with around a thousand residents (including women, children and Chinese), the city boasted three times that many a year later. Sixteen real estate firms and twelve grocery stores were listed in city directories in 1887. Within five years the city's population topped 15,000 and was 27,000 by the turn of the century.

The town's water supply came entirely from wells, and in the spring of 1886 local wells were in danger of running dry because there had been little rainfall. In late May the City Council established a volunteer fire brigade but it was helpless against the holocaust of June 13, 1886. Clearing fires to the west of the town were suddenly whipped into rapacious life by a violent western squall and in less than an hour, Vancouver was in ashes.

Residents escaped to the city wharf at Carrall, along the road to Hastings Mill, to False Creek at Pender and Carrall or

The future of Vancouver was guaranteed less than a year after the fire, when Engine # 374 steamed into the Vancouver CPR station on May 23, 1887. Its arrival elevated the stature of this somewhat obscure settlement, now connected to the rest of Canada by a steel highway that could speed shipment of British Columbia's vast resources to eastern provinces and beyond. Further, the CPR's steamship service from the Orient cinched the promise of Vancouver becoming a world port. Establishment of the sea/rail centre of Vancouver helped shrink the world's trade routes, a development that was fundamental to the continued growth of this west coast city, and essential to the economic health of the new region.

A year after the city was reduced to ashes, the Abyssinia, chartered by the CPR, arrived in Vancouver Harbour with a cargo of silk and tea, its passage from Yokahama taking only 13 days. Total shipping time after being transferred to the rail line was New York in 21 days, and across the Atlantic to London by fast passenger ship in 30 days.

out the Westminster Road and across the bridge to the south side of False Creek. At least 20 people were known to have died but it could have been more due to the crowded condition of the city at that time. Those who survived saved only what they carried.

The next few days proved the legendary pioneer courage and generosity. Before that fateful Sunday was over, residents in Port Moody, the Royal City, Mission and beyond started collecting medical supplies, food, clothing and household goods and by 6 o'clock in the evening a caravan of wagons appeared on the Westminster Road. Lumber wagons delivered tools, nails and material and by daylight on June 14, with ashes still warm and stumps still burning, the rebuilding began. The entrepreneurial spirit was personified by a burned-out hotel operator selling whiskey from a bottle he carried in his hip pocket, serving it in the one glass he had managed to rescue, using a sack of potatoes as a counter.

While the fire devastated the city for a short time, it also challenged residents to rebuild faster. The boom continued. There were 2,000 men working on the CPR rail line from Port Moody to the city, and other CPR projects along the Inlet, but every boat and stage brought more young settlers, eager to be involved in the rebuilding.

Three days after the fire City Council met in a tent at the foot of Carrall Street and first order of business was passage of the original Vancouver Building bylaw, requiring more solid construction and fire precautions. Insurance companies required safety standards to deliver policies so a street clearing program began and all inflammable material was removed from the city. Vivid memories of the devastation of fire on frame construction prompted erection of many of the new buildings in brick and stone. Within three days of the fire almost a dozen businesses were already operating, and within six months it was hard to tell that the disaster had even occured. By New Years Day, 1887, there were 14 office blocks, 23 hotels, 51 stores, 9 saloons, one church, a livery stable, a mill and wharf completed and more construction was under way as far west as Thurlow.

One advantage of Vancouver being a young city is that the camera had already been perfected by the time the City was named, so its growth is well recorded in an important photo collection now housed at the Vancouver City Archives.

Know All Men By These Presents, That We the undersigned have this day voluntarily associated ourselves together for the purpose of forming an association to be known as . The Vancouver Real Estate Board

Object of the Board

First To provide a uniform schedule of commission and charges for conveyancing

Second To provide a system by which accurate and prompt communication can be had between owners of Real Estate and all members of this Board

Third To provide a suitable office for a central office at which all business of the board can be conducted.

Rules and Regulations

Article I The officers shall consist of a President, Vice President Secretary and Treasurer who shall be elected by the board

Article II An executive committee shall be formed consisting

CHAPTER TWO

A REAL ESTATE BOARD IS FORMED

While impossible to confirm it is highly likely that Vancouver, British Columbia, boasts the first real estate organization formed in North America.

On March 14, 1888, less than two years after the city was chartered, representatives of 25 of the real estate companies operating in Vancouver put their signatures to a formal Constitution and Bylaws, a document which gave life to a most unique association. These businessmen, who were all in direct competition with each other, shared a common interest in the present and future orderly development of this young city and in establishing a solid business climate.

The aims and objectives of the first Vancouver Real Estate Board were to promote, encourage and protect the ownership of real property, to give members better ways to market real estate and to provide a uniform schedule of commissions and charges.

At the first meeting, E.V. Bodwell was named President. Elected Vice President was F.C. Innes and Treasurer, H.T. Ceperley. The Executive Committee named at that meeting included D.F. Douglas, W.E. Gravely, C.D. Rand, and R.G. Tatlow. Secretary was John Whitehead.

Organizational meetings had been held in the offices of Ross and Ceperley, and the new executive chose permanent offices which were located above McLellan & McFeeley's store on Cordova Street, at a cost of $25.00 per month rent. Entrance fee for Board Membership was set at $150.00 with monthly dues of $5.00 payable in advance.

Ernest Bodwell had been a paymaster for the CPR and bought land in both Vancouver and Victoria. He was a real estate broker in Victora in 1883 when Walter Graveley arrived, fresh from a survey crew in Winnipeg. Together they arranged to buy a townsite for $8,000, with $1,000 down and full payment by the time the title deeds arrived from England. There was no interest on time payments or charge for title deeds in those days, an era when grass was still growing on what is now Government Street. Their gamble was a success, however, and by the time the deeds arrived from England Bodwell and Graveley had sold enough lots

The companies listed as signatories to the first Real Estate Board were: T.V. Allan & Co.; A.M. Beattie; Bell & Thornton; E.V. Bodwell; Charles Chamberlain; Clements & Farron; J. Devine & Son; Douglas & Hargreaves; W. Fagan & Co.; Frank Granville & Co.; Graveley & Barker; Holland & Archer; Holloway & Lloyd; F.C. Innes & Co.; H.A. Jones & Co.; H.A. Mellon & Co.; M.A. MacLean & Co.; R.D. Pitt; T. Prest & Co.; Rand Bros; Ross & Ceperley; Robertson & Co.; J.W. Sutherland & Co.; Shannon & Hall; R.G. Tatlow & Co.

at $250 each to pay the full amount due.

Hearing the railway planned to move its terminus from Port Moody to the newer Coal Harbour village of Granville, both moved to the mainland in 1885. Graveley bought the first lot sold by the CPR at the corner of Carral & Cordova Street, and moved his real estate office to that site.

Vancouver was young in more than years because its settlers and speculators tended to be youthful. Graveley was just 32 years old in 1888 when he settled down to marriage and a long business career in Vancouver. Because of his early ties with the city, his name was immortalized when Graveley Street was named by Vancouver City Council. A keen sailer, he also founded the Vancouver Yacht Club and was named its first Commodore in 1903. This club became the "Royal" Vancouver Yacht Club by Royal warrant in February, 1906.

Henry Ceperley arrived in Vancouver in 1886 at the age of 35, forming a partnership with A.W. Ross in real estate and insurance. Ceperley retired at the fairly youthful age of 59 in 1910, though he retained Presidency of the company then known as Ceperley, Rounsefell & Company. He was an acknowledged contributor to Vancouver's development throughout his business career. It was well known that his wife Grace was very fond of children and concerned for their safety. After her death in 1918, Ceperley Park Playground was named in her memory and established at Second Beach in Stanley Park with funds from her estate. It was officially opened on June 14, 1924, and 74-year old Henry Ceperley was present at the ceremony. The mansion at 6344 Deer Lake Avenue in Burnaby, once occupied by the Ceperleys, is now the home of the Burnaby Art Gallery.

Arthur Ross, who was Henry Ceperley's partner, had reached Port Moody when it was still the CPR terminus and started a real estate business. Historians credit Ross with a major role in the establishment of Stanley Park, which had been set aside as Government Reserve by Colonel Moody in 1859. During one of Sir William Van Horne's early visits to Vancouver, Ross rowed the CPR chief completely around the forest peninsula in a small boat, pointing out the advantages of securing this large forested tract as a park for the City of Vancouver.

Ross and Van Horne discussed the proposal with Lauchlan Hamilton, who had been elected one of the city's first aldermen while still serving as land surveyor for the railway. Hamilton agreed to put the suggestion before City Council,

*In May, 1886, two lots on the west side of Granville Street between
Dunsmuir and Pender sold for $800. The lot now occupied
by the Hudson's Bay Company (Lot 16, Block 43) was sold in
July, 1886, for $1,000. (Land prices rose steadily; by 1893 the
Hudson's Bay Company paid $2,250 for two lots on the
north-east corner of Granville and Georgia, and in 1900 paid
$8,500 for the two lots adjoining).*

From left, Mayor Hume,
Arthur Jacobson and
City Secretary A.G. Creer.

and Van Horne agreed to discuss it with his influential
government friends in Ottawa. The first resolution of the first
City Council meeting was to authorize the Mayor to petition
the Dominion Goverment that the tract known as Government Reserve be conveyed to the City of Vancouver for a park
and this approval was soon received. The park idea showed
remarkable foresight, considering the years of development
that lay ahead. Vancouver's pride and joy, one thousand acre
Stanley Park, was officially established in 1888, a direct
result of the influence of real estate pioneer Ross and through
the actions of Mayor MacLean, also a real estate broker, and
his Council. Companies operated by both of these brokers as
well as many others in Vancouver, incidentally, prospered
through the years by selling land in the city's West End,
adjacent to the popular new park. Even today a location near
Stanley Park is a sure sale.

Original documents of that first Real Estate Board, presented to Mayor Fred Hume in 1956 by Board President
Arthur B. Jacobson, included a price list of some business
sites in the downtown CPR townsite.

In May, 1886, two lots on the west side of Granville Street
between Dunsmuir and Pender sold for $800. The lot now
occupied by the Hudson's Bay Company (Lot 16, Block 43)
was sold in July, 1886, for $1,000. (Land prices rose steadily;
by 1893 the Hudson's Bay Company paid $2,250 for two lots
on the north-east corner of Granville and Georgia, and in
1900 paid $8,500 for the two lots adjoining).

In early 1886 Hastings Street lots were sold for $750 each
and a section of the site of the B.C. (Electric) Hydro building,
built at Nelson and Burrard in the 1950s, could be bought in
1889 for $470 with $170 down and the balance in 12 months
at an interest rate of 6 per cent.

A businessman could buy lots on Hornby north of the
present Hotel Vancouver for $620 with a $220 cash down
payment, or locate in the blocks bounded by Pender, Hastings, Princess and Campbell, then the heart of the business
section, for $520 a lot, with $186.66 down.

Across the old Granville Street bridge a few sites scat-

along Fourth Avenue were priced at $100 a lot, with $10 down and $5.00 per month payment.

The Board minute book, faithfully recorded in the hand of Secretary John M. Whitehead, shows that pioneer Vancouver Real Estate Brokers were well informed and fully involved in the development of their new city. Today's Board members continue this tradition of civic commitment throughout the fourteen Greater Vancouver communities they serve.

A total of 24 meetings were held before this first association faltered after less than three months. They encompassed eleven General Meetings, eleven Executive Committee meetings and two Special Membership Meetings, the last of which was held on June 6th, 1888, when the members disbanded due to disagreement on the issue of commission sharing with non-members.

Messrs Bodwell, Innes, Ceperley and Rand—determined they could successfully launch a business association, went on to form the British Columbia Mining Bureau on July 4, 1888, but this group too disbanded by agreement on September 25th that year.

In the years that followed, Vancouver experienced various economic peaks and valleys, and while real estate and those engaged in the brokerage business continued to be at the forefront of city development, there was no move to rebuild the original association. After the First World War ended, however, the local real estate community once again joined forces. An association called the Vancouver Real Estate Exchange Ltd. was formed in March, 1919.

Newspapers of the day carried many real estate ads, and also showed that children's ulster cloacks were selling at $ 2.00 each, while ladies hats were priced at $ 1.00 each. Roast was 10-cents a pound and a steak 6-cents a pound.

14

CHAPTER THREE

A NEW CENTURY

After just four years of tempestuous life, Vancouver entered the last decade of the 19th Century. Arrival of the SS Empress of India in Vancouver Harbour on April 28, 1891, was an exciting event which also boosted city trade, employment and growth. This was the first vessel of the Empress steamship line, sailing from England via the Orient. Thus Trans-Pacific service with monthly voyages to and from the Orient was established. For several decades in both boom times and down times, these ships provided jobs for many Vancouverites. A memorial figurehead of the Empress of Japan in Stanley Park is a constant reminder of Vancouver's early bond with the sea and its Pacific Rim trade routes.

By 1892 Vancouver felt the first chilling effects of an international economic recession. A period of depression lasted for several years. Trade contracts with the mills and canneries were cancelled, ships were idled, wages dropped and many people who had been in the real estate brokerage business simply closed their doors.

In 1895 the recession was somewhat relieved by Kootenays mining speculation but it was the Klondyke gold rush in 1898 that did most to pull the city out of the doldrums. Vancouver became an outfitting stop and point of departure for steamships to the northern gold fields. Some of the gold and many of the gold seekers filtered back to Vancouver, and activity in real estate markets increased again.

In 1898, before the local depression had officially ended, J.P. Nicolls, who had been a banker in England, and local investor C.H. Macaulay, established a Vancouver real estate firm that still gives distinguished service to this day. In 1903 the two principals were joined by Ronald M. Maitland, to form Macaulay, Nicolls, Maitland and Co. Ltd. Company founder J.P. Nicolls was very involved in establishing the Real Estate Exchange in 1919, and he is also responsible for recording many of Vancouver's most colourful real estate events.

A comprehensive address by J.P. Nicolls, made to Real Estate Exchange members in 1925, and also his personal reminiscences of over half a century in real estate, published by the City Archives in 1954, provided a wealth of information on real estate values over the years, as well as his insight and first hand knowledge of how historical events often affected these values. We have drawn heavily on these documents for information on early sales and values.

By the early 1900s residential areas had already expanded throughout the West End, Strathcona, Mount Pleasant and Fairview. (Macaulay Nicolls Maitland & Co. advertised in the Daily World of September 23, 1899, four choice lots in Fairview, one a corner lot, for just $300. At the same time a very desirable West End 66' by 132' lot on Nelson, near Broughton Street, was available for just $725.00.)

Downtown property on Granville Street between Robson and Georgia, Lots 15 and 16, Block 53, were sold for $7,000 in 1904. The north-east corner of Granville and Robson, Lots 19 and 20, Block 43, cost developer Mr. Jonathan Rogers $10,500 in 1905. In 1911 he built the Rogers Building, still in use on the north east corner of Granville and Pender.

During that land boom at the turn of the century, American speculators bought large tracts of land in the area of Ninth Avenue and Westminster Road. To promote sales they decided to upgrade street names, so in 1909 Westminster Road became Main Street, and ninth Avenue became Broadway—familiar names found in many major centres around the world, so bound to appeal to the cosmopolite. News reports of the day show that it worked, because all the land sold quickly.

In 1909 a firm called Runnalls & Goodlad, with offices on Park Drive, was advertising "cheap Grandview Houses", a new five-room home on Charles Street for $2,700 with $500 down, a new eight-room home on Williams Street for $4,700 with $1,400 cash required, and a few choice lots on Grant Street at $350 each.

Newspapers of the day were advertising Christmas turkeys at 25-cents per pound, and the Vancouver Opera House was advertising seat price ranges as 25, 50 and 75-cents with $1.00 charged for the best seats in the house. Purveyors of fine clothing in Vancouver were also advertising tailored suits from $20, silk petticoats from $5.00 and elegant evening gowns from $35.00.

Kitsilano was originally called Greer's Beach after its first settler/squatter, Sam Greer, and the CPR wanted a better name for it. Officials asked Postmaster Jonathan Miller to find a more appropriate name, and he chose the name of one of the hereditary chiefs, KHAT-SAH-LANO, modified it to

Money donated by the Carnegie Foundation in 1900 established a library at Hastings and Main which opened in 1903. It is now in use as a popular area community centre.

Motor cars were becoming common sights on local roads by the middle of that first decade, encouraging street building and improvement, and leading to the opening up of Shaughnessy Heights, where a number of fine homes began to rise.

KATES-EE-LANO, then further to KITSILANO, which is the way it first appeared in print around 1905. Despite many historians' disputes over the original Aboriginal spelling, the final result is the same, and by 1910 Kitsilano Beach had considerable residential construction underway.

The city's population was in the neighbourhood of 45,000, but city officials were anxious for more growth. J.P. Nicolls recounted a civic slogan conceived in 1905:

"In nineteen ten, Vancouver then will have one hundred thousand men". Move her! Move her! Who? Vancouver!

It may have started as a dream, but by 1910 some 95,000 residents were counted and the census of 1911 recorded a population of 120,847. (We are assuming that today's politically incorrect use of the word "men" should translate into the more acceptable word "persons", and if that is what the slogan meant, it was a success!)

Motor cars were becoming common sights on local roads by the middle of that first decade, encouraging street building and improvement, and leading to the opening up of Shaughnessy Heights, where a number of fine homes began to rise. The first gas station in the Dominion of Canada was opened at the foot of Cambie near Smithe in 1908, by Imperial Oil company employees, C.M. Rolston, J.C. Rollston, and one J.S. Matthews, who later became the famous and curmudgeonly chronicler of Vancouver's history as City Archivist.

Newton J. Ker arrived in Vancouver as a Land Agent for the C.P.R in 1910. Because of his previous success in developing Rockcliffe Park in Ottawa, he was given the task of planning and vending the C.P.R. Land Grant in Vancouver and was subsequently responsible for the successful planning of first, second and third Shaughnessy, the Oakridge and Cambie areas. The Ker name is still familiar in the real estate industry today.

In 1910 building permits amounted to thirteen million dollars in value, followed by seventeen and nineteen million in 1911 and 1912. Property assessments shot up to over $100 million and taxpayers approved major civic expenditures for schools, improvements to English Bay and Kitsilano Beach. This was the peak of the building boom, and major suburbs surfaced in Kitsilano and Grandview.

Louis D. Taylor, publisher of the Vancouver World newspaper, was elected Mayor in 1910 and—contributing to the building boom—built the "tallest building in the British Empire"—for his newspaper in 1913. Known since 1930 as the Sun Tower, it is still a city landmark at the south east corner of Pender and Beatty, though no longer the scene of newspaper production.

Vancouverites were enjoying the boom time and erecting elegant turreted houses, planting monkey-puzzle trees, hiring Chinese houseboys, joining the Terminal City Club, the Lawn Tennis Club or Royal Vancouver Yacht Club which had been started by pioneer real estate broker Walter Graveley in 1903.

Boom times always increase costs, and newspapers reported Mayor Taylor citing the increased cost of living for suggesting to local taxpayers that he favored a $3.00 per day minimum wage for all city day labour employees.

It seemed those golden days would never end, but J.P. Nicolls' reports show how wrong that feeling was. He said the corner of Granville and Dunsmuir sold in that boom period for $6,000 a foot to the Dominion Bank, and an alley corner on Hastings east near Main sold for $100,000. In 1910 an owner refused $250,000 for a corner of Robson and Granville, but had to settle for a sale price of only $122,500 in 1916. An offer of $125,000 was refused for the corner of Granville and Helmcken in 1912, and sold later in 1917 for $40,000. A 60 foot by 95 foot property on a corner of Cambie and Broadway was advertised at $90,000 and later sold for $8,000.

Hastings at Carral, 1909

Also in 1912, three lots on Main Street near 6th Avenue sold for $75,000, which was around $1,000 per front foot. This was in a period when wages were about fifty cents per hour, and a really good hand tailored suit was less than $40.00.

"Beautiful Point Grey Heights" was being marketed by A.E. Austin & Co. Ltd., from offices at 328 Granville in downtown Vancouver. Two corner lots at 18th Avenue and Collingwood Road, totaling 64.1 feet of frontage, were available for $2,375 and other 33 foot lots along 18th Avenue were $950 each. Terms of purchase were one quarter cash and the balance in 6, 12, 18, or 24 months at 7 per cent per annum interest. People were rushing to buy and build fine houses in an area that would eventually be annexed to the City of Vancouver.

Granville Street, 1912

By this time a swing-span high-level Granville Bridge crossed False Creek, the new Post Office had opened at Granville and Hastings and was doing the fourth largest volume of business in Canada. B.C. Electric streetcars and interurbans were carrying 100,000 passengers a day after extending its interurban lines as far as Steveston and Chilliwack. A new Opera House was completed on Granville Street and 12,000 telephones were in service in the city. The Great Northern Railway had reached Vancouver, there were a total of 52 churches and real estate offices outnumbered grocery stores three to one. The golden years rolled on towards the end of 1912 when another international economic recession slowed the fast forward momentum for a few years.

This recession was felt in Vancouver but not as severely as before because the city now had the resources to survive. Building of the city continued, but at a less hectic pace, and the government did have great expenses in winter unemployment relief. Port traffic was active as the CPR Empress liners, the Canadian-Australasian Line, the Ocean Steamship Co., Mutual Steam Navigation Co., Harrison Line, the Royal Mail Steamship Packet and East Asiatic Line vied for harbour space with Coastal packets, tugs and barges.

The "highest and best use of land" philosophy became West End reality, and apartment buildings started to be built. By 1913 there were at least 50 three-storey multi-unit buildings west of Burrard Street, and the "West End elite" were moving out to more desirable suburban single family locations like Shaughnessy Heights. One of these apartment building developers was real estate and lumber baron, W.L. Tait, who moved his family away from the West End to an ornate Shaughnessy mansion, Glen Brae.

When World War One broke out in 1914, the Admiralty took over the Canadian Pacific Liners and that year for the first time there was a noticeable decline in port traffic.

The Great War brought tragedy to Vancouver. There were streets in the city where every house had a man overseas, and where every block mourned two or three deaths before the

The University of British Columbia opened in shacks and tents on the General Hospital Grounds the fall of 1915, with promises of post-war completion of a Point Grey campus.

Armistice came. There were still effects of recession being felt in Vancouver during the war years and even opening of the Panama Canal, long expected to improve port activity, didn't deliver on that promise immediately due to the scarcity of vessels in the Pacific. The Canal was later to prove a major reason for Vancouver becoming one of the biggest wheat ports in the world, the route increasing both wheat and lumber shipments significantly. Tax sales of forfeited land became common, and several municipalities bought up the land instead of disposing of it on a real estate market which had virtually dried up.

Slowly an economic upsurge came with munitions and ship building contracts. The city had now grown up and away from its frontier past. It was an active industrial city, with a solid working population instead of short-term speculators. But prices were rising steadily and wages weren't. By 1917 the cost of living rose fifty per cent, and the trade union movement flexed its muscles for the first time. Strikes and threats of strikes in various occupations did result in some wage increases, but the post war period in Vancouver didn't see as much labour strife as other parts of Canada because once again there was full employment. After 1918 Armistice celebrations, the city and its residents settled back into the working/building mode. There was a great need for housing as veterans returned and despite high prices for lumber and materials, many homes began rising.

The elements of change were influencing real estate values and altering the face of the city. Elevators made skyscrapers possible. Motor cars and street cars revolutionized transportation so the needed housing could be built further from the downtown area of the city, and accordingly, real estate brokers diversified their services to cover the new needs of investment, management, marketing and sales.

Relatives bid goodbye to the 62nd Overseas Batallion of the Canadian Expeditionary Force one rainy day in March, 1916.

CHAPTER FOUR

A SOCIETY REBORN

Traffic direction, Hastings
and Granville, 1920

In March, 1919, ten local real estate brokers became the first subscribers to a new association called the Vancouver Real Estate Exchange Ltd. Their names were recorded in the Society's first Cash Book on March 13, 1919, coincidentally just thirty one years less a day from when the first Vancouver Board had been inaugurated on March 14, 1888. Exchange entrance fees were set at $25.00 and monthly dues $2.50, with shares offered at $10.00 each.

Members listed included Stanley Burke, R. Kerr Houlgate, J.J. Banfield, A.C. Stirritt, J.P. Nicolls, H.V. Sharples, J.W. Allan and G.L. Edwards. J.M. McFarland, associated with Ceperley Rounsefell & Co, a firm which was a participant in the 1888 Board, was a charter signer in 1919. This firm remained on Exchange/Board Membership lists until February, 1965, chalking up a total of 97 years in Vancouver's real estate history. Another familiar name from the previous century was Exchange charter member H.T. Devine, heir to the firm J. Devine & Son, involved in founding the 1888 Board.

The next month more real estate and insurance professionals joined, including D.W. Reeve, J.H. Griffiths, A.E. Short, C.E. Robson, R.C. Proctor, A.E. Austin, E.B. Morgan, A.F. Lander, H.R. Budd, R.A. Hood, J.R. Waghorn, and J.S. Gall. Associate Membership category with an entrance fee of $10.00 was chosen by A.M.J. English and the Toronto General Trust Corp.

By the end of its first year those listed above had been joined by J.G. Borrie, J.P. Fell, A.P. Hughes, Col. G.H. Dorrell, A. McC. Creery, R.G. Harvey, H.W. Dyson and A.W. Whitaker. These thirty individuals represented 29 companies: Edwards & Ames; J.F. Mahon Estate; Pemberton & Son; A.S. Short Ltd.; H. Bell Irving & Co. Ltd.; London and British North American Co. Ltd.; Griffith & Lee Ltd, Hood Bros.; Andersons Ltd.; E.B. Morgan & Co. Ltd.; Kitsilano Investment Co.; Richards, Akroyd & Gall; Waghorn, Gwynn & Co.; Canadian Financiers Trust Co.; McLaren & Hughes; Macaulay & Nicolls; Johnson & Reeve; A.E. Austin & Co.; Yorkshire & Canadian Trust; Whitaker & Whitaker; Loewen, Harvey & Preston; Turner Meakin & Co.; Royal Financial Corp.; Knowles & Co.; General

Administration Society; H.T. Devine & Co.; Allan & Richards. Nine Associate Members were on the membership list, including A.M.J. English; Toronto General Trust Corp,; Canada Permanent Trust; The Standard Trust Co.; Newton J. Ker of the C.P.R. Land Department; Anglo American Corp. Ltd.; Guaranty Trust Co.; Franco Canadian Trust and Montreal Trust Co.

These members saw their society become a significant part of the business network of the young Vancouver, and established the Board tradition of balanced budgets. At December 31, 1919, with all bills paid, the Exchange bank balance was $860.13.

Henderson's Directory began annual publication in 1889, and by 1919 recorded a total of 173,283 residents in the Greater Vancouver area. The directory listed over 400 individuals and companies offering real estate and/or insurance brokerage, a number of them already Exchange members. Among those listed were some pioneer companies which had been in existence when the city was born, and had joined the first real estate board in 1888. Still doing business in Vancouver some 30 years later were R.G. Tatlow & Co., after whom Kitsilano's Tatlow Park was later named; A. Murray Beattie, auctioneer, appraiser and real estate agent on Cordova Street; E.V. Bodwell, President of the 1888 Board; F. Granville & Co.; J.M. Holland & Co. and Rand Bros.

An eclectic range of insurance coverage was offered in this period of Vancouver's growth, with policies available to cover General Insurance, Accident and Sickness, Fire, Marine, Auto, Burglary, Theft and Larceny, Casualty, Court Bonds, Elevator Liability, Explosion, Fidelity and Surety Bonds, Guaranty Bonds, Livestock, Owners' and Tenants' Liability, Public Liability, Riot and Civil Commotion.

Then, as now, applying for Exchange Membership was a purely voluntary decision. Another firm, H.A. Roberts Ltd., whose principals were to become very influential in Exchange/Board affairs and history, was established in 1918, but did not join the Exchange until 1925.

By the middle of the decade there were 59 individuals registered as members of 58 companies, with a further eight members in the Associate category.

Charter members distinguished themselves in Association service during its first decade; R. Kerr Houlgate, General Manager of Vancouver Financial Corporation in the Yorkshire Building at 525 Seymour Street, was named its first

By January, 1920, when the Exchange held its first Annual Meeting, 25 members paid $2.50 each for the dinner meeting held at the Hotel Vancouver. The Exchange covered incidental costs for that meeting which included $15 for a vocalist and accompanist, $10.00 for typing required in preparation for the meeting, plus $8.80 to provide guests with the very best 25-cent cigars in town!

President, and served three terms through 1921, followed by H.R. Budd, Manager of the London & British North America Co. Ltd. at 626 West Pender, who served in 1922 and 1923. A.E. Austin, who was involved in Point Grey sales long before its eventual amalgamation with the city of Vancouver, was elected President in 1924, J.P. Nicolls in 1926, D.W. Reeve in 1928 and J.W. Allen in 1929.

Geoffrey L. Edwards, another Charter Member who conducted his real estate brokerage from an office in the Williams Building at 413 Granville Street, served as first Secretary of the Exchange at a $30 monthly stipend until April, 1920, when Frank Hoole was employed as Secretary on a permanent basis.

In the Constitution & By-Laws adopted by those 1919 signatories, Exchange members were committed to high standards of practice and to advance the interests of the City of Vancouver and Greater Vancouver area and its citizens by collection and circulation of valuable and useful information pertaining to the purchase, maintenance and sale of real property. Members also agreed to oppose enactment of laws detrimental to real estate ownership. They guaranteed to subscribe funds for education to upgrade the industry, to adopt and enforce sound rules of business conduct among those engaged in real estate and to develop a strict code of ethics for protection of the consumer of real estate services.

The Exchange established numerous Standing and special Committees to accomplish all it had set out to do, and formulated a set of arbitration guidelines to solve commission disputes between Exchange members.

One of the most active Committees of the Exchange was the Valuation Committee, which offered a professional valuation service to civic officials and other property owners at a sliding fee scale depending upon the value determined. In the original Cash Book, the majority of 1919 valuation fees recorded were for $5.00, which indicated subject properties valued at $3,000 or less. Balance of the established scale was as follows: between $3,000 and $5,000-$7.50; $5,000 to $7,500 – $10.00; $7,500 to $10,000–$12.50; $10,000 to $15,000–$15.00. For every $1,000 in excess of $15,000 one dollar was added to the fee if the property was within a 6 mile radius of the Vancouver Post Office, but if located outside that periphery, special arrangements were made.

To inform Vancouver of these and other services of the Exchange, the cash book registers a payment of $39.50 for

R. Kerr Houlgate
President, 1919-1921

Prompted by the advice of the Vigilance Committee of the Real Estate Exchange, a Real-estate Agents' Licensing Act was proclaimed by the Provincial Government in June, 1920.

advertisements in July, 1920, carried in the Vancouver Sun, the Vancouver World and the Vancouver Province.

Prompted by the advice of the Vigilance Committee of the Real Estate Exchange, a Real-estate Agents' Licensing Act was proclaimed by the Provincial Government in June, 1920. Two years later the first real estate license law was established to set minimum standards of practice expected of those licensed under that Act. Vigilance Committee members, always alert to further improvement, proposed an amendment in 1923 that would require all licensees under the Act to furnish a bond. Reasoning for this recommendation was noted in 1923 Directors' Minutes. At that time there was no machinery to cover all fraudulent cases and the Inspector of Real Estate Agents & Salesmen was not always inclined to conduct thorough investigations, so local Exchange members wanted to have more consumer protection in place. The wheels of government often grind slowly, but the Exchange Committee was persistent, and the government of British Columbia finally decreed bonding a requirement in 1927.

The Exchange was born just two years after the federal government had imposed a "short term program" in 1917 to pay mounting First World War costs. Called the "Income War Tax Act", its promise of "short term" duration wasn't fulfilled and all Canadians still pay under the name changed in 1949 to Income Tax Act. This tax and subsequent taxes imposed by all levels of goverment have been conscienciously reviewed and reported upon by Exchange/Board Committees throughout the past 75 years.

Operating from offices in Room 509, Yorkshire Building, at 525 Seymour Street in 1923, the Vigilance Committee dealt with the heavy burden on citizens and property owners from the Dominion's Income Tax and British Columbia's Succession Duty Act. This Act often duplicated charges in other provinces/countries and sometimes had the effect of invalidating titles. It certainly undermined public confidence and decreased potential capital investment in B.C. Even then it was recognized that most family wealth was tied to the value

It was in this period newspaper ads were telling people about revolutionary new products—band-aids were put on the first childhood owies in 1920, and by 1924 Kleenex was keeping their colds at bay. The motorcar was still the reason builders could develop suburban lands, and Vancouverites eagerly visited—and bought—them, driving on the left-hand side in the British custom, until the laws changed to the right on June l, 1922.

of a home and business, and succession duties would discourage new immigrants and investment, so the Exchange launched on-going opposition to this form of taxation, a philosophy that lives on to this day.

Then, as now, the Exchange registered its sincere concern of the ever-increasing cost of government and urged administration cutbacks and national thrift because of its Dickensian observation that the country's expenditure was greater than its income.

Another hot topic of that day which continues to this was equalization of freight rates. Even though the railway was built to open up the west and Pacific region, a 50% "mountain differential" rate was applied to B.C., which was perceived as unfair to British Columbians so the Exchange registered its objection to the higher rate paid at this end.

Aware of the power of advertising, and wishing to advance the interests of this area, the Exchange advertised as far afield as California and other American States in 1923 to promote British Columbia's development and investment opportunities.

Under the guidance of President H.R. Budd, Board members networked with the National Association of Real Estate Boards (NAREB), and Directors travelled to Portland, Oregon, to attend that American Society's annual conference. It can be assumed one of the new ideas brought back from those discussions was a cooperative selling structure, because the term "MLS" appeared for the first time in the August, 1923, Minutes of the Real Estate Exchange.

Licensing education in Vancouver began as a result of the work of a joint Committee of representatives from the Real Estate Exchange, the Insurance/Financial/Real Estate and Legal Bureau of the Vancouver Board of Trade, the Mortgage & Trust Association and the Union of B.C. Municipalities.

These groups jointly sponsored a visit by A.H. Meyers, Director of the Department of Commerce, United YMCA Schools, New York, who was guest speaker at a luncheon held at the Hudson's Bay Company Dining Room on October 15, 1923. Cost of this event, which included luncheon and speaker, was 60-cents per person.

That 60-cents was money well spent, as it encouraged Committee members drawn from all facets of the business community to set up a course in real estate that ultimately comprised 17 comprehensive lectures on the subjects of general sales, insurance, mortgaging, valuation, advertising, rentals, real estate law, Title examination, taxation and ethics.

On January 15, 1924, the Annual Meeting of the Exchange saw A.E. Austin elected President and A McC. Creery as Vice President.

In an address to Exchange members in March that year, Mr. Arthur G. Smith, then District Registrar of Land Titles, warned members that *"unceasing watchfulness is required to prevent ill considered and harmful legislation being passed"*, and suggested it would be wise for the Exchange to be on the look-out at all times to protect the Real Estate business. This was already a Constitutional aim of the Real Estate Exchange, and a legislative vigil that has been maintained until this day.

In November the Valuation Committee advised the City Comptroller that he would be justified in paying anything up to $10,000 for lease of city Water Lots at the foot of Quebec and Ontario Streets. Civic officials depended on the professional advice of the local real estate profession.

That same month the first MLS Committee of the Society, circulated draft MLS forms to all members for comments and suggestions.

Also in 1924, A.E. Austin & Co. was selling Grandview sites, "splendidly situated large size building lots facing on Nanaimo, Kamloops, Charles, Kitchener, Graveley Streets and First Avenue." It was a subdivision of the N.W. quarter of Section 33 in the City of Vancouver, where two lots at the corner of Kamloops and Grant Streets (Lots 17 & 18, Block 5) sold for $550 and another pair at the corner of Graveley and Nanaimo (Lots 8 and 9, Block 5) sold for $800.

A. McC. Creery was elected Exchange President in 1925 and J.P. Nicolls was named Vice President. During the year a joint Committee of members of the Vancouver Exchange, Victoria Real Estate Board and Boards of Trade in Vancouver and Victoria, continued the campaign to amend or abolish the Succession duties Act. The Vigilance Committee also continued its earlier recommendation that surety bonds be carried by individuals and companies in the real estate industry.

Past President A.E. Austin encouraged Exchange members to participate in the 9th Annual Conference of the Pacific Northwest Real Estate Association, scheduled for July 30th, 1925 in Bellingham. The previous year draft MLS forms had been circulated to all members for comments and

A. McC. Creery
President, 1925

A speech made to Exchange members in September, 1925, by A.A. Milledge, Manager of the B.C. Products Bureau, shows today's British Columbian the growth experienced in this province's early years. Milledge said the 1914 value of the province's first industry, forestry, was $35 million, and this rose to $80 million by 1924. He said 72 per cent of all forest product output was shipped through Vancouver in 1924. Agricultural production increased by 120% in the same decade from $26 million in 1914 up to $60 million in 1924. Mining had been somewhat depressed during the Great War years, but increased in value from $30 million in 1914 to $48 million ten years later. Shipments of canned salmon from Vancouver reached a total of 1 and one half million cases in 1924.

suggestions, but they had shown little positive reaction to the Multiple Listing concept. Austin hoped direct contact with American colleagues who used the system might encourage local use. Future events were to show that it took until 1951 to revive interest in MLS, which became an undeniable success within a few years.

In these early years of the Exchange there was constant communication between the local group and the National Association of Realtors in the U.S. The national organization headquarters was in Chicago then, as now, and there are many minuted records of Vancouver visits by the NAR President and Executive Officer, as well as plans for local members to attend the American conferences.

In keeping with its vigilant approach to consumer issues, the Exchange again sent recommended amendments to the Real-estate Agents' Licensing Act to J.P. Dougherty, Superintendent of Insurance in Victoria. In late 1925 these included recommendations to expand personal information on written applications for licensing, licensing fees to be payable at an annual expiry date, more discipline of licensees and again urging bonding for all individuals and companies. In what was probably the first Political Action Committee ("PAC" as today's group is called), a delegation comprised of E. Kerr Houlgate, Colonel Dorrell, A.E. Austin and J.P. Nicolls travelled to Victoria to make a strong industry representation, which was well received by government officials.

In late 1925 the Exchange went on record as favoring the proposed amalgamation of Point Grey and South Vancouver with the City of Vancouver, despite the possibility of a potential rise in taxes to pay for infrastructure, maintenance of roads, sidewalks, street lighting, etc. The amalgamation was finally in place by January 1, 1929, extending city boundaries west to the Strait of Georgia and south to the shores of the Fraser's north arm, and raising Vancouver's population to 240,000 at that time.

Even in those early years, highschool high-jinks were not unknown. As today's real estate practitioner well knows, there are certain seasons (usually the beginning of the school year and graduation) when real estate signs seem to beckon the student population towards graffiti art, sign removal or destruction. This problem was discussed and minuted as far back as 1926.

Elected President in 1926 was J.P. Nicolls, with Col. G.H. Dorrell as Vice President. That year Exchange Secretary

Frank Hoole released total yearly figures for transfers of property which had been obtained from the Land Registry for the five years from 1921 through 1925. The dollar volumes indicated fluctuating real estate values in that period, as reproduced here:

Year	Transfers	Dollar Volume
1921	11,747	$ 20,599,020.
1922	10,766	$ 22,545,200.
1923	9,356	$ 24,194,692.
1924	10,450	$ 22,672,239.
1925	11,797	$ 35,070,727.

Exchange Directors encouraged speakers from all industries to keep them informed on the state of business throughout the province. In March, 1926, a Mr. Wm. McNeil told members that British Columbia grew one half the soft wood supply of Canada, one third that of the Empire and one ninth that of the world. His message then still has a familiar ring today, that "forests should be harvested to a certain extent like any other crop, because if the timber was not used it simply fell to decay". He also pointed out that some reforestation was then being started by lumber companies and advanced the opinion that more lumber should be manufactured here because at that time the U.S. government taxed imported logs but let manufactured lumber products in free.

The Executive Committee proposed amendments to the Legal Profession Act requiring written examinations before new Notarial appointments were made, and also requiring existing Notaries to be examined to guard against unqualified persons making out wills, chattel mortgages and bills of sale.

Later that year the Exchange publicly opposed development of a cemetary in Point Grey, which seemed to have worked as no such facility was ever established.

In a speech to exchange members in 1926 Mayor Louis D. Taylor outlined plans for a suggested Burrard Bridge, which would be put before the electorate for approval. The cost was estimated at $2,500,000. Taylor wanted to improve tourist possibilities for the city and the real estate fraternity enthusiastically endorsed the bridge plan because development was moving west and Burrard Street would be a natural route for a bridge to the south shore and Kitsilano.

At a June meeting of the Association in 1926, Vice President Col. G.H. Dorrell accepted a pre-arranged landmark

J. P. Nicolls
President, 1926

32

telephone call. He was the first citizen of Vancouver to speak from the city with someone at the top of Grouse Mountain on a telephone line which had just been installed.

At that meeting Exchange members heard about development plans for the mountain from William Curtis Shelley, who made his fortune with Canadian Bakeries Ltd., and by 1926 was active in real estate investment. His dream was to build a popular resort atop Grouse, which had been named in 1894 by a party of hunters who flushed blue grouse from the underbrush. One of those hunters was Ernest Cleveland, who later became chief commissioner of Greater Vancouver's Water District, and for whom Cleveland Dam is named.

By the spring of 1927 Shelly's "mountain highway" was completed, made of crushed rock 10 feet deep in some places. It cost $160,000-a princely sum in those days. Despite many hundreds of thousands of dollars of investment, Shelley and his partners were nearing bankruptcy by 1928 and then along came 1929 and the stock market crash. Along with many other investors, they struggled along for a few more years, but by the summer of 1935 the property and everything on it–road, chalet, light and power lines, water and sewage lines, even unfinished buildings, reverted to the District of North Vancouver for non-payment of $20,000 in taxes.

Smoke abatement in the City of Vancouver was studied in 1926 due to what the Smoke Inspector Mr. Scott called the multiplicity of mills and wood burners, steamships, railroad engines and in-house burners in hotels and apartment houses. No solution was found at that time.

The Vancouver Real Estate Salesmen's Association came to the Exchange in August, 1926, asking that commissions be raised to 5% up to $25,000 with 2 1/2% over that sum, from the existing standard of 5% on the first $10,000 and 2 1/2% on excess. This request was refused, and at the same time it was noted that while a customary 50-50 split in commission was recognized by most members, brokers wishing to make changes had their individual right to do so.

Exchange members J.W. Allen and S.L. Seymour were members of the Vancouver Town Planning Commission and in late 1926 informed members of suggested interim zoning regulations to be introduced to taxpayers. At that time it was estimated that 22,000 people lived in the West End, between Burrard Street and the Park, so zoning to include apartment housing was included in areas where it was necessary to raze a good deal of the older inadequate stock.

Rogers building

At the end of that year, further recommendations for amendment to the Real-estate Agents' Licensing Act were made to Victoria, which resulted in Salesmen's Licensing fees being raised to $10.00 annually, and the Exchange once again emphasized its request for the bonding requirement for real estate practitioners and companies.

When the Annual Meeting was held in 1927 Colonal G.H. Dorrel was named President and D.W. Reeve Vice President.

Under his term J.P. Dougherty, Superintendent of Insurance, and Attorney General the Honourable A. M. Manson finally ruled favourably for bonding for all agents. In a meeting with the Exchange Executive Committee it was agreed that license fees of $10.00 for Agents and $2.00 for salesmen be imposed in cities of over 10,000 population and a bonding clause of $1,000 for Agents and $1,000 for salesmen in cities of over 10,000 be embodied in the Act. All agents were required to notify the department when their salesmen left. No personal bonds would be accepted but only bonds by a bonding company satisfactory to the department. Both the Victoria Board and Vancouver Exchange agreed that all applications for licenses would have to be accompanied by the bond. Since its first proposed amendment 1923, the Vancouver Real Estate Exchange Ltd. was finally successful in bringing about the bonding process for consumer protection.

In 1927 an exclusive new area called Jericho Heights was being marketed just above the Jericho Golf Course, now Jericho Beach Park. Two companies, A.E. Austin and Co. and Orr-Hamilton Ltd., advertised the "easy access via the great paved through artery of West Point Grey, Tenth Avenue." Three carlines could be used for access, the Sasamat car which went along Tenth, the Dunbar and Broadway carlines, which were both only three blocks east of the subdivision.

At that time lots sold fast from $700 to $2,400, depending on size and location, despite restrictions that ensured no dwelling of less than $4,000 value could be built on Tenth Avenue, no less than $5,000 on Eighth Avenue or less than $4,500 elsewhere in the area. One quarter of the sale

Largest real estate transaction of the year in 1927
was the sale of the then 16 year old Rogers Building for
one million dollars.

D. W. Reeve
President, 1928

price was required in cash, with four equal payments required in 6-month periods, at 6 per cent interest. Estimated taxes quoted in advertising varied from $28.00 to $100.00 annually.

Elected President in 1928 was D.W. Reeve, with J.W. Allan as Vice President. While amalgamation of South Vancouver and Point Grey with Vancouver was still a year away, Point Grey Realty was urging buyers to see "stupendous bargains" in Dunbar Heights. A six-room bungalow, fully modern, garage in basement, on a 33-foot lot with a fine view was selling for $3,750, with $500 down and the balance on terms to be arranged.

That same year a Mount Pleasant homeowner was selling his own property. He was offering a 7-room house for $3,500, while another owner was advertising an "almost new 5-room semi-bungalow on a 40 foot lot just north of 4th Avenue in Kitsilano", for $5,000.

And on October 18, 1928, Vancouver's first traffic light started blinking red and green at the corner of Hastings and Main.

In 1929, under President J.W. Allan, the Exchange continued to make recommendations to Victoria to fine-tune the Real-estate Agents' Licensing Act. Amendments to establish better background knowledge on applicants for real estate licenses were suggested, along with procedures to detect incompetency or dishonest dealing, and a disciplinary process to deal with such cases were soon in place.

The Marine Building began to rise in 1929 after an official sod-turning ceremony on April 2. The building was formally opened on October 8, 1930, by the Honorable R. Randolph Bruce. Total cost of the land and building at that time was approximately $2,500,000. Built by E.J. Ryan Contracting, this magnificent building rose 304 feet above the Hastings sidewalk, with 18 storeys above ground, and 25 in all from the CPR tracks below. Architects and structural engineers were McCarter & Nairne, and when it was complete, the still stunning Marine Building was the tallest building west of Toronto.

The Exchange undertook pedestrian traffic counts for the first time in 1929, counting walk-by traffic on Hastings, Granville, Robson, Richards, Seymour, Howe, Hornby and Burrard to help establish rental rates for customers considering retail premises in the downtown area.

Colonel Dorrell prepared a standard Agreement for Sale form to be used by all Exchange members, and it was fully approved and in place by the end of 1929.

Unaware of what was to befall the world that very year, the Commission Committee of the Exchange met in June, 1929, to consider a request from the Vancouver Real Estate Salesmen's Association to increase standard commissions to 5% on the first $30,000 and 2 1/2 % on the excess. After many meetings of the special committee, and much discussion, it was finally decided in November that commission rates would increase to 5% on the first $20,000 and 2 1/2% on the excess.

On March 9, 1929, the Vancouver Stock Exchange experienced a record trading day, but on October 29, 1929, the Wall Street Crash was heard around the world. Despite that Black Friday, however, Vancouver's civic authorities, citizens and businessmen didn't seem to immediately understand the economic implications of the market crash and continued approving major civic improvement bonds, such as an expenditure of over $4 million for construction of the Burrard Bridge in December, 1929.

Slowly, however, the penny dropped. Despite considerable building development during 1929, it was soon apparent that the relief rolls were burgeoning, and the destitute were becoming a common sight on downtown streets. Demonstrations and arrests multiplied, and by mid 1930 it was quite apparent that Vancouver, too, had reached the end of its affluent era and was sliding down into what historians would eventually call the world's worst depression.

J. W. Allan
President, 1929

The Marine Building began to rise in 1929 after an official sod-turning ceremony on April 2. The building was formally opened on October 8, 1930, by the Honorable R. Randolph Bruce. Total cost of the land and building at that time was approximately $2,500,000. Built by E.J. Ryan Contracting, this magnificent building rose 304 feet above the Hastings sidewalk, with 18 storeys above ground, and 25 in all from the CPR tracks below. Architects and structural engineers were McCarter & Nairne, and when it was complete, the still stunning Marine Building was the tallest building west of Toronto.

Engineer Major J.R. Grant and architect G.L. Thornton Sharpe of Sharpe & Thompson, started working plans for the Burrard Bridge in 1929. Construction of that bridge started in December, 1930 and it was officially opened on Dominion Day, 1932. When Sharpe began working on the bridge plans he had just completed construction of a two-storey reinforced concrete building for the C.N.I.B. at the corner of Spruce and Broadway–1101 West Broadway, an address that was to play a large part in the future of the real estate association.

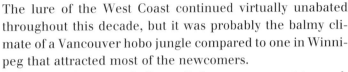

CHAPTER FIVE

THE THIRTIES

The lure of the West Coast continued virtually unabated throughout this decade, but it was probably the balmy climate of a Vancouver hobo jungle compared to one in Winnipeg that attracted most of the newcomers.

In 1930 Vancouver's first relief gangs were set to work clearing brush in Point Grey, but by the beginning of 1931 there were over 7,000 on relief rolls and more were riding the rods into town on every freight train. The "jungles" expanded under the Georgia Viaduct and along the False Creek flats east of Main Street. By the end of the year there were 2,588 families, 175 single women and 4,664 single men on relief. The senior governments had put transients into work camps, which took some expense off the city coffers, but the relief bill for the year was still $1.3 million.

Exchange charter member Newton J. Ker was still acting C.P.R. land agent in 1930 when his sons Alan Newton and Walter Gordon opened the real estate firm Ker & Ker Ltd. That firm set about marketing the many properties in the large C.P.R. land grant, focusing generally on the Shaughnessy area. Newton J. Ker retired in 1936, but his sons kept the family name alive in local real estate circles.

In the middle of 1931 the provincial government took over the sale of liquor, providing an additional source of income for provincial expenses, and Real Estate Exchange members continued to serve the needs of Vancouver clients and customers, though real estate activity was definitely on the decrease.

It was then that 23-year old R.A. (Bob) Pound decided to try his hand at the real estate business. He joined W.H. Moore & Co. at 41st & Granville and became very familiar with the south slope area of Vancouver, an area he considered the most desireable part of the city, even though little was selling in these early depression days. Pound, still hale and hearty at 87 and living with his gracious wife Gladys in Crescent Beach, says it was lucky he'd managed to save a thousand dollars before he became a real estate salesman. If you sold a $400 lot you might end up with around $10.00 in commission, but this could hardly be a weekly or even

J. C. McPherson
President, 1930

monthly experience, and most salesmen and agents too were finding they lived on savings more than earnings during the depression era.

In a rental directory dated August, 1931, the property management arm of H.A. Roberts Ltd. advertised vacancies in many West End apartment blocks. Englesea Lodge, which stood for many years next door to Stanley Park on Beach Avenue, advertised three and four room suites "complete with frigidaire and all modern equipment" for $45.00 to $75.00. Right downtown, the Irwinton Apartments at 777 Burrard—now site of the Vancouver Public Library which in turn is being replaced by a colosseum-like structure on Georgia, opposite the Post Office—had furnished and unfurnished apartments from $45.00 up to $80.00. Furnished houses all around the city were offered for $35.00 and up, with an unfurnished 5 room home on Dunbar Street with hot air heat and oak floors asking a $40 monthly rental. Many empty stores were available, with an 18x60 foot space on Broadway going for $25 per month, or a 14x35 space on Main Street for $20.00.

If anyone was in the buying mood, a large six room architect-designed home on Angus Drive with a view of the Gulf of Georgia, was offered at $8,250. Vancouver prided itself as being a city of home-owners-and in 1931 released statistics to show over 70% of its homes were occupied by owners, and 94% of its citizens were literate.

Exchange Financial statements for December 31, 1931, show that Secretary Frank Hoole's salary of $1,200 was the largest expense registered against income of $2,153.88. Rent and Stenographer cost $557.50 for the year and printing and stationery was $70, with phone charges $95.06.

In 1932 Vancouver was declared Canada's busiest port, but that wasn't enough of an economic factor to prevent assessments from falling and taxes remaining unpaid. The skeleton of the big new Hotel Vancouver, on which work had been suspended, was a constant city skyline reminder of hard times. The centre span of the Second Narrows Bridge had been put out of commission when struck by a ship in

W. S. MacGregor
President, 1931, 1932

In May, 1933, the Exchange organized a "Property Protective Patrol" to monitor the growing number of empty houses in the city. It seems safe to say that early Vancouver real estate practitioners developed and provided this city with the first 'Block Watch' of the century.

G. I. Legate
President, 1933

1930, and it still stood there useless and rusting while idle workers hung around on street corners.

In the winter of 1932/33 the City hit rock bottom. At the Annual Meeting of the Real Estate Exchange in January, 1933, J.P. Nicolls made a motion to reduce the monthly fees from $2.50 to $2.00, and change the requirement of 6-months payment in advance. Members agreed to allow the $2.00 fee to be paid on a month-to-month basis, and some brokerage companies were forced to close their doors.

That winter the government tried to establish what is now known as a "Non Resident Vendor Holdback". The government proposed a deduction at source of 12 1/2% on non-resident rentals and 5% on mortgage interest sent out of Canada, to satisfy Dominion Income Tax Law.

Exchange Past Presidents J.P. Nicoll and Col. G.H. Dorrell launched a protest against this action, saying it would make it more difficult for these owners to pay municipal taxes, and obviously discourage further fresh capital investment in the city. Mayor Louis Taylor eagerly joined the Exchange protest against the holdback, fearing the threat on city income through non tax payment.

In May, 1933, the Exchange organized a "Property Protective Patrol" to monitor the growing number of empty houses in the city. It seems safe to say that early Vancouver real estate practitioners developed and provided this city with the first 'Block Watch' of the century.

Also that year, in an effort to combat "Depression Syndrome", J.P. Nicolls devised a "feel good" scheme. Up to 10 people were chosen before every meeting of the Exchange to stand up and "tell of an encouraging sign that things are getting better". Subsequent minutes don't reflect any spectacular results from this practice, but it can also be assumed that Exchange members tested the theory of positive thinking well before its power was later revealed by Dr. Norman Vincent Peale.

Golfers might be interested in the historical fact that despite the economic depression, Shaughnessy Golf Club hosted the first Canadian Amateur Golf Championship to be played in British Columbia from July 10 to 15th, 1933.

Reviewing minutes of Committee and Membership meetings held in the thirties becomes a deja vu experience when one is conversant with both current Board minutes and universal public complaints of the 1990s.

In 1933 Committees addressed the many factors that were affecting recovery of the economy, and their findings are tediously familiar:

(a) burgeoning educational expenses must be checked.
(b) the increasing burden of health care costs.
(c) increased civic borrowing to meet local expenses,
(d) resulting in a higher level of taxes on real property.

In releasing these facts, Past President D.W. Reeve said real estate taxes in Vancouver provided 86% of the city's total income, and suggested it was high time the Provincial Government started to pay its share of increasing general education costs.

By the end of 1933 economic reality for the Real Estate Exchange was an income just over half of what it received in 1931. The year-end account showed a total income of $1,230.35, and the Secretary's salary had been cut in half—totaling only $600 for that year compared to $1,200 annually in 1931. Rent, Steno and telephone expenses were down by a third, to a total of $440.00, and printing and stationery by half to $36.94.

Charter Exchange Member G.L. Edwards, who had acted as Exchange Secretary Pro Tem before Frank Hoole's employment, was elected President in 1934. A more hopeful mood permeated North America that year when Franklin Roosevelt assumed the U.S. Presidency, but the reality was that the Depression became more severe. There were 34,000 people on relief in the city, tax collections dropped to $10.5 million from the $18 million of 1931/32 and real estate values were devastated.

In the east end a lot assessed at $1,500 would sell for $150 and on Howe Street a property assessed at $30,000 registered a sale price of $5,000.00.

Exchange members continued to address local problems, and worked closely with then Deputy Minister of Labour, Adam Bell, and Jas. Thomson of the Board of Industrial Relations to adopt an acceptable minimum wage for employees in some 700 apartment buildings then registered by

G. L. Edwards
President, 1934

By the end of 1933 economic reality for the Real Estate Exchange was an income just over half of what it received in 1931. The year-end account showed a total income of $1,230.35, and the Secretary's salary had been cut in half-totaling only $600 for that year compared to $1,200 annually in 1931. Rent, Steno and telephone expenses were down by a third, to a total of $440.00, and printing and stationery by half to $36.94 .

Arthur M. J. English
President, 1935

the City License Department. These discussions went on for several years, as consideration was given to market and value fluctuations.

Exchange protests resulted in agreement from the Attorney General's Department that succession duty caveats, which had been registered against properties since 1896, would no longer be enforced against present owners who had bought the property in good faith and were not connected with the succession duty claim in any way.

Then, as now, real estate brokers considered it their responsibility to contribute as much as possible to the community. In December, 1934, in a move to provide some help for the many homeless and unemployed citizens, Exchange Members opted to subscribe $10.00 each for special charitable purposes.

In late 1934 Gerald Gratton McGeer, a vigorous and enthusiastic candidate, was elected mayor of the city. He devised a "baby bonds" issue to finance a new City Hall, which soon started to rise at Cambie and 12th Avenue. Many citizens were aghast at his choice of such a "suburban" location, and the Real Estate Exchange formed a Committee to draw up a protest against the Strathcona Park site, favouring a more central location. While it became popularly known as "McGeer's Folly", sight of the building rising in the midst of the depression generated a positive response from most residents and they proudly attended the opening ceremonies on December 4, 1936. Viewed from a 1990s perspective, the City Hall location is indeed central, and the McGeer choice one of considerable foresight.

In 1935 Arthur M.J. English was elected President. Together with Vice President H.A. Roberts they developed a special paper which expressed a negative view on a proposed Dominion Government assistance program to provide housing.

They appeared before the Economic Council of British Columbia on January 29, 1935, expessing concern on the plight of Vancouver taxpayers, many of whom were unable to pay their taxes and were losing their homes. Investors in rental housing were unable to earn enough to pay expenses. The report urged that all levels of government become fiscally responsible and not engage in either building or providing an artificial stimulus to building where there was already adequate stock; additional accommodation would lower the earning possibility of existing housing even more, and add to the decline in current values. Building activity should be generated naturally from sound and healthy conditions and private enterprize should not be faced with governmental competition, said the petitioners.

This was a year of strife, as strikes, rallys and relief camp demonstrations were experienced across the country. British Columbia's relief bill topped $8 million in 1935, and unemployed people joined the cross-Canada trek to Ottawa.

Exchange Committees continued to work with Adam Bell, Chairman of the Minimum Wage Board, to formulate workable regulations for minimum wages for engineers, janitors and assistant janitors in local buildings.

The Valuation Committee continued its service of providing low-cost evaluations of properties for individuals, companies and governments. While there were civic financial problems that year as lowered values indicated less taxes, the city did collect just over 70% of taxes levied, a better record than many other Canadian cities during the Depression years.

Exchange Committees contributed to such provincial regulations as elevator safety and landlord and tenant matters. Through study and foresight, they also recognized the need for insurance on properties between the offer date and completion date and ways to protect members against misrepresentation by a vendor, establishing some of the recognized practices still in use today.

In January of 1936 H.A. Roberts was elected President and Col. G.H. Dorrell was named Vice President. This administration was active in studying amendments to the Charter of the City of Vancouver, where it related to License fees, tenant's voting list, the question of Wards and license fees. Some provincial cities and municipalities were having a hard time making ends meet, and the Exchange urged the City of Vancouver to live within its income to prevent putting an increased taxation burden on real property.

H.A. Roberts was re-elected President by acclamation in 1937, along with Colonel G.H. Dorrell as Vice President, and immediately had to address the threat of increased civic taxation. The city was urged to renew its efforts to get financial assistance from senior governments.

This year the Exchange recommended to the Attorney General that there was a need for licensing and bonding for both Business Opportunity Brokers and salesmen.

Minimum wage scales for janitors were still being discussed and revised, and the Exchange urged the Provincial

H. A. Roberts
President, 1936, 1937

*One of the lowest prices was for a 6-room home on
West 26th, asking $3,600 (now assessed at $669,000) and
the highest priced 18-room home on Pine Crescent was
selling for $15,000 (now assessed at $949,700).*

Government to restore taxes on Crown Lands to broaden the city's tax base, and that the Dominion pay more of the share of relief costs.

In 1937 the Exchange membership went up to fifty real estate brokerage companies, with ten other Associate member companies in the insurance and trust field. Business had improved somewhat because the monthly membership fee was restored to $2.50, after having been reduced to $2.00 four years earlier, and the Secretary Frank Hoole was given a salary increase up to $85.00 from the $50.00 monthly he had accepted during the deeper part of the depression. Late that year the Exchange also agreed to an increase in office rent to $40.00 per month for Room 807 in the Yorkshire Building at 525 Seymour Street.

The Canadian Pacific Railway Company Land Department was actively marketing homes in its Shaughnessy land grant. An original typewritten price list for over a hundred and twenty homes dated November, 1937, shows the C.P.R. offered brokers a commission of 5% on the first $5,000 and 2 1/2% on the remainder, but no commission would be paid unless the sale was approved by the Advisory Committee of the railway. The houses could not be shown inside except to bona fide purchasers and "tenants were not to be unnecessarily disturbed".

One of the lowest prices was for a 6-room home on West 26th, asking $3,600 (now assessed at $669,000) and the highest priced 18-room home on Pine Crescent was selling for $15,000 (now assessed at $949,700).

In January, 1938, the Annual Meeting of the Exchange saw Colonel G.H. Dorrell named President for a second time and F.A. Cleland Vice President.

Throughout this year Committee members kept a watching brief on Landlord and Tenant Act amendments, Succession duties, and paid particular attention to a report on Dominion and Provincial relations which would be submitted to the Rowell Royal Commission set up to study this matter. An Exchange delegation appeared before this Commission in Victoria on Tuesday, March 22, 1938, to present a brief on taxation and the undue burden imposed on the City of Vancouver and the need for more assistance from senior governments.

Members discussed False Creek zoning or in-filling with the Town Planning Commission, along with arterial street widening and new zoning regulations.

Even then the high cost of advertising was the bane of a real estate firm's existance. At a meeting in May, 1938, it was first suggested a boycott of local classified ad pages be conducted, but this was amended to take the form of a letter of protest to be included by each Board member on the occasion of payment of their next advertising invoice. News blues often surfaced, as Exchange members took issue with reports on real estate matters, so a Committee of Past Presidents J.P. Nicolls, G.L. Edwards and A. Rout Harvey was appointed to watch for and correct the offending statements when they appeared.

In late 1938, Exchange Minutes reflect a completely opposite point of view to what was later to become a hot housing issue in the '90s. Broker members were expressing concern about the SMALL houses being built in neighbourhoods of better houses, thus destroying values. This situation was to be discussed with the City and its Corporate Counsel.

F.A. Cleland was named President in 1939, along with Vice President W.H. Mowat.

In March the Exchange agreed to cooperate with the Junior Board of Trade in contacting owners of property for which they were agents regarding a general cleanup of the route to be taken during the expected visit that year of King George VI and Queen Elizabeth.

Exchange executives again found it necessary to object to expected tax increases to be imposed by the City, saying that at that time—March, 1939—assessment values were too high to encourage investment in property; a six per cent net income must be accrued to make investment attractive. This was still a depressed period, and a heavy social burden rested on civic shoulders. To help restore tax equity, Exchange members were vigilant in disclosing anomalies such as little or no tax paid by the luxurious new Hotel Vancouver as compared to other hotel properties in the city.

In June of 1939 the C.P.R.'s C.W. McBain told Exchange members that in return for the some $90 million in land grants received by the C.P.R. in 1886, the railway had already paid to date more than $150 millions in taxes and had repaid

The Guinness family investments included a large tract in West Vancouver which had been named British Pacific Properties. A bridge, which was already started to cross First Narrows, would give speedy access within a year. This crossing, named the Lions Gate Bridge, cost just over $6 million when completed in 1938. In a presentation to the Exchange in March, R.W. Keyserlingk, Manager of British Pacific Properties, said the company expected one thousand homes to rise there within the next ten years and asked for the cooperation of Exchange members in selling the lots at a commission of ten per cent, because the company wanted to do as little of the selling as possible.

F. A. Cleland
President, 1939, 1940

In September 1939 the Exchange also reminded the provincial legislators that in 1888 the government had paid one hundred per cent of education costs until Vancouver insisted on paying a portion of same to have input into educational matters. By 1939 Vancouver taxpayers were burdened with sixty-two per cent of educational costs and it was felt that more provincial revenue should be provided, with the suggestion of a sales tax (food excepted) advanced. In the opinion of the Exchange, a sales tax would mean all citizens would pay a fair share of educational expenses, taking them out of the category of a land tax.

all its loans with interest, something which no other railroad had ever accomplished.

During this year the subject of Business Brokers' licenses had still not been resolved, as the government was still suggesting licensing through amendments to the Real Estate Agents Licensing Act and the Exchange was still registering objections to that move.

The Exchange also dealt with the subject of Shaughnessy Heights restrictions and put forth a case for modification to allow remodelling of larger buildings into suites or duplexes, and many meetings with the Shaughnessy Heights Property Owners Association were held.

Business may have been going on as usual locally, but on the international scene more serious events had erupted into World War 2, with Europe in a full state of emergency, and England's Commonwealth nations girding to support the cause.

A special presentation to Exchange members by Mr. Howard Green, local Member of Parliament, in October, 1939, outlined the powers of the federal government during this state of war, and emphasized that Canada was more united than at any time since World War One. Industry across the country had mobilized to provide the needs of the military then building across the country, and the government had taken a strong stand against profiteering. The agriculture and lumber industries were deemed most important, and shipbuilding would be developed, so Canada would end the war in a much better position than when it entered.

This remark may have been prophetic, but did not reveal to any listener just how many years of war and horror would have to be endured before that "better position" would be realized.

CHAPTER SIX

THE FORTIES

F.A. Cleland was appointed President of the Exchange for a second consecutive year in 1940, and E. Leonard Boultbee was named Vice President.

At that time Vancouver was experiencing a small boom, as the city got its share of wartime economic activity. Building permit values rose from some $6 million in 1939 to over $8 million in 1940, and rose again in 1941 to $9.2 million, which included construction of 2,125 new homes.

After the "phoney war" in Europe erupted into full blown conflict, war industry began to expand in Vancouver, and with it came the problems of growth.

Vancouver Real Estate Exchange officials were kept busy reviewing various situations which were predictable results of both the depression years and the growing national war effort. During those early war years Vancouver still supported a large number of citizens on relief, and the city proposed a new Bylaw to force maintenance of rental properties. Further, the federal government imposed a "rent standstill", through its Rental Control Administration.

Rental surveys were carried out with the cooperation of the Associated Property Owners Association. President Cleland agreed to serve on the Executive Committee of this group because of the common goals and concerns held by members of both groups. The joint review of existing rents and operating costs was helpful to both local and national government administrations. A special brief was sent to the City of Vancouver, noting that long-term rentals to Depression Relief tenants, coupled with the wartime freezing of rents, caused many hardships for property owners who could not come up with funds for all improvements deemed necessary by the city.

Another cause for concern was that Vancouver City's real estate department staff advertised city owned housing for sale or rent, undercutting the market rates of private properties represented by owners or real estate agents.

In those days of Vancouver development, licensees putting together a real estate transaction were often required to go one step further than the actual sale. Many lots were sold to people who then needed help with building plans and contracting, so the salesman would arrange the full package. At that time a fine 1,200 square foot home could be built for approximately $3.00 per square foot.

Sales licensees were not members of the Exchange, so Bob Pound, then a 9-year real estate veteran, was instrumental in forming the Vancouver Real Estate Salesmen's Association in 1940. He also served as its President during a short two-year existence. This group compiled data on the activities of unlicensed agents and salespeople and appeared before the Vancouver Real Estate Exchange to outline the problems that might occur if unlicensed sales people were allowed to serve the public, and asked help in stopping the practice. The Association also asked the Exchange to support its request for payment of the Exchange minimum commission of $25.00 per lot to salesmen who arranged a sale on any of the city's tax-sale lots.

Monthly meetings of members of the Exchange, held in the York Room of the Georgia Hotel, attracted full houses of 50 or more members each month. This attendance and member commitment allowed fast passage of new or amended Bylaws, as notice of motion could be given one month, followed by full discussion and voting at the next meeting. One such amendment in March, 1940, established a commission scale for property management services at a rate commensurate to the amount of work involved, with a minimum of $5.00, and for collecting rents a minimum monthly charge of $1.00 was set.

That year members established a practice still used today in one form or another—Agents' Opens and tours; the Programme Committee launched a "fair market evaluation plan" for selected properties by having several agents give their own value estimate at a monthly meeting, followed by full discussion of their reasons for valuation by all those present.

In the spring of 1940 the Exchange was again asked by Adam Bell of the Minimum Wage Board to become involved in a Committee studying a request for revision and regulation of janitors' wages.

Exchange members on the Committee chaired by Bell included E.L. Boultbee, M. Davidson, J.F. Kelly, S.V. Smith and J.P. Roberts. Previous rental survey information was expanded to include the different sizes and requirements of rental buildings, the work loads and perquisites of current janitorial staff members. Many hours were spent in meetings with representatives of the Trades & Labour Council, Stationery Steam Engineers and Building Owners and Managers. After much deliberation, the Exchange proposed an increase of 10 per cent in the existing minimum wage for janitors with a $5.00 minimum daily payment.

In June that year Exchange members took time out to play—golf, that is. A golf tournament held at Point Grey Golf and Country Club proved a perfect time for Vancouver licensees to socialize with those from the New Westminster Real Estate Exchange and the Bellingham Realty Board.

In November Exchange members observed a moment of silence on the loss of J.W. Allan, one of the ten charter members in March, 1919.

Leonard Boultbee was named President and A. Rout Harvey Vice President at the 1941 Annual Meeting. Business Brokers licensing again became the subject of meeting action. Members of the Exchange, the Better Business Bureau and representatives of both the Provincial and Vancouver police met to discuss this licensing, knowing the public would welcome the protection of licensing and bonding of business opportunity brokers. The Better Business Bureau introduced some $83,000 in questionable transactions brought to its attention in the past 9 months. All agreed to gather briefs for Attorney General the Honorable G.S. Wismer, who agreed with their concerns and urged the Committee to continue its strong lobby to get the legislation passed that fall. Despite much work towards this end, it was to take more time.

It was proposed to tighten up the Real-estate Agents' Licensing Act administration, by cooperation between the city, which issued business licenses to real estate companies in Vancouver and the Provincial government. They agreed to exchange lists of qualified licensees to help identify firms or persons who had not obtained licenses and bonds.

This year Exchange members got wholeheartedly behind the war effort and started a drive to sell War Savings Certificates, but also kept a watchful eye on other legislation coming down thick and fast. Briefs were sent to the Oil Controller to consider real estate firms exempt from gas rationing, and—on behalf of their landlord clients—also addressed fixed coal prices and the need for a reasonable supply to be kept for civilian use.

An Exchange Committee also tried to forestall the federal

E. L. Boultbee
President, 1941

Excess Profits Tax, where highest income received by real estate licensees in a four-year period was to be deemed to have been received in each of those four years, resulting in inequitable taxing. The Exchange sent a brief to the Minister of National Revenue, asking for exemptions already granted to Insurance Agents and Lawyers, whose annual income fluctuated as much as that of real estate brokers.

Federal wartime Rent Control had been introduced to prevent gouging, but according to many owners, it restricted repairs and maintenance because rents were set from ten to fifteen per cent too low. Arbitrations accelerated and many new valuations needed, but the low housing vacancy level became a real concern as the year advanced. Low rent levels were blamed for the lack of any new investment in rental housing. A 15% non-resident holdback on rentals was inequitable, and the Vancouver Real Estate Exchange endorsed the idea of a locally based Committee to deal more effectively and expeditiously with housing matters on a local level.

A wartime legacy was a $50,000 Armoury built at UBC in 1941. This was also the year that the provincial Liberal and Conservative parties agreed to a Coalition government, which reigned for the next decade.

City coffers were suffering, however, because the Dominion Government was taking over more and more city property for the war effort. The city lost tax revenue as the senior government didn't pay tax, nor did it even pay the full cost of civic services. The Exchange and other ratepayer groups strenuously protested when the city sought to rectify its economic position by removal of the 20 Mill limit and the raising of the mill rate, which would impact sorely on already strapped property owners.

But it was not only the city and citizens who were seeking extra funding. After much deliberation, Exchange Executive placed a dues increase before the membership, and it was finally approved late that year that Membership Dues be raised to $35.00 per annum, and a charge of $2.00 per salesperson, payable quarterly, be imposed for companies with two or more salesmen. It was also decided a membership drive would assist the Exchange's fortunes as new members began to attend.

On December 7 that year, the Japanese attacked Pearl Harbour, and a new level of activity was added to the agendas of this and any other civic group—war

Things moved fast during the early war years, and Vancouver's population rose to 275,400 in 1941. Some 20,000 of those people were working in the shipyards and thousands more in the Boeing Aircraft plant on Sea Island. New industries developed as iron foundries completed bigger ship castings than ever before and new plywood techniques were developed for airplane manufacture. Skilled workers flocked to the city.

preparedness. Board members acted quickly to focus on safety, fire prevention and emergency actions, cooperating with local wardens of the Air Raid Patrol (ARP) to determine precautionary measures and coordinating the necessary disaster training for janitorial staff of residential and commercial buildings with the Building Owners & Managers Association.

In January of 1942 A.R. Harvey and W.C. Atherton were named President and Vice President of the Exchange, inheriting the on-going attempt to ensure a level of licensing to monitor the actions of Business Brokers. Many war related problems such as gas rationing, building supplies priorities and, of course, rent control, continued on the agenda. A local representative was appointed by the Administrator of Housing Rental from Ottawa, however, and it was hoped that local disparities would be settled more quickly. J.S. McGuire, appointed Rentals Control Officer, tried hard to dispell Exchange members' perception that he held undue bias for the tenant, which resulted in growing difficulty for building owners. An example, pointed out by Howard Meakin, was that notice to vacate required from the owner was three months, but only one month from the tenant. Meakin suggested requiring three months rent in advance, and McGuire agreed this could be done if in writing.

The Valuation Committee was asked for an opinion of value on expropriated portions of the Airport on Sea Island. After considerable discussion and study of sales in the vicinity, a February meeting of the Committee determined the value of portions of Section 36, Block 5N, Range 7W, (parcel one of 31.07 acres and parcel two of 4.40 acres) at $800 per acre, or the total for the two parcels, $28,376.00.

Rising city taxes were a concern, and once again there were complaints around the board room table of escalating costs to operate the school system.

In February, 1942, after much study and discussion, Exchange Officials—like so many other groups in the city—resolved that due to the enormous danger of hostile attack it was advisable that all those of Japanese descent regardless of age or sex, be removed from the Coastal area to prevent their support of Japanese invaders in the event of an attack. As history shows, action was taken on this suggestion, and those of Japanese origin were sent to Interior and Prairie points.

In April a letter was sent to Ottawa protesting the manner in which a newly introduced War Risk Insurance was being

A. Rout Harvey
President, 1942-1944

organized. The Exchange said the government should assume liability for all bomb damage instead of planning to set up another bureaucracy and imposing high premium costs which would have to be paid by residents of both the vulnerable east and west coast areas.

Committees continued to work with Rental Control officer J.S. Maguire to reduce the complications existing in rent control, such as terms that required an owner to give the tenant a longer notice period than the tenant was required to give the landlord.

Exchange Minutes of May, 1942, reveal the first local reference to a national association. Harry A. Roberts was noted to have suggested that "a national Canadian Board would be useful" in dealing with national issues.

Later that month a joint committee of representatives from B.C. Electric, the Board of Trade and Regional Government traffic, several city aldermen and Vancouver Exchange members met to discuss staggering work hours to relieve traffic congestion that had increased over 26% from the previous year.

The Exchange agreed to try the suggested 4:30 closings in an effort to spread rush hour traffic away from the existing 5 to 5:45 p.m. time slot. This new "travel window" from 4:30 p.m. to 6 p.m. would give street cars time to make two trips instead of one in rush hour. In real estate offices that often meant salesmen manned clerical needs after 4:30 as support staff observed the new hours.

Effects of the global war were affecting many areas of life now. Milk deliveries were seriously cut back due to gas shortages, and the Wartime Prices and Trade Board proposed cutting hours for retail stores. The Exchange sent letters of protest to Ottawa and the city, saying there were already many vacant stores and restricting business hours further would surely lower the profit margin, already hit by rationing, shortages and price controls. The Retail Merchants Association countered by trying to restrict licensing of any new stores to protect its members' current level of service. These subjects were hotly debated during the next months. Mayor J.W. Cornett cast blame on business opportunity brokers selling retail stores with non existant goodwill, and Board President A. Rout Harvey was quick to outline the years of on-going but so-far unsuccessful attempts by the Exchange, the Board of Trade, City and provincial police to establish licensing legislation for such

Austin Taylor, Chairman of the B.C. Securities Commission, appointed Past President Leonard Boultbee as Chief Administrator of the Japanese Interior camps for a three year period. A veteran of the First World War, Boultbee was considered the man with the knowledge and energy to locate inland sites for the over 11,000 Japanese Canadians who were removed from coastal areas. He was lauded by colleagues and government spokesmen, but more significantly, his charges all spoke highly of his administration and his personal concern for their comfort, health and happiness. Over thirty years later, when many of those who had been interned were scattered far and wide across Canada, their high regard had not wavered. At the time of Leonard Boultbee's death in early 1977, the Japanese Community collectively reiterated its accolades of Boultbee's supportive administration.

Due to wartime activity, most bottom lines were much
improved from the previous decade, and the Exchange
was able to increase Secretary Frank Hoole's salary
to $100 per month, a welcome move since that salary
had been reduced drastically during the Depression.

individuals as a consumer protection.

In August, 1942, the City Electrical Department required installation of new wiring in older existing buildings to prevent condemnation. An Exchange delegation—the voice of reason then, as the Board so often is now—made the point that while some older buildings may be at risk, most wiring was perfectly satisfactory and in any case, it was almost impossible to get replacement material in wartime.

At the same time Reverand W. N. Byers, Secretary of the Lord's Day Alliance, expressed concern about the industry practice of Sunday home inspection. The Executive Committee agreed to discuss this matter at the next full meeting of Exchange members. After full discussion, it was recommended but not required of all members that they refrain from holding Sunday inspections.

Exchange executive dealt with many questions from all levels of governments due to the all encompassing expertise gathered by real estate brokers, investors and property managers. The Regional War Labour Board again requested assistance on the question of janitors' wages. The Exchange recommendation was that an increase was justified for janitors in buildings where heating had changed from oil to hand-fired coal.

At an October general meeting an address on recent trends in legal cases involving commissions gave Exchange executive concern that various listing forms then in use by Exchange members were not as valid as had been believed. This led to much consultation, many Committee meetings and study sessions, finally leading to a uniform Exclusive Listing and Open Listing form for use by members of the Real Estate Exchange.

Due to wartime activity, most bottom lines were much improved from the previous decade, and the Exchange was able to increase Secretary Frank Hoole's salary to $100 per month, a welcome move since that salary had been reduced drastically during the Depression.

These were the days Vancouverites had to depend on lots of sweaters for warmth. The Fuel Control Board and the

Rental Control Board cooperated to announce a reduction in acceptable heat in business and residential buildings. Tenants were told heat levels would be kept between 64 and 68 degrees Fahrenheit for the duration. Many meetings were held between the Exchange and the various wartime bureaucracies set up, as Exchange brokers tried to clarify the requirements on rent controls notice on both the tenant and landlord side, the problems when a new owner became landlord, and penalties or recourse in case of tenant sub-let, theft or outright fraud.

At the Annual Meeting of the Exchange in January, 1943, A. Rout Harvey was named to a second consecutive year as President, and H.E. Bond was named his Vice President. The Executive was immediately immersed in discussions with Russel S. Smart, K.C., the Real Property Administrator in Ottawa. His new federal Housing Conversion Plan involved government leasing housing for conversion into two or more living units for the duration and a further three year period after the war ended.

Past Presidents A.M.J. English and D.W. Reeve, along with S.V. Smith, E.B. Cameron, J. Walker and Exchange Secretary Frank Hoole studied the plan and made various recommendations. Smart wanted the Exchange to survey available properties and submit this information, but the Executive recommended the government advertise directly to owners to get them to join the plan. It was noted many privately held 6 to 10 room older homes in the $3,000 to $6,000 bracket were most suitable for conversion, but a large number had already been converted under Vancouver city by-laws by that time. The federal department was also given professional advice on equitable lease return if they wished to encourage more owners to join the plan.

More immediate in its effect on consumers was the new wartime rule that 12 months notice must be given to tenants, so a delegation from both the Westminster and Vancouver Real Estate Exchanges met with Donald Gordon, Chairman of the Wartime Prices and Trade Board to outline the many inequities for owners of rented property. Gordon, however, was adamant, and no changes would be made during the war years.

The Wartime Housing Authority was acquiring city property and building houses at that time, but the Exchange was concerned that the government was not paying its fair share of taxes. It was known that North Vancouver had lost consid-

Concerned that severe wartime housing restrictions would erode property rights and seriously damage the real estate profession, Exchange executive joined with others across Canada and agreed to become members of a new Canadian Association if dues were not too high. Having a unified national voice for the real estate industry was as important then as now. The Exchange noted it favoured a type of Associate Membership at a fee of around $50.00 per annum, because only Dominion matters would be referred to this group.

erable tax revenue through the Wartime Housing scheme, and the Exchange continued to monitor and register concern about this situation. Lumber, which was in such short supply, seemed to be released for this government housing but not for private sector construction, and letters of protest were sent to the Board of Trade, local Members of Parliament and the Controllers of Timber and Construction.

The Construction Controller was R.J. Lecky, who was also Secretary of the Building Construction Industries Exchange in B.C. In a speech to the brokers, Lecky said under wartime control licenses were required for all private sector building projects, but projects paid for directly by the government were exempt from licenses. There were shortages in building materials, particularly for private builders, while the government was building "temporary" wartime housing under the National Housing Act. All interested groups were working together to try to solve this housing supply problem. The Home Building industry lobbied Ottawa, spoke to C.D. Howe and—like the real estate industry before them—proceeded to organize a national association (now called the Canadian Home Builders Association) which would voice its needs more strongly with the national government.

Despite problems those war years visited upon citizens of Vancouver, a vigorous and generous war effort continued. Many real estate and insurance brokers were advertising: *"chase the huns with victory guns—buy victory bonds, the best investment for postwar homes and happiness"*

The Pacific Northwest was intrigued and excited about the building of the Alaska highway in 1943 and another housing phenomenon became part of the local lexicon— pre-fabricated housing. Architect C.B.K. Van Norman told Exchange members that President Roosevelt had ordered 45,000 pre-fabricated houses to assuage his country's housing shortage. A Vancouver plant produced most of Canada's excellent pre-fab product, and these had been shipped as far north as Alaska and east to the prairies and Ottawa.

Even in 1943 a common complaint was both the level of assessment and late receipt of notices. Some owners received their tax assessments as late as December 29th and deadline for registering appeals was January 4th. The Exchange took this problem to the City Assessor and eventually this period was lengthened to the benefit of owners.

It was about this time the Exchange arranged with the Town Planning Commission to have its zoning maps available to broker-members on a regular basis, and this continued for the convenience of practitioners well into the computer era of the last decade.

That year the Exchange and other Associations and businesses working in the city of Vancouver were given the opportunity to register to vote in civic elections.

By mid-year the war was at its height but Vancouver businessmen—including Real Estate Exchange members—started holding meetings to discuss recovery plans for post-war years. It was recognized that an unusual shifting of population might occur, leaving some Canadian towns empty and others straining at their borders; employment, production and distribution must be maintained at a high level to start reduction of the huge Dominion war debt; war time restrictions would have to be relaxed gradually and attention given to filling a heavy demand for consumer goods while preventing inflationary pressure.

In early 1944 A. Rout Harvey was named President of the Real Estate Exchange for an unprecedented third consecutive year, Harry E. Bond named his Vice President. This was again a year of struggling with the ever changing regulations of wartime rent control, supply and service lacks and limitations. An example was real estate salesmen being denied the privilege to purchase either new or second hand tires because their work was not considered essential. It was also a period the Exchange started discussing examination, courses or experience in a real estate office as prerequisites of licensing.

Affordable housing for the working man was then—as now—a special goal. Many property owners were still complaining about the building of SMALL houses on lots next to their homes, feeling this "under-development" would cause a decrease in the value of their own larger properties.

The Exchange continued to meet with the Rental Control Board of Canada to keep in touch with ever–increasing regulation and also worked closely with the National Bureau of Statistics which was gathering data for use in allowable rental rate increases.

A growing city population put pressure on housing development and Exchange member-company H.A. Roberts proved to be an innovator by introducing the first prefabricated subdivision to the Vancouver home buyer. In a dramatic one-day demonstration in April, 1944, the first home in a new 30-home subdivision called "Orchard Grove", was raised in the Fremlin/Laurel area, north of 70th Avenue and east of where the first South Granville White Spot was located. Started at 9:00 a.m., high-speed construction saw carpenters, plumbers, electricians and roofers working together to install solid two-inch exterior walls, fit windows, complete the indoor fireplace plumbing and wiring, shingle the roof and build the chimney. Exterior work was completed by 6:00 p.m., when window boxes complete with flowers were attached, part of the front garden turfed, bedding plants in full blossom planted in their beds, while Hudson's Bay employees busily placed furniture in this brand new show home.

To compare these home prices to those of today would require considerable skill to factor in economic differences in dollar and housing values between 1944 and 1994. However, 50 years ago the total building program, land and 30 houses, was brought to market at an overall cost of $125,000, selling from $4,600 up per unit. Driving through the area today, what appear to be one or two of the original houses can still be seen, but most have been replaced by apartments, duplexes and larger homes.

In September, 1944, C.E. Purnell, President of the fledgling Canadian Association of Real Estate Boards headquartered in Toronto, spoke to Exchange members on difficulties suffered by property owners through imposition of wartime rental control. Many rents had been frozen at levels common in the depression era and had not kept even with the cost of living so small investors were being hurt financially. He also noted that following the Veterans' Land Act, brokers might be prohibited from dealing under the National Housing Act and this right must be established. Purnell said that eastern Real Estate Boards had been asked to appraise properties for the Veterans Land Act amounting to millions of dollars without payment because it was deemed their "patriotic duty".

Because of these national threats to the industry as a whole, Purnell asked that Vancouver brokers join CAREB as active members and contribute to efforts addressing these inequities. The past year's Affiliate Membership in the national association was reconsidered because of these and other Dominion-wide problems expected when the war was finally over. At a monthly meeting on Wednesday, October 11, members of the Vancouver Real Estate Exchange agreed join the Canadian Association of Real Estate Boards at an annual fee of $5.00 per member. It is understood that the Victoria Real Estate Board and New Westminster Real Estate Exchange members took the same step and became CAREB members at that time, strengthening western representation.

Late in that year executives of the Vancouver Exchange and the Victoria Board started discussions on amendments to the Real-estate Agents Licensing Act, touching on such matters as unqualified salesmen, the potential problems of part time licensees, and suggested increases in bond requirements. Later a delegation of Vancouver, North Vancouver, New Westminster and Victoria practitioners were given a good hearing in Victoria and promises were made to "tighten up the Act" as soon as possible.

The Exchange also addressed major problems in both the Veterans Land Act, 1942 and the War Service Grants Act, 1944, which restricted real estate agents from receiving any remuneration when their services were requested by sellers dealing with veterans as purchasers. The Government insisted it did not wish to deprive brokers of commissions, but only to protect veterans from unscrupulous practitoners.

The 1945 Exchange Directorate, under President Harry E. Bond and Vice President W.C. Atherton, continued the campaign for more rights under these federal acts, and Bond joined the CAREB Directorate as a Western representative. Despite cooperative argument and continued debate on this matter, there was no overall solution. Finally, Section 33 was deleted in 1946, following an Exchange suggestion that commission be reduced to 5% on the sale of farms to Veterans only, under the V.L.A. The Act also prohibited agents from charging commission on the sale of land owned by a veteran and this restriction was not repealed until 1959.

During these war years Vancouver was bursting at the seams and housing shortages were everyone's concern. Due in part to shortage of contruction materials, the Controller of Construction would approve construction of homes of an estimated cost of $1,500 or less and 528 square feet without Federal licenses required, but this created a hardship on

One gets a 1990s flashback reading Exchange minutes of 1944. The subject of illegal suites and the broker's responsibility towards both seller and buyer were the subject of many discussions. Conversion of homes in one-family dwelling zones made it necessary for brokers to educate their salesmen on the bylaws and full disclosure that the suites were not legal in one-family districts. This same situation faces today's practioners in every community.

those who wished to build more substantial housing. At a February meeting Len Boultbee reported that in the previous week ten permits for homes over $1,500 had been issued, but one hundred for smaller homes below that value had been approved. There was a real concern that too much low quality housing would result.

By special request of Housing Administrator, Air Vice Marshall L.S. Stevenson, Exchange President Harry Bond became a member of his Advisory Committee. A new Shelter Order # 484 was proclaimed to protect the tenancy of those already housed or in need of alternate accommodation to stop outsiders from freezing out older tenants and to prevent overcrowding in already congested neighbourhoods. Availability of cooking facilities was one of the main determinants authorizing a unit for use as housing.

Soon young men would be returning from the Service, marry and need housing. The Administrator asked real estate brokers to help pinpoint available housing and urged people to not occupy more room than they actually needed.

Soldiers who were former Vancouver residents would be given every assistance and a housing permit without question, but those moving here from other areas would not. In those days it wasn't simply a matter of visiting Vancouver and deciding to buy a house. If a newcomer was occupying rental "domestic accommodation" he might be authorized to obtain a house, but living in a hotel or tourist cabin would not establish that eligibility. Cases such as employees moved in by employers were reviewed on individual merit.

These were difficult times, both for residents and real estate practitioners, but those professionals kept working for everyone, liaising on a regular basis with the Emergency Shelter Administrator, Civic Planning and Parks Committee, Construction and Builders Association, Controller of Construction, the Board of Trade and the Town Planning Commission. It was the combined work of all these groups, sharing expertise in all housing and business aspects, that helped ease the transition from wartime conditions to peacetime living.

Because of real estate activity, delays in the Land Registry procedure had been increasing and by mid 1944 were causing a three-day lag in registering liens against properties. Exchange members were urged to keep a watch on this situation and make several searches before paying out any monies. Vancouver Sun classified ads from May, 1945, show

H. E. Bond
President, 1945

A housing crisis had even hit University of British Columbia at that time as returning servicemen and other students searched for living accommodation near the campus. Army huts were eventually employed to house some 1,500 student veterans in both single or family accommodation. They were also used to provide extra lecture rooms for the burgeoning student body, bouyed by returning servicemen with educational gratuities from a grateful government.

a west side 25-year old six room home on 18th Avenue near Cambie for $5,150 and, for those willing to go further afield, a "seven room modern home on ten acres in Burquitlam, lots of outbuildings and fruit trees" for $4,500.

In the depths of the depression, the Exchange Entrance fee of $25.00 for new members had been suspended due to hard times, but in April of 1945 it was reinstated because then potential new members were quite able to pay.

By the time V.E. Day had been celebrated in 1945, landlords had endured frozen rental rates since early January, 1940. In a report to the Rental Control Board in mid-June, the Exchange addressed many inequities and suggested first that at least a 15% increase on the basic rentals would give owners an adjustment that would recover costs. During that five years, many tenants who rented at frozen rates, sub-let at two or three times the controlled rate, while the owner was still required to pay increases in taxes and other costs on his lower income. The Exchange suggested this profiteering by tenants should be eliminated and also asked for an end to the "seasonal notice" which meant tenancies could not be terminated in winter.

As can often be the case, a few "fly by night" companies were taking advantage of the post-war activity, some of which was driving prices of housing up. At an Exchange meeting Len Boultbee told of warning a returned service man he was paying $1,500 too much for a home, but housing shortages forced the buyer to pay it anyway. F.A. Cleland told of a house he evaluated at $3,500 but the owner insisted on asking $5,200. Cleland refused to show it at that price but another agent did, and sure enough, the age-old market force of sharp demand and not enough product caused the home to sell within a week at the inflated price.

To combat this type of activity and undignified real estate advertising that was beginning to appear, the Exchange decided an ad campaign of its own should be conducted. It wanted the public to know that many qualified, ethical real estate agent-members of the Exchange were available, and the public would protect itself by employing these reliable firms.

A recently demobbed air force veteran, S.W. Taylor, was introduced to Exchange Executive on September 10th, 1945, as the newly appointed Superintendent of Insurance, with responsibility for the Real-estate Agents' Licensing Act, and Registrar of Companies. He discussed amendments to the

Real Estate Agents' Licensing Act that had been suggested by the Victoria, North Vancouver, New Westminster and Vancouver real estate associations, and these discussions set the stage for many industry procedures still observed today.

Regulations for business brokerage where real property, chattels and goodwill were included were formulated. All real estate agents would be required to prove financial capability, salesmen would work under the direction of an agent, and be required to mention the employing agency's name in all advertising. At that time the required bond in communities with a population of 10,000 or more was $2,500 for the agent and $1,000 for salesmen.

It was suggested that a salesman work in that capacity for a minimum of two years before an agent's license would be granted and in 1947 an Order-in-Council was passed approving that procedure. It was also suggested that a real estate agent must have a place of business other than his residence in centres of over 5,000 population, set up a trust account and keep a complete record of receipts and disbursements for immediate access at the Superintendent's request. It was also suggested at that time that full particulars of all sales be recorded and both parties to any transaction must be supplied with all such documentation. Finally, no agent or salesman would take net listings, only listings at a gross price out of which the vendor would pay the agreed commission. In 1946 the Act was amended, permitting regulations to be established for qualifying license applicants and the further amendments were passed by the Legislature in 1948.

The War Transit Control was withdrawn, Vancouver stores were extending their open hours to 5:30 p.m. once more, and businesses again wrestled with the matter of staggered closing hours. Pedestrian traffic counts, which had been started at major downtown locations by the Exchange, became more important than ever as population increased.

The Canadian Association was addressing post-war regulation and legislation in Ottawa and-in a minuted passage that sounds all too familiar even today-was asking for a dues increase from $5.00 per member to $7.50 plus the establishment of a "fighting fund" of at least $100,000 with which to continue its political action. One active local participant was John Roberts, younger brother of 1936/37 President Harry Roberts and a recently returned veteran

B.C. Electric had not been able to add or update equipment during wartime and downtown workers created a heavy load at rush hour.

himself, who joined CAREB's Committee to oppose the Veterans Land Act as then written.

In 1946 W.C. Atherton was appointed President, along with Vice President Gordon Bell. It was this administration which created the Honorary Life Member status, with the first individual so honored A.M.J. English, a founding member of the Exchange, who had recently retired after 27 years of membership.

The Exchange was diligent in keeping watch on local assessments and civic activities. Street widening was being proposed on Robson Street and the city engineer had no plans to pay compensation for the 7 feet he needed. A Committee was struck to study and deal with this matter, and another was still working on Rental Controls, which had not yet been entirely eliminated. A new form of Interim Receipt was adopted, and the Exchange expanded its recently initiated Discipline Committee, investigating complaints about the actions and ethics of its own members.

Motor traffic was mounting as manufacturers were again selling to the civilian market, and B.C. Electric was planning to introduce Trolley Buses and take up the streetcar tracks. Ironically-nearly half a century later, city officials are considering reactivating streetcars by using the CP Rail corridor along the south shore of False Creek so streetcars can run between the Main Street SkyTrain station to Vanier Park. This would reduce auto traffic and give transit riders quick access to the popular destinations of the Vancouver Museum and Planetarium, Granville Island and Science World. Because of increasing auto density in 1946, a brand new innovation was tried in the downtown core—Parking Meters were installed for the first time, and one nickel in the slot bought one hour's parking on downtown streets.

Returning veterans, protesting the lack of housing and slow government actions on their behalf, occupied the old Hotel Vancouver, then standing un-used at the corner of Granville and Georgia.

Rent control was still in place and again Exchange members sent briefs to government agencies to try to effect increases on rent levels that had been set in 1940.

Dean Mansell and J.C. McPherson headed the Exchange in 1947, and once again the subject of Sunday opens was raised. The Exchange wrote to all three local papers asking that mention of Sunday showings be eliminated from any future real estate advertising, and members were again

W. C. Atherton
President, 1946

asked to refrain from this practice which upset many citizens. We're told by some members who still remember those days, the practice of real estate was somewhat "loose", in that few vendors would sign listings and it was "open season" on most of the generally open listings the salespeople were trying to serve.

A move towards all-day Wednesday closings by the Retail Merchants' Association was perceived by Exchange members as a threat to downtown business and property values and an encouragement to cross-border shopping.

At the Annual Meeting of 1947, Superintendent Taylor addressed Exchange members on the question of licensing. He reviewed the number of licenses, saying that in 1938 there had been 900 licenses registered throughout B.C., but by the end of December, 1946, there were 4,350 licensed agents and salesmen. He recounted the difficulties of controlling this number, outlined some new regulations and asked for Exchange cooperation in setting up a better regulatory body.

The Vancouver Exchange hosted its first CAREB Conference in October, 1947 and planning started early. Topics of interest to the times included Immigration, covered by Colonel C.C. Merritt and Federal Taxation and Real Estate, the subject of Mr. Leon Ladner. That year the Convention Commmittee had to budget $105 for rental of the Hotel Vancouver's Mayfair Room during the three day conference.

An Exchange Committee revised the Interim Receipt form adopted in the previous decade to clarify the requirement of commission payment by owners. It was approved and put into circulation in mid September, 1947.

In April of 1947, Provincial Income Tax had come into being, with a 5% tax on companies being collected for the province by the Dominion. These early post-war years were fraught with economic concerns. A suggested five-day week made some think costs would go up and production down, schools and colleges were overcrowded and the housing supply was still very limited.

Dean S. Mansell was named to a second term as President in 1948 and Stanley V. Smith was elected Vice President. This administration decided to change the name of the Exchange, returning to its original 19th century name of Vancouver Real Estate Board. Solicitor R.H. Tupper gave assistance at that time and the firm he helped found, Bull, Housser and Tupper, has acted for the Board ever since. Approval of the

Dean Mansell
President, 1947, 1948

Membership was given on St. Patrick's Day—March 17, 1948, and memberships were transferred from the Vancouver Exchange to the Vancouver Real Estate Board as soon as incorporation under the Societies Act was completed, which happened by the end of the month. Exchange shareholders automatically became Board members and remaining Exchange assets reverted to the Board. Frank Hoole, who had been Exchange Secretary for 28 years, was appointed Board Secretary.

Further amendments to the Real-estate Agents' Licensing Act were under constant study, as this group had committed itself to continuing self-scrutiny and professional improvement. In March, John P. Roberts, who at that time was a Regional Vice President of CAREB, told Directors there were Provincial Associations in Ontario, Alberta and Nova Scotia. Forming a provincial association should also be considered in British Columbia to strengthen licensing laws and to represent the industry's views to legislators in Victoria.

Many Lower Mainlanders well remember the Fraser River floods of 1948. Indeed, 1948 was a year when flood disasters occured in Alberta and Manitoba as well, but of course locally, everyone concentrated on B.C. flood relief. A quota of $15,000 was set for the real estate and building owners and managers' group to raise, so a group of canvassers was assigned to visit each member company for donations.

Board members then, as now, agreed to an Arbitration process to resolve commission differences between offices. As always, the Board continued its watching brief on civic assessments, and as part of its mandate, on commission scales as related to the current state of the real estate market.

A Committee consisting of Past Exchange Presidents Len Boultbee and J.C. McPherson and Board Vice President Stanley Smith prepared a commission change resolution which was approved by the membership on November 17th, 1948. Rates set at that time changed little until competition policy abolished the right of Associations to set fee and commission standards. Commission scales were amended to 5% up to $100,000 and 2 1/2% over that amount. Standard fees were also laid down for inventories, negotiating tenancies, preparing tax returns, etc. The scale of minimum fee for valuing non agricultural property or acreage was set at $10.00 if the value was $3,000 or less; rising $2.50 in stages of value until a $20.00 charge would be levied for valuation of properties between $10,000 and $20,000 and an extra

$1.00 charged per thousand of value over $20,000.

The Board's Valuation Committee set a scale of $3.00 per $1,000 of value when it was required to evaluate civic or private property. A commission rate of 5% on the full sale of farm properties was also set at that time, but it was the practice of brokers to negotiate a higher commission based on distance and value.

By the end of 1948 there were still long delays in land registry, and in a December speech to Board members, Registrar H.L. Robinson stressed the need for extreme care to prevent frauds but mostly the need to correct documentation that had been sloppily done by real estate practitioners. He urged members to teach their salespeople not only HOW to complete the documentation, but WHY, so they would be more careful.

In 1949 Stanley Smith was named President and Leslie C. Creery Vice President. This administration continued to liaise with the Superintendent and Minister on the Real-estate Agents' Licensing Act, helping to prevent part-time licenses being granted, and checking that proper offices were being maintained and advertising guidelines observed.

Formation of a B.C. Association of Real Estate Boards was discussed with Boards in North Vancouver, New Westminster, Surrey and Victoria and this Board agreed to provide the initial $150 for registration, to be recovered proportionately from those other Boards, and it was in place by year-end.

At the same time, the Superintendent of Insurance was setting up an Advisory Committee to establish regulations and amendments to the Real Estate Agents' Licensing Act. Of the seven members appointed, four were from the Vancouver Board, including Messrs S.V. Smith, L.C. Creery, D.S. Mansell and E.P. Taylor. The other three represented New Westminster, North Vancouver and Surrey.

As the decade drew to a close, members were saddened by the resignation of Frank Hoole due to declining health. Hoole had served as Board Secretary for 29 years. In recognition of his loyal service, Board directors decided to supplement Hoole's retirement income up to a total income of $100 monthly, and he was named an Honorary Life Member of the Board. Mr. Tempest deWolf was named Secretary at that time, and a new era of change and development began.

S. V. Smith
President, 1949, 1950

CHAPTER SEVEN

THE FIFTIES—
A COOPERATIVE
DIRECTION

Opening ceremonies for new
Granville Bridge, February,
1954.

A copy of classified
advertising in the Vancouver
Province newspaper of
February 9th, 1950, shows a
three bedroom and den
Kerrisdale home, lot 100'
by 360' with annual taxes of
$250 offered clear title
at $14,000. A four-bedroom
nine-year old Marpole home
with separate garage was
$10,000.

KERRISDALE
3 BEDROOMS AND DEN
QUALITY — SECLUSION
We are completely sold on this
impressive well located home. It
offers both charm and personality and
the plan is most interesting especially for entertaining. The usual
modern cabinet kitchen and gener-
ously tiled bathroom found in the
better type home, master bedroom
is downstairs and is twin bed size,
lovely living room 17'x24', a view
dining room, 12'x18'. The den or
playroom on the main floor is a
honey, 25' long with a separate entrance to the back garden. 2 excep-
tional bedrooms up, oil air condi-
tioned heat. The lot is one of the
finest in the district. Imagine! 100'x
360' and taxes only $250. The sale
price is $14,000 for clear title. Phone
Mr. Oliver, KE 4675R or Mr. Harold
Robinson, KE 0771M for preview.
P.S. You will agree this is the
home to raise your family in, also
a home to be mighty proud of.

The new decade began with President Stanley V. Smith and
Vice President Leslie C. Creery named to second terms by
acclamation.

The question of married women obtaining real estate
licenses came up for the first time during on-going discussions of Real-estate Agents' Licensing Act amendments in
January, 1950, but no action was taken at that time. This
subject had been a point of contention for some Vancouver
women who aspired to join the industry.

Also in January that year the question of a Cooperative
form of listing to circulate property information to members
with a guarantee of cooperation was again raised by John P.
Roberts, who always attended NAR conferences with a view
to adapting good American ideas for use by his Board.

Real estate boards were being formed in other areas, and
Frank Hoole, with his long-time Vancouver Board Secre-
tarial experience, was called in to assist. One such Board
formed in 1950 was in West Vancouver, joining other Lower
Mainland boards in Vancouver, North Vancouver, New Westminster and Surrey. Hoole also served as a Secretary to the
B.C. Association of Real Estate Boards.

The then Central (now 'Canada') Mortgage and Housing
Corporation, operating under the National Housing Act, was
still trying to solve the veterans housing shortage and a fairly
substantial building program had been announced. Board
members E.P. Taylor, R.A. Pound, and W.E. Fowler kept a
watching brief on the housing planned around the city, a
good amount in the Fraser area, and gave their opinion that
it was penny wise and pound foolish to build these houses
without attics or basements. Building a house with basement
only added $350 to the cost of building one without, and it
would give the family so much more expansion room, laun-
dry and bad-weather play facility. Another objection was
that CMHC planned this housing to be all rental, instead of
giving the veterans an opportunity to buy with their accumu-
lated gratuities. Eventually however these homes were sold
by the government, and predictably, the new owners spent
much more than $350.00 to provide themselves and their

families with the "luxury" of a basement for the needed storage/laundry/play area that could have been provided so easily and economically in the initial building.

By March that year John Roberts submitted a comprehensive report on a cooperative form of listing. This was circulated to member-companies and agents were asked to discuss the process with their salespeople to get a consensus. The Committee worked hard through the year to interest the general membership and finally in November, a separate Cooperative Listing Bureau under the wing of the Board, but without its financial assistance, was established with John P. Roberts as Chairman.

The Real Estate Agents' Licensing Board was functioning by June, 1950, to act in an advisory capacity to the Superintendent on matters of qualification, experience and suitability for the real estate profession. This new Board also proposed a probationary "learners" category and urged development of standard listing and offer forms. A crackdown on disciplinary procedures was undertaken and Mr. Tempest deWolf, Secretary of the Vancouver Board, was assigned as its Secretary as well. The Licensing Board set up educational qualifications with plans for a correspondence course for all license applicants.

In early 1951 Leslie C. Creery was named President and Jack Kelly his Vice President.

This administration engaged Alan G. Creer, a youthful World War 11 veteran who was then completing accounting articles. Alan was appointed Assistant Secretary of both the Vancouver Real Estate Board and the Real Estate Agents' Licensing Board, and thus began a professional record that would result in 38 years of much heralded service to the real estate industry. In the fall of 1951 Tempest deWolf resigned as Secretary of the Real Estate Board and Creer was appointed in his place. He was also giving Cooperative Listing Bureau Secretary Jean Montgomery a hand with this new sales system, with responsibility for reporting its progress to Vancouver Board Directors. deWolf continued as Secretary of the Licensing Board.

Early that year an adjustment of fees and dues brought the Board annual dues from $35.00 to $45.00, plus $1.25 per sales licensee (up from 50–cents), all payable in equal quarterly payments. Annual dues set for Associate members (those active outside the Board's jurisdiction) was $10 annually and $5.00 annually for their sales people, also payable in

Leslie C. Creery
President, 1951, 1952

Alan G. Creer
Board Secretary 1951-1988

*The Federal Government had announced a final end to
the War time Rent Control by March 31, 1951, but the
Board was alerted that the Provincial Legislature was
prepared to continue such control.*

equal quarterly payments.

Sunday selling returned as a subject for concern in
February, 1951. In the opinion of the Real Estate Agents'
Licensing Board, Sunday selling was illegal under the Lord's
Day Act. When the question was put to Board members, it
was agreed unanimously that Sunday selling be prohibited.
As not all licensed real estate brokers belonged to the Board,
this would prove to be a contentious subject among licensees
for years to come, with Sunday "showings" continuing
and paper work always dated after midnight on the
Monday date.

The Federal Government had announced a final end to
the War time Rent Control by March 31, 1951, but the Board
was alerted that the Provincial Legislature was prepared to
continue such control. The four Lower Mainland real estate
Board Presidents, along with Past Vancouver Board President Dean Mansell, who was then President of CAREB,
journeyed to Victoria to offer a plan of gradual removal of
control measures to avoid chaotic rental conditions. By
year-end there had not been movement from the Province,
but in the spirit of the Board's aims and objectives of protecting both the rights of private property owners and of those
who rent property, the Board had once again voluntarily
followed its mandate of suggesting equitable rights for
tenants and owners. This attention to legislation that could
affect its clients and customers is still carried out by today's
Board Directorate.

Since its inception in 1919, Exchange/Board members
had offered a valuation service to individual and civic groups,
and at the end of 1951, the Board President was to report that
this voluntary activity by Board members had netted $1,400
for Board funds that year. Another voluntary activity undertaken by Board members was a series of Vancouver Night
School lectures entitled "So You're Going to Buy a House?",
which was most popular and the beginning of many such
speakers' series in the future.

Board Director Arthur B. Jacobson was fond of golf so
decided in 1951 to revive an annual Fall Golf Tournament

*A second consecutive Presidential term was awarded
to L.C. Creery in 1952 and first order of business
was circulation of the First Annual Report of
the Cooperative Listing Bureau, which appeared to
be a success in progress.*

started by S.E. Peters of the Real Estate Exchange but not
held in several years. That event is still held annually though
now expanded to both a Spring and Fall tournament, a Ladies
tourney and a Seniors' session to accommodate all those who
wish to participate.

In late summer that year the idea of a Salesmen's Committee to take an active part in Board affairs was considered
for the first time and investigations into the matter began.

A second consecutive Presidential term was awarded to
L.C. Creery in 1952 and first order of business was circula-
tion of the First Annual Report of the Cooperative Listing
Bureau, which appeared to be a success in progress.

John Roberts reported that the bureau was launched
early in 1951 with a membership of only nineteen willing
participants, who each subscribed $30.00 to finance its early
operations. Monthly dinner meetings were scheduled and a
growing spirit of cooperation could be observed as attendees
discussed the merits of listed properties. Quality of listings
improved as the year progressed, and the listing broker's
share of the commission was set at 2 1/2% and the Cooperative Listing Bureau's share at 1/2%. That first year the
Bureau handled a total of 360 listings and effected sales
totalling $803,975.00 with total commissions distributed to
the membership over $52,000. What's more, by year-end
there were THIRTY NINE members, (ten of whom had
not been Board members previously) more than double
the charter membership of nineteen, and the bureau had
not had to touch the initial subscription fees by those
first members.

It was evident after the first year that Cooperative
Listing would be a definite membership attraction, provide
a much-needed cooperative attitude to the industry, as
well as a visible public benefit provided by the real estate
brokers' association.

The Legislative Committee of the Board that year dealt
with drafting a new Interim Agreement Form in cooperation
with the Standard Forms Committee of the Real Estate
Agents' Licensing Board and made recommendations for

J. F. Kelly
President, 1953

amendments to strengthen the Real-estate Agents' Licensing Act. Art Jacobson had also initiated discussions with the Notaries Association and the Attorney General to seek the appointment of more real estate agents as Notaries.

The Social Credit Party came to power for the first time in 1952, and the Board executive immediately began taking up the cause of rent restrictions with this new government.

In this period Boards were allowed to set standard commission and fee schedules, and the Arbitration Committee was required to hear a number of cases where members had cut fees to obtain listings. This situation no longer exists, as Competition legislation prevents real estate boards from setting specific commission and fee levels.

J.F. Kelly, who had been named Western Regional Vice President of C.A.R.E.B. at the October 1952 Conference, was named Board President in 1953 and John P. Roberts was elected Vice President. At the Annual Meeting held in January, members heard of the growing success of the Cooperative Listing Bureau. External advertising in newspapers, on radio and TV began to spread the word about cooperative listing/selling. Interestingly, the "new" electronic kid on the block, KVOS Television, charged $14.00 a minute, while veteran radio broadcaster CKWX charged $18 per minute for the ads that informed the public of this new cooperative concept.

After its first year of operation thirty nine member-firms had joined the bureau, but by the end of 1952 over ninety were using its services despite an increase in membership fee to $50. Evidence of its growing importance to the industry was the year-end dollar volume of property sales, which had reached an unprecedented two million dollars! Board membership had increased to 130 from 100 just two years before and it was believed the Cooperative Listing Bureau was largely responsible for this rise.

Late in 1952 the Real Estate Agents Licensing Board issued a proposal for a "Real Estate Brokers Licensing Act", referred to as a 'consolidation of the present Real Estate Agents Licensing Act and regulations and amendments which had been suggested', with a reply requested by December that year. Vigorous protest arose about many suggested provisions of the proposed Act and also on the short time allowed for its study, so the Licensing Board agreed to defer its submission to the government until complete study had been possible. By early 1953, however, the Licensing

Stanley Smith, who had been Board President in both 1949 and 1950, took on the job of Chairman of the British Empire Games Committee in 1952, and took every opportunity leading up to the 1954 date to speak to his Board colleagues and elicit help and cooperation for this epic event. It still stands out in sports history as the time Roger Bannister and John Landy broke the 4-minute mile for the first time.

Eventually the Board set up a steering Committee to organize housing for the many visitors who arrived for the games.

Board did have in place a new procedure for applying for licenses under a correspondence course. In March, 1953, a special Committee was set up to study the authority and responsibilities of the Real Estate Agents' Licensing Board, which many thought to be more extensive and intrusive than had been understood upon its formation and there was a concern that powers granted under the legislation could lead to abuse.

The 1953 Executive, Messrs J.F. Kelly, J.P. Roberts, H.P. Bell Irving, J.H. Davies, B.C. Elliott, A.B. Jacobson, D.W. Meakin, J.L. Tennant and F.B. Urquhart, were joined by the following appointed members: Gordon Bell ; C.W. Bradley; Harold Chivers; Walter Baker; Harold Gavin; A.R. Harvey ; Herbert R. Fullerton and Chairman, B.I. Sperling. Past President Dean Mansell joined the Committee, along with two other Past Presidents, Leslie C. Creery and Stanley V. Smith, who were members of the Real Estate Agents' Licensing Board. This Special Committee became known as "The Sperling Committee", and its voluminous findings were delivered to all Board members in July, 1953.

The Sperling Report, and additional motions by Herbert R. Fullerton, were both critical of many aspects of the Licensing Board and its powers, which were perceived to be equal or greater than those of the Superintendent in the licensing of agents and salesmen. These reports also criticized the authority of Tempest deWolf, the former Board Secretary, and his financial involvement in the Realty Training Bureau. Not all on the Vancouver Board's executive agreed with the Sperling report in its entirety or Fullerton's motions, but at a lively special meeting on September 23, a majority of 79 Board members agreed with the criticisms and suggested further impartial study to a negative vote of only 29 members. This overturned the Board Executive's recommendation that the Attorney General implement the proposed act and regulations.

The general membership was informed of all deliberations, and full written documentation was circulated to all members and other real estate boards in the province. Executive called for an early Annual Meeting so the membership would have the opportunity to elect a new executive, as half the former executive had resigned due to the dissention. Resignations were received from Messrs S.V. Smith, L.C. Creery and J.F. Kelly (all past presidents) and also from Messrs H.P. Bell-Irving, D.W. Meakin and J.P.

Roberts. Four vacancies were filled by appointment of Messrs Herbert R. Fullerton, H.G. McRae, R.A. Pound and R.G. Patterson, who would hold office until the scheduled Dec. 2, 1953, special Annual Meeting.

At that Annual Meeting Colonel Herbert R. Fullerton was elected President and R.A. Pound Vice President. Also elected were Directors Harold Davies, H.G. McRae, B.I. Sperling, A.B. Jacobson, J.J. McCarthy, H.B. Itter and R.G. Patterson, a slate that favoured change through an independent licensing process and improved industry standards.

Members were kept informed of the opposing viewpoints; those who preferred continuation of existing licensing procedures and those who wanted new regulations and increased scrutiny and education for applicants for licensing. This group felt an improved system should be conducted by a full time Superintendent with advisory service by a Board of members elected from the real estate industry throughout the province.

The B.C. Association of Real Estate Boards passed a motion in May, 1954, calling for an impartial study into the administration and operation of the Real Estate Agents Licensing Board to be conducted by the Attorney General, an idea originally suggested by the Sperling/Fullerton reports of the year before. Believing it was important to the future benefit of both the general public and the real estate industry, the Sperling motion had recommended well known lawyer T.G. Norris, Q.C., be assigned to this important task and the B.C. Association of Real Estate Boards went on record as approving this recommendation. The Norris appointment was finally confirmed by late summer, 1954, and his investigation was underway.

While all these Licensing Board concerns were major agenda items, the Cooperative Listing Bureau had continued its successful climb, as each month saw more listings processed and more sales registered. The Bureau was administered by a Committee of members and an appointed elected Board representative.

By early summer of 1953, after much investigation, the Board was able to offer a Crown Life group Life and Medical/surgical plan to all members wishing to apply, probably the first such service in a real estate association.

Due to the membership increase in both Board and Cooperative Listing Bureau, more staff and space were required. By mid-1953 membership was 115 and still grow-

Colonel Herbert R. Fullerton
President, 1954, 1955

ing and the bureau was completing over half a million dollars in business each month. Because of space problems due to this increasing workload, effective December 1, 1953, the Board had secured 1400 square feet of space in the Seymour building at 525 Seymour St., on a three year lease at a monthly rental of $212.50. By the time of the move, membership stood at 159, with 130 Active & Financial Members, 27 Associate and 2 Honorary Members. The Cooperative Listing Bureau was contributing up to $800 per month to the Vancouver Real Estate Board's general revenue by year-end.

The new administration set out a more fully rounded and effective Committee system in early 1954, requiring each Committee to meet at least once monthly, with either Secretary Alan Creer or Assistant Secretary Jean Montgomery, to be in attendance and prepare minutes. Now in larger premises, with more Committee meetings to be accommodated, Creer's request for a new Boardroom Table and chairs at a cost of $115.00 was approved.

The Cooperative Listing Bureau set about planning a pamphlet that would outline the rules and regulations of the service. And to maintain interest, a sales contest was planned for the first time in 1954, where 4 points were awarded for each $100 in commission earned and 2 points for every monthly dinner meeting attended. A total of five cash prizes—$300, $200, $100, $60 and $40—were offered, with an additional $100 for the salesman listing the greatest number of properties sold by others and $100 for the salesman selling the greatest number of properties listed by others.

More and more North Shore companies were making Associate Membership applications to the Vancouver Board bringing the Associate Members number up to 41. It was obvious these companies were interested in listing houses in the fast rising North Shore suburbs. Access to those suburbs would become easier via the planned new Second Narrows bridge, an alternative to the Lions Gate. In early 1954 President Fullerton had written to the Presidents of both the North and West Vancouver Boards, suggesting an amalgamation so Cooperative Listing services could be provided to a "Greater" Vancouver Real Estate Board membership. This suggestion started a series of meetings which continued for several years.

As the use of the services of the Coop Bureau grew, so did the situations that needed scrutiny. And thus began development of the Rules and Regulations all MLS users follow today:

Viewed from the basis of today's frenetic activity in the
MLS Department when 550 listings per DAY is
not unusual, the Coop Bureau's early 1954 jubilation
at receiving 270 listings per MONTH may read
like a non-item.

"In the event of a sale, the Selling Broker may place his sign on the property with that of the Listing Broker by affixing the Co-op SOLD sign to both signs."; A photography charge of $3.00 for each improved residential listing was established, using a system of stamps applied to the listing contract; "At all times the Selling Broker has the right to accompany the Listing Broker when presenting offers"; Commission split set at that time was 3% of the sale price to the Listing Broker, 4% to the Selling Broker and the Listing Broker was responsible for paying the Bureau charge of 1/2% of sale price.

Staff of the Board/Bureau as 1954 began was Secretary Alan Creer, Assistant Secretary Jean Montgomery and 3 clerical employees, but by February as listings and membership increased, it was necessary to take on one more staff person. Staff typed listing contract information on specially printed four-corner stencils for in-house printing on green perforated stock, using a Multilith machine.

Viewed from the basis of today's frenetic activity in the MLS Department when 550 listings per DAY is not unusual, the Coop Bureau's early 1954 jubilation at receiving 270 listings per MONTH may read like a non-item. But considering this youthful marketing system was just over 3 full years old and total Board membership less than a tenth of that existing today, it was indeed a success story. The Cooperative listing plan was gaining more and more favour, and the Bureau celebrated its first "Million Dollar Month" in June, 1954.

Objective set out for the Education and Library Committee was to make available for agents and salespeople a series of courses of a practical and useful nature, with a final aim of establishing a degree course at UBC. There had also been prior discussion about a "Real Estate Institute", much like the Insurance Institute, which supplied advanced courses of study. This would be entirely independent of any educational plans put in place by the Superintendent for pre-licensing examinations. Harold Davies, who would become Board President in the next decade, was Chairman. A rough draft of proposed Institute aims and syllabus were soon in place.

There had been talk for some time about lockbox use, but it hadn't been followed up because it was felt neither vendors or salesmen would use such a system, but finally, in February, 1954, the Bureau purchased twenty lock boxes and eighty extra keys. The boxes would be offered for use by members at a returnable deposit equal to their cost, ($5.00) but the keys were only available by purchase at 75-cents each. At this time it was also noted that increased listings resulted in increased photography requirements, so Ted Cholowski, who had been taking coop pictures on contract, was given a staff position, one he would hold until his retirement some 20 years later.

It should be noted that throughout the years of Exchange/Board existence, By-Laws of the association were constantly updated, rules of the Cooperative Listing Bureau, and Standards of Practice for all members were being developed and expanded. Ballot questionnaires would be sent to all members, and upon their completion the majority replies would be calculated. As membership increased, and more and more companies took advantage of access to the Complaints and Discipline and Arbitration procedures to settle differences, the situations revealed provided necessary research fodder for a Code of Ethics. This was developed by the Legal and Legislative Committee chaired by Ben Sperling, who also drew upon the Codes of Ethics of the National Association of Realtors and the Canadian Real Estate Association, consolidating the most specific points for the Vancouver Board's business code. After studying others in existence, the Legal and Legislative Committee also established a form of Salesmen's Contract which was used by Board members for many years.

This too was the year the Board first established a "blanket bond", starting at $10,000. This excess cover was later increased to $100,000 and continues at that level today. A Board library was set up, and along with a list of real estate publications suggested by N.A.R.,it featured a complete set of Vancouver City Bylaws, and city zoning maps plus a subscription to the Journal of Commerce's Daily Real Estate Record, so property ownership records could begin to be organized at the Board level.

It was now considered by all involved, that the authority for and the aims and objects of the Cooperative Listing Bureau should be incorporated under the Constitution and By-laws of the Board, instead of operating independently under the Board umbrella. This would mean any Board member who agreed to abide by Coop Bureau Rules and Regulations could participate at only the costs of such fees as were then required for service. A May 21st address by W.H. Shorthill, President of CAREB, gave members a talk on the benefits accruing to members of the operation of a successful Cooperative service. In trying to protect the name Cooperative Listing Bureau, the Board discovered that under provisions of the Cooperative Associations Act it was restrained from use of the word "Cooperative", so in August, 1954, business began to be carried out under the name "Multiple Listing Service of the Vancouver Real Estate Board", protected provincially and federally for use by this Board.

A letter from the City Assessment office, received by Board executive in mid-1954, was a complaint about the number of calls from real estate licensees the department was forced to answer. A thorough check of the membership revealed that a good number of the calls to city hall were being made not by members but by lawyers and non-members. The Board still urged its members to keep their calls to City Hall to a minimum, but because this information was important to members the Board started investigating ways of providing data such as the ages of properties from City water connection records, and the Journal of Commerce Daily Record of real estate transactions through the Land Registry Offices. It was from this first initiative that a full-fledged Statistical Department was started.

Other major matters of concern were payment of commissions to licensees by the City of Vancouver, which the Property Department wanted to discontinue. This issue continued through many meetings with civic authorities and was finally resolved in June, 1955, when the City agreed to continue to pay commissions to licensees selling city properties, but capped that at 5% on sales up to $20,000 and 2 1/2% on any balance above that amount. The Board was also working with CAREB on the nation-wide problem of non payment of commissions by Central Mortgage and Housing Corp. for sales of housing built under the National Housing Act. CMHC said it deemed the "contractors' profit", which had been calculated into the selling prices, sufficient to include real estate commission.

The Board raised $1,100 in subscriptions from members to fund the "six-day shopping week" campaign as licensees had always felt the Wednesday afternoon closing was detri-

*A great deal of time was spent in 1954 by the Board of
Directors revising and updating the Constitution
and Bylaws, and after a number of special meetings
and revisions, these were finally approved January 11,
1955, and became effective March 1 that year.*

mental to the business areas of the city.

At the 1954 conference of the Canadian Association of Real
Estate Boards a total of $15,000 in voluntary contributions
was gathered for the Ontario Hurricane Relief Fund, $500 of
which was donated by the Vancouver Board.

Throughout the minute book records of Board meetings
of the past, it becomes evident that years of volunteer Board
duty usually preceded a member's election to higher office.
This also included those serving in the early years of the
Cooperative Listing Bureau/Multiple Listing Service Committee. Two participating members who helped write the basis
of MLS Rules and Regulations still observed today, were
Messrs John Roberts and E.S. (Ted) Henderson, both slated
to become Board Presidents and Honorary Life Members.

A great deal of time was spent in 1954 by the Board of
Directors revising and updating the Constitution and By-
laws, and after a number of special meetings and revisions,
these were finally approved January 11, 1955, and became
effective March 1 that year.

At the Annual Meeting on February 8, representatives of
182 companies (in person or by proxy) were noted present.
There is no printed membership list but the numbers
recorded for that year were 225 Active and Financial (voting)
members, so the proportion of attendance to membership
was very good at the Hotel Vancouver's banquet rooms that
night. The election process saw Colonel Herbert R. Fullerton
returned as President for a second term, and R.A. Pound as
First Vice President. The new Bylaws called for the appointment of four more Directors when they became effective
on March 1.

While salespeople were not Board members, the Agent
members had always paid a fee to the Board on behalf
of each sales licensee employed. In 1955 names of salespeople
employed by Board members began to be recorded seriously
and efficiently on a Seely Card Wheel and plans for an official
Salesmen's Division to function as a Standing Committee of
the Board were soon underway. The addition of this Division
brought 1,134 Salesmen-members under the Board

In 1955 names of salespeople employed by Board members began to be recorded seriously and efficiently on a Seely Card Wheel and plans for an official Salesmen's Division to function as a Standing Committee of the Board were soon underway.

umbrella, and along with 225 voting members, 115 Active Associate Members,(a new category of membership for other nominees of associated firms) 59 Associate Members, and 7 Honorary Members, for a startling total membership of 1,540 members of the Vancouver Real Estate Board. (In 1954 before the Sales Division was officially established, 700 sales employees were recognized by 185 Board members, and in 1953, before salesman-registration began, the Board Membership was 159 in total.)

At a monthly general meeting held April 7 at the Commodore Cabaret, results of the Salesmen's election revealed the first elected President to be A.J. Steeves of Macdonald Realty and Vice President elected was D.B. Allen of Pemberton Realty Corp. First meeting of this elected body was held on April 26,1955. At this organizational meeting, the Salesmen Directors set goals of education, sales promotion and clinics on marketing Multiple Listings, advertising and social functions to promote friendship and cooperation among the l, 400 members. At the first of a series of monthly dinner meetings held in the Georgia Hotel on July 7, however, only 57 members were welcomed by Division President A.J. Steeves, Board President Fullerton and Vice President Jacobson.

The Board was assuming more Committee, community and Divisional responsibilities, and at the same time demands on the Multiple Listing Service were increasing. From the previous year when the first "million dollar month" was observed, in April of 1955 that production figure was more than doubled, with a dollar volume of $2,340,000. registered.

To accommodate this added work load more space was required so the membership was asked to help in the search for up to 5,000 feet of ground floor space with parking for up to 30 cars. The location chosen was 883 Howe Street, a small building of approximately 2,500 square feet with basement storage and parking lot, rental of $550 per month, and the offices were relocated by mid June that year.

Regular golf tournaments were still being enjoyed by Board

1955 was also the year for the old Exchange "notarial seal" type crest to be updated to the more stylized circle with B.C. map and REALTOR ribbon that became the Board's identification for some 35 years until the current skyline logo was adopted in 1990.

members, with the 1955 Spring tourney booked for June 3 at Peace Portals, at a price of $5.00 per ticket for golf and dinner. That summer another social event that was to endure for many years was born-a family picnic, which was first held at Belcarra Park by the Salesmen's Division and continued at varying Lower Mainland locations for the next 15 years. In December, 1955, the Salesmen's Division held the first of a successful series of "Snowball Frolics" at the Commodore Ballroom, an annual event that was to continue into the mid-'70s when the growing popularity of Geographical Division holiday events began to decrease ticket sales and it was cancelled in favour of the smaller social occasions held within Division members' jurisdictional territory.

New Honorary Life Members named in May, 1955, included R.A. Hood, Howard Meakin, J.P. Nicolls, D.W. Reeve, and H.V. Sharples. All were 1919 charter members of the Vancouver Exchange and Nicolls and Reeve were Past Presidents of the Association.

Bonding requirements changed this year, with new bond levels set at not less than $4,000 for agents and $1,500 for salesmen in communities with a population of 10,000 or more.

In September, after many months of revision, a fully amended Constitution and Bylaws and a schedule of Minimum Commissions and Fees were approved by voting members representing 60 real estate firms. Largely housekeeping to keep abreast of changing and expanding business, the new Bylaws also brought into effect a voting and balloting system that allowed for mail-in votes for Board elections from that day onward.

An increase in fees applied to licensees by the Canadian Association of Real Estate Boards that fall saw a proportionate increase in Board fees. As a result, Active and Financial Membership dues rose to $50 annually: $35 for Board dues, $10 for CAREB dues and $5.00 for B.C.A.R.E.B. dues. Salesmen members paid $12.00, $5.00, $5.00 and $2.00 allocated for these same three categories. Associates who used the Multiple Listing Service paid $50 or $10.00 without the use of MLS. At that time Property owners had the privilege of joining the Board at annual dues of $15, and Honorary Life Members were charged no dues.

As the year drew to a close, Vancouver City Council proposed a million dollar money by-law to local property owners, so the Legislative & Public Affairs Committee circulated the membership with bylaw background and of 115 ballots returned there were 94 in favour of opposing the Bylaw. In answer to this clear mandate from the membership a series of half page ads in the three local newspapers (Sun, Province and News Herald) were produced to give the public a clear picture of the city's action. Further minutes do not indicate if Board ads ameliorated the city's action, but the L. & P.A. Committee had set the stage for many future such campaigns-such as more recent well publicized opposition to the Property Purchase Tax when it was introduced in 1987 by B.C.'s Social Credit Government. While unsuccessful in changing the legislation at that time, the Board's moves did show the public it was taking a responsible stand on its behalf.

The new year of 1956 saw the first mail-ballot election, with Arthur B. Jacobson elected President, and under provisions of previous By-law changes, three Vice Presidents elected were J.F. Kelly, G.H. MacKenzie and R.G. Patterson.

Board Secretary Alan Creer and his Assistant Secretary Jean Montgomery were now supervising nine other staff members as the Board's activities and Multiple Listing Department kept growing by leaps and bounds. Neil McLeod, accountant, who had been hired in 1954, was slated to carry out a long-time service of 33 years until his retirement in 1987, a record that was to become characteristic of many Board employees. First Board Secretary Frank Hoole, had started this loyalty feature in 1920 and gave over 29 years of service, but that record would be broken in 1988 when Alan Creer retired after 38 years. Photographers Ted Cholowsky and Jimmie Kakutani each contributed over 20 years service, Lorraine McKeen of the Statistical staff served 30 years before her retirement in 1989. Still employed and following the same long-service style of Board staff are Public Relations Director Anne Broadfoot, 32 years; executive Secretary Patsy Heath and photographer Bill Haywood, 29 years; Secretary Pauline Treiglaff and Accounts Receivable clerk Colleen Nicoll, 21 years; Connie Steele, MLS Opens, 20 years; Diane Hall, MLS Supervisor, and receptionist Sabine Carleton, both have 19 years of continuous service. Associate Executive Officer Brad Scott has served 16 years, Training Director Jean Huish 15 years, Accountant Sandra Halprin 13 years and Executive Officer Larry Buttress served 13 years before his recent departure, while Ulrika Beauchamp, relief receptionist has been with the Board over 11 years.

Elected President of the 1,229-member Salesmen's Division in 1956 was D.B. Allan, who reported to the Board's

Arthur B. Jacobson
President, 1956

The Board's by-laws were revised to provide for
Divisional membership of groups operating outside the
City of Vancouver. Annual elections of a Divisional
Directorate would entitle its President to sit on the
Board's Directorate as Divisional representative.
Agents would become active voting members in the
Vancouver Board, and their sales employees members
of the Salesmen's Division.

Directorate. Bert Edwards was named its Vice President.

The Norris investigation was continuing and by May of 1956, Colonel Norris had a skeleton of the new Act and Regulations which he wanted to discuss with the Board's Legislative Committee.

North Vancouver Real Estate Board executives had been conducting on-going meetings on amalgamation with the Vancouver Board since the original invitation made by President Herbert R. Fullerton in 1954. In the first quarter of 1956 success was achieved. The Board's by-laws were revised to provide for Divisional membership of groups operating outside the City of Vancouver. Annual elections of a Divisional Directorate would entitle its President to sit on the Board's Directorate as Divisional representative. Agents would become active voting members in the Vancouver Board, and their sales employees members of the Salesmen's Division. Geographical Divisions would retain autonomy in matters of policy and practice of the civic or municipal governments in their area. As more people joined the real estate business, and more recognized the merits of Board membership, the 1956 total membership grew to 1,652.

Since the name Multiple Listing Service had been legally protected it was of some concern to Board Directors that the New Westminster Board was using that protected name without Vancouver sanction. A Liaison Committee was established to formulate an agreement on use of the term, on jurisdictional boundaries and on the potential problems of dual listings and Board compensation in the event of a sale. This Committee began negotiations toward what has become a cooperative working arrangement between the Vancouver and now Fraser Valley Real Estate Board.

Multiple Listing had already been adopted by the Victoria Board in 1955 and later a request for assistance in setting up such a plan by the Nanaimo Board made the Vancouver Committee realize this extended availability actually enhanced public understanding of the Multiple concept to everyone's benefit.

The Multiple Listing Service Committee wrestled with a

problem they obviously didn't solve because it is still of concern today—incomplete listings. Because listing values were still in question the MLS Committee had considered hiring an appraiser for all listed properties, but decided to involve all viewing members through use of pre-printed forms at Open Houses where individual licensees would record their value opinions. The Committee also investigated hiring a "field man" to be on tap at individual company sales meetings to explain and promote the use of Multiple. At that time, while the use of Multiple was increasing, the western section of the city was still not participating in any measurable way.

The Education Committee was discussing a proposed two year real estate course with Dean McPhee of the Commerce Faculty at UBC. The Committee also agreed to cooperate with the Department of Psychology towards developing a series of aptitude tests that might determine sales ability for future real estate licensees. Pre and post licensing training either by lecture or correspondence was also being discussed at this time and this recommendation was passed on to the Norris Commission. This Committee also made a point of expanding the stock of the library of real estate related publications, which was then maintained at the Board office.

Jean Montgomery, who had been Assistant Secretary at the Board and Cooperative Listing Bureau for 6 years, retired in May, and was replaced that year by George Nelson Muir, whose experience included having his own Point Grey real estate company. Thus began another long-term service record, as George worked faithfully to further the growth and prosperity for the Board for over 20 years until his own retirement in 1978.

Always aware of its duty to be involved in civic affairs, the Board once again made a commitment of a $1,500 donation to the Civic Development Commission and for the third year accepted responsibility as volunteers to collect for the Community Chest (now known as United Way.) Planning was underway for the 1957 CAREB conference which was to be hosted by Vancouver. By nature real estate practitioners are biased in favour of ownership of real property, so it was in 1956 that a Building Fund was established for such time as the Board could buy or build its own premises.

The subject of Sunday selling came up regularly each year, and the new Salesmen's Division Directors were in favour of the Board taking a stand to bar such activity,

George N. Muir
Associate Secretary
1957-1978

It was also mid-1956 that the Board first decided to publish local maps, and the Stats & Survey and Multiple Listing Committees cooperated to make sure known real estate boundaries were identified on the map. This "overlay" remains the basis for today's area codes, still produced as location boundaries and coded for efficient computer access to areas and sub-areas.

G. H. MacKenzie
President, 1957

suggesting a 6-day week for all salespeople. Because a ballot-questionnaire sent to members didn't show a conclusive majority in favour of such action, further study was committed. A second ballot questionnaire in July returned a higher number in favour of Sunday closing, but still further study was requested by Directors. There was also a great concern about part time salespeople in the profession and the Salesmen's Division went on record in 1956 as being in favour of stricter controls.

J. Ross Ker, grandson of Exchange charter member Newton J. Ker and son of Alan N. Ker of Ker & Ker Ltd., was called to the B.C. Bar in the early '50s and spent some time in Ottawa as Assistant to the Honorable Ralph Campney who was then Solicitor General and Minister of National Defense. Upon the death of his father, J. Ross returned to British Columbia in 1956, took out real estate licensing and assumed management of the firm, joining the Board at that time.

In September, 1956, President of the West Vancouver Real Estate Board, E.S. (Ted) Henderson, an Associate Vancouver member, wrote to Directors with his Board's desire to become a Division of the Vancouver Board. One great concern was Sunday selling, which was prohibited in West Vancouver, but Board President Jacobson undertook to circularize Vancouver members to abide by those West Vancouver rules, and further ballot-questionnaires led to a full vote on the subject at the next membership meeting, where it was again defeated.

The Norris report had been delivered and he described the existing act as a "totally unsatisfactory piece of legislation" and also said that "certain of the present regulations are ultra vires and generally not suitable for the purposes for which they are intended." The B.C. Association of Real Estate Boards commenced a detailed study of the report and drafting a suggested new Real Estate Act for submision to the Government.

Gordon H. MacKenzie was elected President in 1957, along with three Vice Presidents including H.P. Bell-Irving, Harold Itter and J.F. Kelly. Assigned to represent the Board on B.C. Association of Real Estate Boards were Art Jacobson, Herbert R. Fullerton, Fred Urquhart, J.D. Barlow, D.E. Rivers and Charlie Brown, many of whom had worked on both the Sperling Report and towards improvement of standards of pre-licensing education through UBC courses.

Early in this year the West Vancouver Real Estate Board became a Division of the Vancouver Board, and all members of that Board who previously held Vancouver Associate Status automatically became Active voting members. John Hawkins had been named President of that Board so became a Director of the now enlarged Vancouver group. By year's end, the growing Board membership had reached 1,765.

One of the early actions of the new Directorate was to study and recommend approval of the draft new Real Estate Act and it was then sent to the Attorney General of the Province for legislative action. The Norris report recommended formation of a Real Estate Council and Institute of B.C. Real Estate Agents.

The B.C. Association of Real Estate Boards proposed the formation of a new Society, the Real Estate Institute of B.C., which would contain three Divisions: The REALTOR Division, which would replace the B.C. Association of Real Estate Boards, the Provincial Division, which would act as the vehicle to elect members to a Real Estate Council and the Professional Division, an organization of professional members with the designation R.I.(B.C.).

The REALTOR Division is now B.C. Real Estate Association. Need for the provincial Division was obviated by changes in the election procedure for the Real Estate Council, and membership in the Real Estate Institute requires graduation from the UBC Diploma Course.

The Real Estate Council now has the responsibility for issuance of licenses, maintenance of records, transfers and the authority to discipline real estate agents and salespeople. The Council also acts in an advisory capacity to the Superintendent of Real Estate and advises on real estate education through the Faculty of Commerce at UBC.

The Main Branch of Vancouver Public Library still maintains one of the most extensive real estate information collections on the Lower Mainland, in part because the Board's own Library of publications was donated to the section a few years later when it became too onerous for staff to handle, but also due to a donation from the Board which is still given annually, most recently in the amount of $2,000. The Library still honors access to all Board members, regardless of office location. Whatsmore, today the Vancouver Public Library is not the only such facility to receive a grant since a generous annual donation is now also made to each main Library in the other 13 communities served by Board members.

With the consent of the Attorney-General and approval of other B.C. real estate boards, the Education Committee

Education continued as a major theme at the Board, and the Committee negotiated an agreement with chief Business Librarian, Aileen Tufts, of the Vancouver Public Library to create a Vancouver Real Estate Board section within the Business Reference Division in the new Library building, then just opened at Robson and Burrard. All Board member-firms would be given library card access regardless of suburban location and a $1,200 grant was given to assist in the purchase of real estate reference books and periodicals for this section.

*With the consent of the Attorney-General and approval
of other B.C. real estate boards, the Education Committee
finalized plans for a pre-licensing course for new
applicants through the Faculty of Commerce at UBC,
which was to be in operation by mid 1958.*

finalized plans for a pre-licensing course for new applicants through the Faculty of Commerce at UBC, which was to be in operation by mid 1958. This first course consisted of 15 two-hour lectures, 60 hours of reading and assignments and 70 hours of on-the-job training.

The first reference to 100% of commissions paid to salesmen who in turn were charged a desk rental appear in the March, 1957 minutes. Solicitors' advice was sought and the Directors prepared to change Bylaws to prevent this practice. At a well attended Special Meeting in May, after several amendments were made and defeated, the voting members chose to pay their salespeople a basic scale of no more than 50% of gross commission earned and any bonus given would not exceed 10% of gross commission. It was also established that all salespeople in the employ of Board members must immediately apply for membership in the Salesmen's Division. That Division, incidentally, took immediate umbrage at these bylaw changes that for many years proved to be a point of contention between corporate agents and salespeople.

Despite an increase of 150% in the membership entrance fee—up to $250 in 1957—there were still 60 applications for membership, of which only 3 were rejected. The Committee was outlining a proposal for Probationary Membership to be presented to Directors.

Multiple Listing showed another steady increase-in 1957 there were 3,430 sales of the 10,652 listings taken, and dollar volume rose to $38,578,382. Varied advertising in the form of newspaper display, billboards, match folders, and city maps helped spread the word about MLS.

Comparable sales figures are integral to the service given to clients and customers today, but it was only after a few years of records from the Multiple Listing Service were available that this marketing advice could be offered. An "Appraisal Assistance" service was started by filing the records of listings and sales complete with listing and selling prices, age, lot size, downpayment and other pertinent details to which inexperienced salespeople could refer for comparative purposes in the neighbourhoods represented. This further extended the services of the Statistical Department which existed until the late '80s when hard-copy data was no longer necessary. Today's fast-paced VANDAT menu of over 30 on-line programs with everything from an active listings search, comparable sales search, residential market analysis, telephone cross reference, municipal statistics and many more, give the sales force an awesome amount of information in the least amount of time.

The year 1957 can be remembered for a number of achievements. The Convention Committee hosted the largest conference that C.A.R.E.B. had ever held, and this was to become a regular experience each time the Vancouver Board agreed to host a national conference, up to and including the most recent in 1988. All Canadians enjoy a Vancouver visit, so it's an "easy sell" location.

The monumental task of establishing a Chair in Real Estate at UBC was accomplished by three real estate boards- Vancouver, new Westminster (now Fraser Valley Board) and Victoria pledging a total of $50,000 over a five-year period, ($30,000, $10,000 $10,000 respectively). The prime movers behind this initiative were the late Colonel Herbert R. Fullerton and Education Committee Chairman Charlie Brown. It was arranged that Professor Philip H. White from London University would arrive in mid-1958 to administer the program.

H. P. (Budge) Bell-Irving
President, 1958

Two founding members—J.P. Nicolls and H.V. Sharples died in 1957, and three Past Presidents were welcomed as Honorary Life Members, J.C. McPherson, F.A. Cleland and W.S. MacGregor.

An important milestone for members was the provision of Errors and Omissions Insurance, once a prohibitive cost for individual members, to be purchased through the Board at reasonable rates.

At the Annual Meeting held in February of 1958 it was announced that H.P. (Budge) Bell-Irving was elected President, assisted by Vice Presidents Charlie Brown, Harold Chivers and J.F. Kelly. These officials were to oversee two of the most progressive events in real estate history; (1) passage of the new Real Estate Act, effective June 1, 1958, a culmination of some seven years of effort, consideration and research on the part of this Board's elected members, and (2) the first salesmen's pre-licensing course at UBC, which comprised twenty two-hour lectures given daily throughout the four-week course, plus a daily assignment based on the lecture. The Committee was urging a complete correspondence course for the convenience of sales hopefuls in rural locations, and this was finally available in 1959.

By this time there were seventeen employees at the Board, including Secretary Alan Creer and Assistant Secretary George Muir. Staff continued to grow as the membership and its demands grew, and space was again becoming strained at 883 Howe Street. Board officials concluded early in the year that the Building Fund now had adequate reserves to consider purchase of a permanent home for the Association, and the search was on. Then, as in the 1993/94 new Board construction period when all members were given the opportunity to sell the existing building, all Board members were encouraged to bring forth proposed locations.

Founding member R.A. Hood, given Honorary Life Membership in the Board in 1955, passed away and another Honorary Life Membershipwas bestowed upon George L. Fowler, an Exchange member since 1934 and a Director from 1941 through 1946.

Because the Multiple Listing Service was drawing listings from further afield, the photographic field had to change to meet the need, so was expanded to a radius of 30 miles from the City Centre, to include suburbs within that periphery. An additional photographer named Jimmie Kakutani was employed and a darkroom installed for in-house processing. Jimmie also joined the ranks of long-time Board employees, taking MLS pictures through all seasonal weather conditions until his retirement in 1981.

Having done stellar work on real estate education for members of the profession, the Education Committee turned its attention to the public, and took over extensive public courses offered through the night school program of Vancouver School Board. Subjects covered everything from how to buy, finance, convey, maintain and insure a home, to the structure of the real estate industry, civic governments and the assessment, taxation and services they impose/provide.

In mid-1958 one W.W. Reid, affiliated with the Canadian Labour Congress, became self-proclaimed President of Canada's first Real Estate Salesmen's Union organized and chartered by 12 salespeople who were not members of the Board's Salesmen's Division. Reid was invited to a question and answer session with the Salesmen's Division. Over 150 sales people attended a July 16 meeting at the Stanley Park

The Sunday closing issue was still simmering. Reverend H.T. Allen of the Lords Day Alliance again appealed to the Board to impose Sunday closings, but the Board's reply was that until the Lords Day Act was applied and enforced equally to all—non-Board members, builders and for-sale-by owners alike—it would not deny its members the right to hold Sunday Opens.

Pavilion but prevailing opinion that day must have been the general desire for freedom from regimentation which brought most people into the real estate business. After a heated debate where more questions were asked than answered, there was a call for a show of hands by all those in favour of the union. Not one hand was raised. Naturally the Salesmen's Division had to take some action, and at a subsequent meeting in August, an unprecedented 655 members attended to hear of actions and suggestions in progress from the elected Salesmen's officials. These included investigation of a separate Salesmen's Association registered under the Societies Act, and a proposed by-law amendment from the joint Broker-Salesmen's Committee for a non-refundable drawing account for all sales employees. This proposal was subsequently defeated by a decisive negative vote from Board members, who did, however, approve an increase in salesman-representation on the Board's Directorate. Requests for certification by the sales forces of several member-companies were successfully opposed by the Division.

The Sunday closing issue was still simmering. Reverend H.T. Allen of the Lords Day Alliance again appealed to the Board to impose Sunday closings, but the Board's reply was that until the Lords Day Act was applied and enforced equally to all—non-Board members, builders and for-sale-by owners alike—it would not deny its members the right to hold Sunday Opens.

In 1958 a petition from seventeen brokers in the Burnaby area that they be allowed to organize a Division of the Vancouver Real Estate Board was approved, and so the Board's membership increased once again, ending the year with 295 voting members, 166 Active Associate members, 1,481 Salesman members, 37 Associate and 7 Honorary members for a total of 1,986, some 221 higher than at the end of the previous year. John B. Haddy of Gilley Real Estate was elected the first Burnaby Division President.

The Statistical and Survey Committee compiled much more informational data to be used by members, reports of starts, completions, population and N.H.A. reports, Mortgage registers, and also negotiated publication by the Journal of Commerce of a Daily Real Estate Record of all conveyances, Agreements for Sale, Mortgages, assignments, quitclaims, deeds and releases registered in the New Westminster Land Registry office. It had already put the same record in place covering the Vancouver Land Registry office. And plans were proceeding for the first publication of Real Estate Trends in Metropolitan Vancouver, with publication planned for 1959.

The Multiple Listing Service was still growing, as Bill Harrison, the Board's field man attended sales meetings and made personal canvasses at offices. The listings were being printed and mailed to companies at that time. This was the year some success was finally achieved with some hard to convince west side licensees, and there was a decided increase in commercial, industrial and revenue properties being listed. As a result, the year ended with the largest volume to date, at $39,467,486, and a sales to listings ratio of 25.5%.

Many plans initiated the previous year were completed in 1959 under direction of new President Charlie Brown and Vice Presidents Harold Chivers, J. Ross Ker and J.P. Roberts.

A substantial vote of 132-4 showed membership approval of the final decision on a Board premises. After investigating buildings at Bute and Melville streets, 8th and Granville and Burrard and Drake, the favoured purchase was a building at Broadway and Spruce. While upholding the right of property ownership and encouraging the purchase of property—inherent in the reason for real estate boards having been formed—the Vancouver Board was the first in British Columbia to have achieved the financial capability of ownership of its own building. Previously owned by the C.N.I.B., this two-storey reinforced concrete building had been designed and completed in 1929 by Thornton Sharpe, the Burrard Bridge Architect. This building provided plenty of room for the Board's requirements, plus allowing for several rentable areas to help defray expenses. For thirty four years this was to be home base for the real estate association, until it moved into its especially designed building at the corner of 8th Avenue and Spruce Street in mid-1994.

In 1959 the Education Committee saw over 850 pre-licensing students, 600 from the Lower Mainland alone, go through the new correspondence training under Professor Philip White of UBC. Thus began development of real estate education that has become the envy of almost every Cana-

Charlie Brown
President, 1959, 1960

dian province and most American States, often copied but never equaled. The three-year diploma course was under way, a $500 scholarship was offered for the first time and the Vancouver Library real estate section soared to a total of 800 volumes. Testifying to its popularity, there were on average 560 volumes on loan at all times.

Bert Edwards was serving a second term as President of the Salesmen's Division, which was now five years old and an established Standing Committee of the Board. He saw salesmen sitting in on Complaints & Discipline meetings and able to have access to Board Arbitration proceedings. The Annual Snowball Frolic was a continuing success, as the Commodore Ballroom's springy dance floor accommodated some 650 happy sales celebrants each December.

This was a time when Boards and Associations could set standards of commissions and fees. While the standard then was 5% for exclusive properties and 7% for multiple listings on the first $100,000 of value and 2 1/2% on value beyond, there was a movement from the industry to increase the minimum commission to 6%. A special Committee was set to study and discuss the matter with members from the New Westminster and Victoria Real Estate Boards as well.

The Multiple Listing Committee made several changes for improved service to members. Arrangements were made for members to either pick up their listings at the Board premises or at a pre-arranged pick-up point so save waiting for the listings to be delivered through Canada Post.

A mechanical McBee sorting system had been installed to enable members from any area to find out from the Board all the MLS listing numbers for houses of a certain type in any desired district. Sounds like a fifties' forerunner to the Active Listings Search on VANDAT today.

As the Multiple Listing Service became more used and more sophisticated, its Rules and Regulations had to be reviewed constantly and amended to meet changing conditions. In 1959 the listing period was extended from the existing thirty days to two months, which remains the minimum listing period today. Cancellation due to lack of action was eliminated and equal rights for sold signs on property for both listing and selling broker were established.

This was the year that vendors began to get a copy of the picture of their house, enclosed in a specially printed frame thanking them for listing their property and outlining what kind of service to expect through the Multiple Listing Serv-

Spring of 1959 saw another tradition born-the first issue of Real Estate And Business Trends, a monumental 200-page book filled with important business trends and statistical facts. Still eagerly sought thirty five years later, and now called MetroTrends, 1,500 copies of that first edition sold at $5.00 plus provincial Tax, about the same number still in demand annually at today's $33.00 plus PST and GST.

Facelift for 1101 West
Broadway

ice. This inspired public relations gesture was continued through the sixties and seventies before the sheer volume of listing made it impossible to continue.

The Multiple Listing Service Committee proudly announced that the Service had once again out performed its previous year. In 1959 total sales volume was $41,570,749, just under the $42,000,000 goal the Committee had set at the beginning of the year. That sum represented $2,700,000 in total commissions distributed to Board firms, despite the effect a "tight money" situation had on all business that year.

As the Board prepared to turn the corner into another decade, the Education Committee planned advanced Appraisal Training and extending night school classes for the public. Having purchased 1101 West Broadway, the Board looked forward to a permanent home to ensure the Board's efficiency and financial security.

CHAPTER EIGHT

THE GOLDEN SIXTIES

The 1959 Executive was returned by acclamation in 1960—Charlie Brown as President, with Vice Presidents Harold Chivers, J. Ross Ker and J.P. Roberts. The year began with planning for renovations to the new building under chairmanship of Harry Gillespie of Gillespie Investments Ltd.

Television had flickered on in most households, the Kennedy era dawned and flower power immigrated from San Francisco to bloom brightly in Vancouver. Dr. Rose, a Professor from the University of Toronto, told CAREB Conference delegates in 1960 that the decade would be the "golden Years of real estate" due to coming of age of the large crop of "war babies" born between 1939 and 1945.

European immigration was also adding to the Canadian population and at that time the "average Canadian family" was getting larger, increasing demand for new housing. This, said Dr. Rose, was the foundation for the "golden sixties" ahead for the industry.

Economic conditions across Canada in 1960 weren't as "golden" as Professor Rose had prophesied, but financing for the Board building was successfully conducted through a Debenture Issue to members, paying an interest rate of 8%, with National Trust Company appointed Trustee for the Debenture holders under the Trust Deed. Renovations were carefully and economically handled. As President Charlie Brown said in his Annual Report, "it required all the belt-tightening that any first-time home buyer is faced with..." and this husbandry assured a small surplus of revenue over expenditure for the year.

The B.C. Association of Real Estate Boards appealed to its members to approve a resolution to the Attorney General to introduce legislation to make it lawful for homes to be shown between the hours of 1 p.m. and 6 p.m. on Sundays. Reasoning was that buying a home is a family affair, and due to the sociological structure of life, Sunday is often the only day the family has together. Board Directors adopted the Resolution. Finally, in 1963, Provincial authorities gave assurance that drastic action would not be taken against those showing houses for sale on Sundays.

The controversy over Sunday Opens resulted in more weekday Opens, particularly during this selling period when a lot of extra effort was needed to complete home sales. Sometimes three and four weekday Opens would start in the afternoon and last throughout the evening. It was not unusual to list a home after the vendors had been required to move, leaving maintenance of the property to the good offices of the licensee who, of course, did it to present a desirable property to buyers. It could take several seasons to find a buyer, and many real estate salesmen at that time could diarize months of duties—shoveling the walks in winter, painting the trim and porch steps in early spring, installing awnings for summer and even mowing the lawn.

(One such 1960 West Side sale on Athlone was described to this writer. After faithful maintenance, showing 97 possible purchasers and 67 agents through the property, it sold for $19,500. VANDAT shows three subsequent sales for this property in the past 34 years, the last one in 1993 for $849,000.)

There is nothing contemporary about the illegal suite question, because as far back as the '50s Vancouver City Council was in regular contact with the Board on that subject as well as other zoning matters. During the sixties the Legislative and Public Affairs Committee of the Board spent many hours considering this question with city representatives. It wasn't until the last half of the 80s that a solution was finally reached between members of various municipal councils and the Board. To comply with disclosure requirements, the catalogue listing must identify if unauthorized accommodation is contained, but for external advertising the only two phrases allowed are "Fully Finished Basement" or "partially finished basement".

Four new Honorary Life Members were named in 1960, including Past Presidents H.E. Bond, E.L. Boultbee, A Rout Harvey, and H.A. Roberts.

The Multiple Listing Committee had a busy year but one not as financially successful as those before. For the first time since its inception, the Service registered a decrease instead of increase over the year before.

Monthly award dinners were continued for top salespeople and a new category for high unit volume was introduced. A new extension agreement form for renewing or extending existing listings was introduced, and a $5.00 refundable listing fee (on payment of the sales' assessment) replaced the $3.00 photography fee. But Canada's economic woes affected the buying public that year, as would be the experience on future occasions.

The 1960 sales volume totalled $38,924,071.00 from the sale of 2,970 properties, down from the previous year's

*This was the first full year the Board had its "home",
where the Education Committee had a good
sized auditorium for seminar offerings, and where
staff could function more effectively.*

Harold Chivers
President, 1961

$41,570,749. The "average" MLS transaction price was $13,105. At this time there were some 45 local real estate boards in Canada operating Multiple Listing Services, and the volume of transactions reported to CAREB in 1960 was $445,000,000. Vancouver's dollar volume represented 9% of that total. (At the end of 1993 total sales reported to CREA by its member Boards was $51.5 billion. One of 117 reporting Real Estate Boards, Greater Vancouver-the second largest Canadian Board-reported a $9.4 billion dollar volume, which represented 18% of total 1993 Canadian MLS sales)

Harold Chivers from Burnaby became President in 1961, the first president elected from outside the confines of Vancouver city. He was assisted by Vice Presidents Denys Back, J. Ross Ker and J.P. Roberts.

This was the first full year the Board had its "home", where the Education Committee had a good sized auditorium for seminar offerings, and where staff could function more effectively.

The three geographical Divisions instituted MLS Open House Tours, which encouraged more listing on the Service and promoted comradery among licensees from all around the Divisional areas. North Vancouver Division used a caravan bus accommodating from 35-40 persons each tour, and there was a measurable improvement in MLS sales. The West Vancouver tours didn't work as well, and the caravan was cancelled, but plans were soon underway to schedule a special Open House Day, and its success is obvious in that it is still held 33 years later.

The Board practised what it preached by using Multiple Listings to inform all members of leasable space in the new bulding and was successful whenever excess space was available.

Perhaps it was the economic slowdown that precipitated a problem which has never been entirely solved—that of part-time salespeople being allowed by Agents to work at other endeavours. The Board undertook to inform its own members, but also made a recommendation to the Real Estate Council that it circularize all Agents to draw to their

In his Annual Report for the year, President Chivers
chided those Board members who, while in a minority,
were "unscrupulous" in their method of financing proper-
ties, offering large "bonuses", to take advantage of
unwary investors, and those who advertised that they
would buy homes when indeed they did not.

attention the pertinent section of the Act forbidding this, and
the penalties for failure to comply.

A special Dual MLS Committee was wrestling with both
the economic and logistical possibilities of a system of dual
Multiple Listings between members of Vancouver and New
Westminster Boards.

In mid-1961 the Commission split was changed to 3 1/2%
to the Selling Broker and 3 1/2% to the Listing Broker, who
paid the MLS fee. Despite this encouragement to selling
salespeople, the year's production again showed a down-
ward trend, achieving $35,155,062 for the 2,847 sales, and a
percentage of sales to listings of 24.5%. This $3.8 million
reduction from the previous year corresponded proportion-
ately to a drop in sales personnel during the same period. In
1960 there had been 1,369 salespeople in the field, which
dropped the next year to 1,187.

In his Annual Report for the year, President Chivers
chided those Board members who, while in a minority, were
"unscrupulous" in their method of financing properties,
offering large "bonuses", to take advantage of unwary investors, and those who advertised that they would buy homes
when indeed they did not. They applied what he termed a
devious method of financing which was unprofessional and
not becoming to a Board member. Another problem he
focused upon was that of members who accepted Multiple
Listings at unrealistically high prices, knowing the vendor
would eventually have to take much less in price and terms.
This practice of discouraging other members from selling
the property was directly contrary to the true concept of
M.L.S., which is meant to be an equal sharing of knowledge
among members for the benefit of all.

1961 had been a fiscally difficult year because of a drop in
Multiple Sales, legal expenses due to a difficult case arising
from the discipline of a member-firm, a sales tax assessment
for production of Multiple Listings, and extra costs associated
with acquiring, renovating and opening the new building. All
Board Executives and volunteer Standing Committee members continued to work as hard as ever to keep the ship afloat,

right to the point of paying for their own lunches when they attended meetings. Before pounding the gavel to start the meeting, each Chairman would collect the 75 or 80-cents required to pay for the sandwiches. Indeed, some Committees opted to "brown bag" their own meal rather than pay up-front.

As the year came to an end, the B.C. Real Estate Act was amended to limit charging the business tax on real estate licenses, and also to permit trust companies to enter the real estate brokerage business. Originally the trust companies employed unlicensed salespersons but through the efforts of the Vancouver Board and other B.C. Association of Real Estate Boards members, this was amended to require licensing.

As 1962 dawned, President Kennedy was warming up the Cold War and setting up the Peace Corps., and the Vancouver Board elected its youngest-ever President, J. Ross Ker, a third-generation member of the Board, grandson of charter member Newton J. Ker, C.P.R Land Agent.

Vice Presidents that year were Denys H. Back, John L. Boultbee and J.P. Roberts. Treasurer was Harold Davies, and together with the Finance Committee, he began to deal with the financial woes. One of the first things dealt with that year was in passing the protected marks, "Multiple Listing Service" and "M.L.S." to C.A.R.E.B. Pending prosecution by the Cooperative Association of Canada, the Canadian Association of Real Estate Boards had to drop the terms "Photo Coop" and "Cooperative Listing", as did VREB eight years previously. The Vancouver Board had protected the term "Multiple Listing Service" in 1954, but now willingly assigned rights to that term to CAREB, upon its undertaking to pay the costs originally incurred for protecting the mark.

The Real Estate Salesmen's Association # 1570 was still in existence, and the Board's Salesmen's Division was now into its eighth year. The Association made application for Minimum Wage protection to the Board of Industrial Relations, but the Vancouver Salesmen's Division, along with New Westminster and Victoria Sales Divisions, were successful in defeating the application. Their argument was that to subject real estate salesmen to minimum wage legislation would replace their traditional independence and freedom to set working hours. The principle of salesmen paid on the basis on commissions on sales was considered incompatible with the concept of set wage scales by opposing salespeople.

Among the many civic subjects investigated by the Legis-

J. Ross Ker
President, 1962

Individually members enjoyed a banner year as the level of activity increased. The value of applications to register Deeds and Mortgages in the various Land Registry offices throughout British Columbia soared to $867,560,783 in 1962 from $669,520,776 the year before. The Vancouver Land Registry alone released figures of $285,439,778 in 1961 and $322,431,741 the next year.

lative and Public Affairs Committee is one of those "the more things change the more they remain the same" items–the amount of time in certain cases before civic authorities would issue a development permit! A constantly recurring theme, this is a subject still on the tip of a developers' tongue as we reach the mid-point in the '90s over 30 years later. As each year's population growth creates more official problems, it seems, official wheels grind more slowly.

The position of MLS "field man" had been eliminated in 1960 but when Director Henry J. Block took over as Committee Chairman in 1962, he filled the "fieldman" role on a volunteer basis. During the year there wasn't a member-company which wasn't visited, with the result that new life seemed to be breathed into the MLS system. A series of meetings with members' salesmen generated enthusiasm, and an MLS News page was introduced so members could exchange extra listing information within the membership. A pamphlet called "The Magic of Multiple" gave potential vendors all the reasons to list Multiple.

Individually members enjoyed a banner year as the level of activity increased. The value of applications to register Deeds and Mortgages in the various Land Registry offices throughout British Columbia soared to $867,560,783 in 1962 from $669,520,776 the year before. The Vancouver Land Registry alone released figures of $285,439,778 in 1961 and $322,431,741 the next year.

Vancouver Board's MLS sales represented a significant part of those Registry figures with $44,829,789 in sales volume for 1962, an increase of 28% over the previous year's volume. Vendor and developer sales were also represented in the registry figures. The previous high MLS year had been registered in 1959 when over $41.5 million in sales was realized. There was still a long way to go in convincing Board members that Multiple would work as well or better than exclusive listing, but progress was being made because in 1962 the number of listings increased to an all-time high of 14,630. The most satisfying statistic to all concerned, however, was that the sales to listings ratio rose to 26%, highest level ever.

Successful Multiple Listing sales, while profiting the vendors, buyers and sales people involved, also benefited the Board in its time of need. Considering its obligations for payment on the new building, the Finance Committee was pleased to report income for 1962 of $50,000 more than in 1961, a result of successful MLS activity.

Past Board and CAREB President, Dean S. Mansell was proclaimed an Honorary Life Member in 1962.

It should be noted that since its inception, the Exchange/ Board had maintained a Complaints and Arbitration procedure, both of which became more structured and active after introduction of the Multiple Listing Service, which had clearly set rules and regulations. Not to belabour the point that the Committees met and wrestled with many problems, it should be observed that this process is still working for the benefit of members and the public. The Complaints & Discipline Committee—now called Business Practises—has investigated and resolved many public and member complaints as has the Arbitration procedure helped settle financial disputes between members. Few industries/Associations can look back at such a successful record of settlement accord from within their own ranks.

John P. Roberts—the "father" of the Multiple Listing Service—was named President in 1963, assisted by Vice Presidents, John L. Boultbee and J. S. Wood, and Treasurer J. Harold Davies.

J. P. Roberts
President, 1963

After a financially successful 1962, the new year started with a good product inventory—2,022 units representing a gross value of over $37,000,000. The Board's financial position was also strengthened because all extra rentable space in the new building was occupied that year and activity on the MLS was brisk. These contributed to the fact the Directors were able to completely retire the first mortgage on the building by year end, after only three years of ownership.

During this year the subject of creation of a Real Estate Education Foundation was first raised, and a fund-raising Committee was appointed. There was little support for such an institution at that time, but the interest didn't subside, and the Real Estate Institute Education and Research Foundation was underway a year later funded by grants from all British Columbia Boards. Vancouver gave $6,000 in 1964 and promised $5,000 annually in future years providing funds were available.

Through the years when the Association had the ability to

*The Multiple Listing Committee announced the first
"Quarter Million Dollar Club" achievers this year from
their individual MLS production figures for 1962.*

set or change commissions and fees the subject often arose
of a schedule that would increase commissions to a flat 6%
from the existing 5% and 7%. It is significant that the
majority of Board members regularly voted in the negative to
this suggestion and despite sharp economic fluctuations
through the years the rate remained at 5% (7% MLS) set on
the first $100,000 of MLS listed properties and 2 1/2% on the
balance. Competition legislation now prevents Boards from
setting a standard commission rate. The company or individual's cost of providing service is now entirely the decision
of that licensed entity and clients are urged to negotiate a
satisfactory arrangement for realty service.

In August of 1963 a new statistical newsletter called
"Trend News" was introduced by the Statistical and Survey
Committee, a useful publication filled with MLS statistics,
housing starts, apartment vacancies and office, commercial
and industrial statistics. The Multiple Listing Committee announced the first "Quarter Million Dollar Club" achievers
this year from their individual MLS production figures for
1962. Seven salespeople were lauded for having sold properties totaling more than the magic $250,000 goal, and this at
a time when the average MLS transaction was $12,518.

The following year the number of Quarter Million Club
achievers more than tripled and eventually, as average
residential transactions on Multiple rose in value, a "half"
and "million" category were introduced. In the early '70s it
was recognized that the name of this achievement category
was often misunderstood, as the public assumed it to be a
category of "total earnings", not "total sales volume." To
correct this misconception the name was changed to Medallion Club, which is still very much a Multiple achievement for
up to ten percent of those using the Service. Qualification
levels are set annually based on market activity and "average" transaction values. One per cent of qualifiers can achieve
top status of "President's Club" for outstanding sales success.

Because many local residential properties required upgrading and National Housing Act Home Improvement Loans
were set at only $4,000, the Board endeavoured to have this

One of the first accomplish-
ments this year was the
formation of the first
Commercial, Industrial and
Investment Division by
Past President, John P.
Roberts, who also served as
the first President of that
Division.

loan limit doubled and the amortization period extended from the traditional five years. After the Board's resolution was forwarded to the Minister, a letter received from Central Mortgage and Housing informed members about an amendment not generally known, rarely published and rarely admitted by lending institutions-the maximum term allowed was actually ten years. This fact helped Board members inform both homeowners and lenders of the longer-term payback of 10 years, and potential homeowner-borrowers benefited by needed home improvements amortised over a more comfortable payment period.

Long involved on advising labour ministers on fair compensation for janitorial workers, in 1963 the Board again launched a successful protest against new minimum wage orders that would negatively affect both apartment owners and the janitorial people themselves. Working closely with the Provincial Government Labour Department, a Board Committee's factual statistics helped establish a satisfactory minimum janitorial wage based on the number of suites involved in each building.

For many years professional public relations counsel had been supplied to the Board on a retainer basis, but in late 1963 Mrs. Anne Broadfoot joined the staff on a half-time basis to conduct media relations and produce a monthly REALTOR magazine. This half-time position became full time by the end of the decade and as the Board grew, so did public relations and communications requirements. That busy department now has four full time staff members.

A Multiple Listing Sales Comparison picture catalogue was published for the first time that year and was valuable in helping establish realistic prices. The first issue sold out a 725 print-run at $1.50 plus tax per copy. Subsequent editions were published each six months.

At the end of 1963, the Multiple Listing Service again achieved gains. Dollar volume reached $47,981,042.00, an increase of seven per cent over the previous year.

Seventy eight years after Magistrate John Boultbee prepared the incorporation papers for the City of Vancouver in 1886, his grandson John L. Boultbee was named President of the Vancouver Real Estate Board in 1964. (He had been preceded 22 years earlier by his father, Leonard Boultbee, President in 1941.) He was assisted by Vice Presidents Walter Brown and J.S. Wood, with J. Harold Davies as Treasurer.

A Broker-Salesman Committee was established to exam-

John L. Boultbee
President, 1964

ine in depth the problems affecting productivity that were common to both salesmen and agents, with particular reference to the high ratio of salesmen to the population in the Greater Vancouver area at that time. (There were 2,259 persons licensed as salesmen in British Columbia at that time. While no confirmed Greater Vancouver figure for 1964 was found, the Vancouver Board's share of those was in the neighbourhood of 1,200, and approximately 28% of these were female. In mid-1994 the Salesmen's Division boasts a total of 8,354 members, 4,964 male and 3390—or 41%—female)

Then graduate student of UBC, Stan Hamilton, was employed to conduct a survey relative to production of the sales force. Survey results showed a high level of low-income salespeople; 28.2% earned under $3,000 annually at that time; From $3,000—$5,000—27.7%; From $5,000 to $7,000—19.7%; From $7,000 to $10,000—17.1% and only 7.3% of licensees earned more than $10,000. The Joint Broker-Salesman Committee continued to meet and consider these facts.

Early in 1964 what was called "a pioneer move in the mortgage field" was announced by the Bank of Nova Scotia, Aluminum Co. of Canada and the investment house, Greenshields Inc., who had incorporated the Mortgage Insurance Co. of Canada (M.I.C.C.), which allowed borrowers up to 83 1/3% mortgaging. Conventional lenders gave 66 2/3% and the balance by Central Covenants Ltd., owned by MICC and 22 other lenders, mostly trust and insurance companies. The loans were insured by M.I.C.C. at rates a quarter of one percent above conventional rates prevailing in any community, with those insurance premiums adding only one quarter of one per cent. It was in late 1993 the industry learned that after nearly 30 years of existence M.I.C.C. would no longer be insuring high ratio mortgages.

In 1964 Vancouver was one of two British Columbia Boards to be awarded the highest honor then given by the Canadian Association of Real Estate Boards. Vancouver and the Okanagan Mainline Boards were given OSCAR designation for "maintenance of exceptionally high standards both within the real estate industry and the community".

When the $25 million Port Mann Bridge opened in mid 1964 it forged a major link in the Trans Canada Highway system and guaranteed residential growth in the Fraser Valley. The Board has always been responsive to growth patterns, and ready to meet the increasing needs of members.

An IBM automated system was introduced in 1964, so major details of all listing contracts (MLS number, address, listing/expiry dates, physical characteristics, etc.) were recorded on IBM punch cards. This eliminated time consuming hand-recording handling of listings. It also enabled the Board to prepare more and different information programs for members, such as availabilities by price range, number of rooms, area, or any sequence requested by members. When a property sold, the appropriate card was pulled and selling data punched in, so monthly sales pictures could be completed faster.

This system was also the basis for faster MLS billings to member-brokers and formed a monthly automatic accounting system, eliminating the "pink slip" which had formerly been the invoice. The 402 IBM Accounting machine also replaced the cumbersome Addressograph method of maintaining membership records, reducing the time to prepare a Salesmen's Division Membership list from four hours to just one hour.

J. Harold Davies
President, 1965

Sound like a precursor to today's data systems? Of course it was. Vancouver Board administrators were always in the forefront of better business methods, and were soon to became known as pioneers in real estate computerization in Canada.

The Annual Christmas Luncheon for Board members had been moved from the Georgia Hotel to the Tudor Hall in the new Board building in 1961. By 1964 the demand for tickets was so heavy that two luncheons were held on subsequent days to satisfy this holiday spirit and eventually it was moved back to the Georgia Hotel to accommodate the members. It is now held at the Bayshore Inn.

More efficient Board office service and an increasing acceptance of Multiple Listing by both members and public helped sales volume rise that year. But 1964 was also a year of rising employment and increasing retail trade right across Canada. Some of that benefit came to the Board, as Multiple totals rose $8.5 million above the previous year, for a dollar volume of $56,548,419.

By the mid sixties there was a "building boom" all over Canada, and Vancouver was receiving its share. Skylines were changing as apartment buildings rose in the West End, Kitsilano, Kerrisdale and North Vancouver.

At the Annual Meeting in early 1965, J. Harold Davies was installed President, with Vice Presidents J.S. Wood and Alf Buttress and Treasurer M.J. Wenaus.

Quarter Million qualifiers were always recognized at the Annual Meeting in those early days, and when the third annual awards were made total qualifiers numbered 65—double the previous year.

The Joint Broker-Salesman Committee under Past President John Boultbee had worked hard to answer the Board's concerns that a large number of salespeople in the industry did not earn a proper living. The Committee recommended that the membership approve a provision of a minimum weekly non-refundable drawing account of $50.00 per week for all members of the Salesmen's Division, which numbered 1,286 individuals in 1965. A series of Agents' discussion groups, however, proved negative and the suggestions were put on hold.

It is an idea that could be investigated again, and one that is being used to the advantage of staff of a large Pennsylvania-based real estate firm. Thinking that if his agents could enjoy a stable monthly income their sales performance would improve, Howard Hanna Real Estate Services introduced an "Income Advantage Program" in early 1994. Agents can receive a monthly cheque for up to 50% of their previous year's monthly earnings as a draw against future commissions if they had earned at least $25,000 in commissions and referral income during the previous year. According to the Real Estate INSIDER, the program has been a resounding success, with sales agents actually increasing their previous year's income by an average of 11.8%.

By the mid sixties there was a "building boom" all over Canada, and Vancouver was receiving its share. Skylines were changing as apartment buildings rose in the West End, Kitsilano, Kerrisdale and North Vancouver. The economy and the population of Greater Vancouver were rising, and downtown Vancouver's arterial streets were getting ever more congested with vehicular traffic. The City of Vancouver decided to establish stringent parking require-

In 1965 the first five $500 annual scholarships were offered to members' children planning to attend post secondary education in B.C. In the past 29 years, those first five winners have been followed by 140 other academically inclined children of Board members to graduate in a diversity of disciplines. Annual review of needs has brought the award up to a more appropriate 1994 sum of $1,500 each and it can now be used for attendance at any accredited North American institution.

ments for new commercial development in the area west of Burrard Street which threatened to seriously curtail development in that area.

The I.C.I Division commissioned a Parking Survey by nationally recognized Traffic Engineer Mr. J.R. Walker. His report said an existing over-supply of downtown parking space which was also under-priced were major factors encouraging people to eschew public transit and drive their cars downtown. Walker's report revealed the reason for a steadily deteriorating transit system, which in 1946 carried 118,995,994 passengers with a Greater Vancouver population of 400,000. In 1964 it carried only 54,536,645 passengers while the population had doubled to 800,000. In an improving economy more people bought more cars, and due to the sub-economic parking fees they drove daily in one-passenger cars to park all day in the city core, adding to arterial congestion and the demand for more highways.

While a great deal of public attention and acclaim was generated by this report, Civic authorities and planners gave it very little attention and the congestion continues to this day. The only thing that has changed is the cost of parking-which, while higher, is still not at a level to adequately discourage vehicle congestion in the downtown core.

The Board purchased Lots 8, 9 and 10, Block 334, on the southwest corner of Spruce Street and 8th Avenue, immediately across the lane behind the Board's building. This property was used for many years as a surface parking area for Board members. Quarter Century clubbers will recall how carefully the 1965 blacktoppers worked around the 50-year old Cherry Tree. The protected tree continued to bloom throughout the years until 1992 when it was removed for the new construction. The sheer foresight of that earlier purchase decision was welcomed by more contemporary Directorates, who were able to use this space to build a complete new Board building, opened in 1994, the year of celebration recognizing 75 years of continual service from this association.

A plan put in motion in 1965 by the Public Relations Committee chaired by Director Fred Russell, was to achieve far more attention than the Parking Survey, and achieve public acclaim for the Board for over two decades. Spurred by Committee member Ted Henderson, Russell encouraged publication of a four-colour pictorial representation of Greater Vancouver, photographs taken by Board photographer Ted

Czolowski and copy written by staff public relations officer Anne Broadfoot.

A fiscally careful Finance Committee finally gave permission for a print-run of 7,500 copies instead of the 15,000 proposed, conditional upon pre-selling at least half that number before going to press. The Committee held a "name the book" contest, with each entry required to be accompanied by an order for at least two books at a cost of $3.50 each. Winning entry, *Through Lions Gate*, was submitted by 1964 Salesmen's Division President, Bill Clarke, and production was soon underway.

Two new Honorary Life Memberships were awarded in 1965 in recognition of their collective encouragement and introduction of new educational opportunities for Vancouver real estate practitioners. So honored were Past President Col. Herbert R. Fullerton, and Professor Philip H. White of UBC.

Financially, 1965 was an excellent year and the Multiple Listing Service registered a 27.3% advance over the previous year, recording a dollar volume of $71,989,379.00.

This financial success was to be carried through 1966, when M.J. Wenaus was named President, Alf Buttress and Bert Edwards Vice Presidents and J.S. Wood Treasurer.

As the year began economists were publicly worrying about a "financial famine" due to a diminishing supply of mortgage money, but because of the Board's improved financial situation, the $5.00 Listing Fee was removed for a trial period and an equal commission split between lister and seller established. That Listing Fee was never imposed again.

The Economic Council of Canada said that household-formations were setting new records each year, and these must have helped Multiple Listers and sellers in the previous year because when Quarter Million Club qualifiers were announced, there were 117, up from 65 the year before.

From its inception the Multiple Listing Service had always had a strong following from those who sold on Vancouver's East Side, followed in volume by North Vancouver, but after Burnaby's new Simon Fraser University held its first classes in late 1965 and the Lougheed Mall started to develop, a

M. J. Wenaus
President, 1966

110

flurry of building and selling activity in new housing developments made the members from that large municipality true MLS competitors. Board use and loyalty by Burnaby-based brokers was increased after that year's election, too. M.J. (Huck) Wenaus was only the second Board President to come from surburban ranks, having been preceded in 1961 by Harold Chivers, also of Burnaby.

In a special ceremony that year the Burnaby Division's President, A.G. Toppings, accompanied by Board President Wenaus, presented the University's geography department with a giant 5 foot by 9 foot mosaic map of the Lower Mainland.

Because the Board's Tudor Hall was often not in use during the evening, it was donated to various non-profit groups and organizations such as B.O.M.A., for meetings Monday through Thursday when janitorial staff was on duty. Again, always upgrading, the Board's long-time receptionist Barbara Coughlin had to learn to "dial not plug", when the old plug and cord telephone board was replaced with a fully automatic switchboard. Today's telephone user might view that system as the "buggy whip of communication", but it was a "giant step" buggy whip on the road to today's technology.

Probably the most successful event this year was the June release of *Through Lions Gate*, culminating almost two years of effort on the part of the Publicity & Public Relations Committee. The book was acclaimed by the press and public, but particularly by members, who snapped up copies a dozen at a time to give as client and customer gifts. The first print-run of 7,500 was depleted in less than a month and a second printing ordered to satisfy demand. The Greater Vancouver Visitors and Convention Bureau named President Wenaus "Man of the Month" for July on the strength of this "significant contribution to the tourist industry in Greater Vancouver". Dedication in the book was "A pictorial tour of Greater Vancouver, published by the Vancouver Real Estate Board and dedicated to its citizens."

Throughout the years this popular publication was revised seven times to stay up to date on all developments and

111

facilities. It has been distributed to princes and plain folk, Consuls and clients and customers, business associates and relatives around the globe. The last revision was completed in preparation for Expo '86. During its lifetime over 200,000 copies of this book have been circulated around the world and it holds the distinction of being the first four-colour pictorial book ever published in Canada. It came off the press one year before the 1967 Canadian official Centennial book, "Canada in Colour", which, incidentally, asked for and received permission to reprint three of the Board's TLG pictures.

All real estate licensees were now required to be bonded under the new B.C. Security Bonding Act, and in 1966 B.C. established a Grade 12 educational qualification for Licensees. This requirement was dropped by the Provincial Government in 1981, but in 1994 an English Proficiency requirement was imposed by the Real Estate Council.

The discussion on a name change to more appropriately describe the area served by Board members had started in 1964, but it was not until 1966 that approval of the change to "Greater Vancouver Real Estate Board" was received from the Registrar of Companies in Victoria. Final change, then, was subject to approval of the membership. This was received, early the next year, and May, 1967, the name of the association officially became Greater Vancouver Real Estate Board.

In 1966 the MLS Committee was pleased to report a banner year for the Multiple Listing Service, with sales that topped $90,000,000, an increase of 25.6% over the previous year. Retiring President Huck Wenaus reported to members that by the end of 1966 the Board was completely unencumbered, and was already starting to build an adequate liquid surplus in case of future periods of austerity. This financial security was in no small part thanks to Wenaus himself, who had served two years on the Finance Committee, one as Treasurer and Chairman, and carefully handled the Board's resources to the best advantage. To ensure this would continue, 1967 Directors voted him Treasurer again in his Past Presidential year, ensuring on-going fiscal responsibility.

Alfred Buttress was named President, with Hugh Clee and Bert Edwards serving as Vice Presidents. One of the first acts in respect to consumer protection in 1967 was restoration of the excess cover bond in the amount of $100,000. It had been abandoned in 1962 due to the "tight money" situation of

Alfred Buttress
President, 1967

*One of the first acts in respect to consumer protection
in 1967 was restoration of the excess cover bond in the
amount of $100,000. It had been abandoned in
1962 due to the "tight money" situation of the building
renovation period.*

the building renovation period. This bond is over and above
the coverage granted by the surety bonds required for licensing and even today is held by the Board as trustee for the
clients of members. Payouts as a result of wrongful or dishonest dealing on the part of a member in a real estate transaction are recoverable by the bonding company from the
member involved.

To continue to be successful frequent review of programs
and regulations must be conducted, and thus it was that a
number of changes were made to the M.L.S. Rules & Regulations. The assessment payable to the service upon sale of a
listed property had been established as a percentage of
the selling price not exceeding .5% on the first $100,000.
This fee was now made a variable one with a maximum of
$500, so the assessment could be set at a rate that fluctuated
with market conditions. This resulted in substantial savings
to the Membership, and is still in existence today. During
the past five years, in fact, Board members have enjoyed
the lowest assessments in the history of the Service despite
some minor variations.

Copies of *Through Lions Gate* were still much in demand,
with Canadian Pacific Airlines and other companies buying
many copies to give to clients, along with choice of typescript
transalation available in German, Italian, French and Japanese. The Publicity Committee also formulated a program
where non-profit and educational organizations could get
limited numbers of free copies for distribution.

The staff's work load was increasing as Board Committees
became involved in many community projects, so in May
Peter Watkinson was employed as an Assistant Secretary to
work with the I.C. & I Division, Legislative & Public Affairs
and Education Committees. After military service Peter spent
nearly 20 years with the Board of Trade's Civic and Governmental Department before becoming a Board staff member.
He retired eleven years later in 1978.

OSCAR merit awards had been received regularly, and in
1967 CREA awarded it to the now "GREATER" Vancouver
Real Estate Board.

*Canada had just embarked on its "second century" as
a united nation, despite a geography spanning one
of the world's largest continents from Atlantic to Pacific.*

President Alf Buttress went to City Hall to argue the case
for higher density, more intensive use of land and a supply of
homes in the "middle income" bracket. (Then $6,000 to
$7,000 per year) The Strata Titles Legislation (now Condo-
minium Act) had been passed the year before and as the city
population grew, the Board felt the City had a unique opportunity to use city-owned land in the south-east corner of the
community for a large multi-family development instead of
single family lots. The Champlain Heights moderate-cost
housing development exists today as one result of this type of
civic involvement by the Board.

Family picnics at Birch Bay were still a mid-week summer
hit, with at least 600 adults and children from a relatively
compact membership in attendance. That fall another large
contingent of Greater Vancouver members took advantage
of attending a CAREB Conference hosted in Vancouver by
their home Board.

Ten years earlier in 1957 the Social Credit Government
had started a series of Home Owner grants to relieve property
tax woes, starting at $28.00 per year and rising to $120
by 1967. Along the same lines, the first in what would become
a series of housing incentives was initiated, the B.C. Home
Acquisition Grant with a basic grant of $500 for buyers/
builders of housing. All these buying incentive grants were
rescinded in 1983, except for the B.C. Second Mortgage
which was a repayable loan. This initiative too was abolished
in 1993.

Rising employment and a high demand for housing helped
the Multiple Listing Sales Volume soar to never before
reached heights-topping 1966 by 44% and more than breaking the One Hundred Million barrier to record $130,187,897.
Membership in the Quarter Million Club rose to 300
members as the growing awareness of Multiple's magic
was brought home to more and more members who, in
turn, advised more and more listers of the wisdom of cooperative selling.

Bert Edwards scored better than a hat-trick in 1968. He
had been named President of the Salesmen's Division in

Bert Edwards
President, 1968

1959, elected a Director at Large in 1964, Vice President in both 1966 and 1967, and the next year topped the vote as President. Hugh A. Clee was named Vice President and Treasurer, and F.E. Russell Vice President. Canada had just embarked on its "second century" as a united nation, despite a geography spanning one of the world's largest continents from Atlantic to Pacific.

Bert made a prescient statement at the Annual Meeting of the Real Estate Institute that year—computers will never replace salesmen! Even a quarter of a century ago everyone was studying the new technology expectantly, but it was soon realized that no matter how good the data derived from a computer, there would still need to be a human analysis of the facts. That is still true today, when technology has reached a zenith of efficiency and performance, but only as a tool to the licensee who must analyse and perform the selling/buying miracle.

In 1968 two new real estate boards were established in British Columbia—the Northern Lights in Dawson Creek and the Northwest Real Estate Board in Terrace, bringing the total Boards to ten in the province at that time. These Boards represented 3,170 licensed B.C. salesmen and 970 agent licensees.

When the City indicated it would seek Legislative approval to ensure proposed expropriation for Block 42-52 redevelopment, the Board publicly opposed the "principle of expropriation of the property of one private party by the City of Vancouver or any other authority for the benefit and use of another party."

It was a busy Legislative year as the Board made a representation on Bill 66 in respect to Landlord & Tenant Act, made a submission to the federal Hellyer Task Force on Housing and Urban Development, and studied the then very new South Side of False Creek development proposals. The Board's responsible role in many major civic issues brought about a growing public awareness of its willingness to take a balanced stand on important issues that affected not only the business community but the general population as well.

This year the Board started a tradition of weekend radio editorial features that was to continue for more than ten years. Called "Getting Involved", the series used subject matter that varied from traffic jams to house prices, legislation to zoning and development problems, getting out the vote to getting out the pollution. These regular broadcasts

115

emphasized the fact that Realtors—like other taxpayers—had a stake in the future of Greater Vancouver and that common concerns should be recognized. This series was so popular that five years later frequency was increased to three times per week, under the title *"You and Your Real Estate"*, voiced and recorded by then Past President Ted Henderson. The Board received letters of praise from listeners as far away as Alaska and Florida, who agreed with its hard-hitting editorial comment.

A Committee of Real Estate professionals began to work with a Committee of Secondary School Teachers on a text on Home Buying, and T.L.G. pictures were again recycled into the Board's first *"Through Lions Gate"* calendar. The calendar offered for use by members retained that name through 1992, when it was changed to reflect the Board's new logo.

In 1968 Federal Treasury Board Chairman Ed Benson announced legislation that would allow a substantial increase in the portion of a wife's income that could be applied towards making a couple eligible for NHA mortgages. Single women were rarely approved for mortgage financing, regardless of income, but their "peripheral" role in the family unit was more recognized with this legislation.

In 1968 the West Vancouver Division decided to gild the lily of Canada's most beautiful municipality, by planting a number of flowering trees on the boulevards and verges of West Vancouver. Since that time an annual beutification project, as varied as beach-view benches, a hand-carved totem for the City Hall, or welcome signs at the entrance to the municipality, continues to be donated by the hard-working Realtors who show pride and love for the area in which they live and work.

Dowdy downtown Granville Street took on a new look in the summer of 1968 as a result of special Board sponsored meetings between City planners, tenants and owners in the area. "Theatre Row" had to be made more attractive and user-friendly, it was decided, so wider side-walks, benches and planters were added. This transformation was superceded in later years by major underground mall development and the no–auto Granville mall. Vancouverites celebrated the opening of the new Centennial Museum and H.R. MacMillan Planetarium in Kitsilano.

Three people were named Honorary Life Members in 1968 —B.I. Sperling, Leslie C. Creery, and Stanley V. Smith.

It was also the year that one member was mourned. Howard

West Vancouver Division welcome signs at the entrance to the municipality.

116

Meakin, a founder of the Real Estate Exchange, and at 84 still an active member of the Board, had operated Turner Meakin & Co. Ltd. since it was formed in 1912, eventually joined by his sons Arthur and Dudley. In 1964 grandson Howard Meakin Jr., son of Dudley, became licensed. Dudley is retired, Arthur —soon to celebrate 50 years of licencing—and his son Dennis, licensed in 1972, operate the brokerage end of the company and Dudley's son Brian, licensed in 1981, administers the Property Management division. There are many instances throughout the Board membership where family licensing equals or exceeds the record of the organization they helped build and maintain.

By the end of 1968 the average transaction on the Multiple Listing Service was $20,500, up almost 49% in the past five years. The variety of properties sold, their locations and values reflected the growing popularity of Multiple. Dollar volume of sales zoomed to $169,687,960, a gain of 30% over the previous year. This volume was achieved through sales of 8,239 properties, compared to 7,299 the previous year. The Quarter Million Club had begun special social occasions for agents and salesmanagers during the year, because they were the people who could most influence staff salespeople to use MLS.

As the new year dawned, financial pundits were predicting rising mortgage rates for 1969. On January 1, they stood at 8 3/4%, with a threat of rising to a then unprecedented 9 1/4%.

It was into this somewhat troubling economic climate that Hugh Clee assumed Board Presidency, with administrative assistance from Vice Presidents Fred Russell and Henry Block, and Treasurer and Past President, Bert Edwards.

In late 1968 brokers serving the growing residential and commercial areas of Richmond-Delta had asked to join the Board, so 1969 started out with an official Richmond-Delta Division, whose first elected President, Norman Macdonald, served for the first two years, sitting on the Board's Directorate with the other Divisional Presidents.

A Secondary School teaching text, released early in the year, was an instant success with Lower Mainland school teachers and soon requests were being received from schools in other British Columbia centers. Other Boards agreed to circulate them, and some even copied the idea—with permission—to enhance their own public images. This text was constantly updated to reflect both federal and provincial

H. A, Clee
President, 1969

housing initiatives and amendments until early in the '90s, when the Board felt this should be undertaken by BCREA's education department. In retrospect this seems a shame because in its 23-year existence the text, which became known as *Home Ownership—a Basic Guide*—was given free in class sets to any school requesting it, which meant a circulation of at least 1,000 copies per year. From the beginning a Speakers' Roster was put in place, with professionals who were willing to lecture and answer questions when the text was being used. Many students who learned the rudiments of real estate from the Board and its emmisaries this way, became happy customers/clients of an industry willing to take the mystery out of their real estate transaction with full information on this complex subject.

Throughout the year the Board continued to cement a rapport with the Civic administration by assisting their decision making with reports on Transportation, Low Density Housing regulations, the city's Five Year Plan, and False Creek planning. In its reply to the city's "Issues" questionnaire, many of of the Board's suggestions have come to pass through the ensuing years—a downtown conference centre near the hotel concentration; Fairview Slopes development to be compatible with False Creek; Chinatown be kept as a distinctive area; rehabilitation of Gastown and retention of high West End density; establishment of a regional Transportation Authority and approval of special commercial developments in major apartment buildings.

The Board also made an in-depth study of the Real Estate Act section dealing with sub-divisions, and issued its findings to the Realtor Division (forerunner of the B.C.R.E.A.) and the Real Estate Council. And in answer to many member-requests, radio advertising was expanded to include Multiple Listing commercials.

The Provincial Government changed its Home Acquisition Grant of up to $1,000 (less Home-Owner grants) to a $5,000 Second Mortgage Loan at the 1969 Legislative session. This amount varied with the difference between cost and the amount of the mortgage and was repayable at a rate of 8 3/4% over a period not exceeding the length of the first mortgage.

The first Guide Map was produced in 1969, 32 pages of maps and information on the Board's coverage area. An arted bird's eye look at the Lower Mainland formed its wraparound cover, and this art was later reproduced in a poster-

In 1986 the Burnaby Division established MLS tours to cover the Coquitlam area,and by 1971 the Division's name became the Burnaby-Coquitlam Division. After jurisdictional changes agreed between the former Westminster County Board and Vancouver were established in 1973, the Division became Burnaby-Coquitlam-New Westminster Division. This same accord changed the name of the Richmond-Delta Division to Richmond-South Delta Division, with North Delta jurisdiction going to the now Fraser Valley Estate Board. Because of their desire to have the advantage of MLS, many offices in outlying areas wanted to join the Vancouver Board. In the early '70's Directors amended Board By-laws, extending the area served bythe Board to make it possible for brokers in such locations as Squamish, Whistler and the Sunshine Coast to become members.

As the year came to a close construction of new houses was up in British Columbia—54.4% higher than the year before, and wages were up too, to an average $129.05 per week, the highest in Canada.

size ready for framing at 50-cents each. Primary school current-events/geography teachers around the Lower Mainland soon started calling on the Board for free copies because it was a perfect "overview" of where students lived. It seemed many students in West Point Grey were totally unaware of where Port Coquitlam fitted into the metropolitan area-another perfect teaching instrument had been produced. Mayors of all communities represented on the map were presented with framed copies for their offices.

Inflationary pressures had buffeted the country throughout the year, partly due to some unusually high labour settlements, notably one in the building trades. To match the trend, "average" MLS transaction values rose by 14.8% in one year—from $20,500 at the end of 1968 to $23,600 the following year. Sales volume rose more than the average price-by 16.5%, and the Service registered an astounding $197,000,000 for 1969.

The framework for more change had been set in motion that year, with a Computer Committee considering a Realtron Computer Services proposal from C.A.R.E.B., along with other suggestions from U.B.C. which had previously conducted much market research using the Board's punch cards. Another name change for the Board to "Real Estate Board of Greater Vancouver came under consideration.

As the year came to a close construction of new houses was up in British Columbia—54.4% higher than the year before, and wages were up too, to an average $129.05 per week, the highest in Canada. Next nearest rival was highly industrialized Ontario with $118.12. His Royal Highness Prince Phillip officially opened the East Wing annex of the Vancouver City Hall on his cross–Canada tour that year.

CHAPTER NINE

THE SEVENTIES—RIFT AND RESTRUCTURING

Frederick E. Russell
President, 1970

The year 1970 began in a celebratory mood, as British Columbia, Quebec and Ontario were the three participating Canadian provinces at Expo '70 in Osaka, Japan, and the province had already put plans in motion for major Centennial Celebrations for the following year —1971— one hundred years of belonging to Confederation.

Following hard on the heels of the inflationary trend in the sixties, serious commission agitation began among some Salesmen's Division members. For two previous years some salesmen had begun to lobby against Article 32A of the Constitution and Bylaws which limited commission payment to no more than 50% of gross commission earned by salespeople. In 1968 one George Shaw had been elected a Division Director, and his role was to become one of some concern to the agent members of the Board.

Doom and gloomers were worrying about a 15% hike in hydro rates and rising food and shelter costs. But the Economic Council of Canada was the "gloomiest", saying spending by the three levels of governments in Canada had doubled in the past decade, reaching $24 billion, one-third of Gross National Product, and projecting another doubling to $43 billion, or 37% of GNP by 1975. In 1939 Government spending was only 16% of GNP and by 1952 had risen to 22%.

Fred Russell was elected President, with Vice Presidents Henry Block and Bill Harrison. Treasurer was W.T. (Bill) Moore. But a quirky economic climate was not the only potential problem that year.

At an Extraordinary General Meeting of Board members, commissions payable to salesmen had been limited to a 50/50 split, along with a retroactive bonus of up to 10%.

In early April dissention built within the Salesmen's Division. George Shaw and a number of other members styling themselves as a "Policy Committee" circulated notices to secure support for their "manifesto":

(1) to change the Salesmen's Division to an autonomous body within the Board (not a union);

(2) to ensure a commission structure of not less than 60% of Gross Commissions;

(3) to regulate the influx of new people into the industry;

(4) eliminate any agent influence from the Salesmen's Group and

(5) that the current elected Salesmen's Division Directorate be forced to resign.

The existing elected group refused to resign but did ask Board Directors for stronger influence within the Board, and—referring to the 1965 attempt to introduce one—that a system of non-refundable drawing accounts would both regulate the inflow of new licensees and also satisfy financial needs of the sales force.

The Executive Committee of the Board met with the Directors of the Salesmen's Division and the Policy Committee, which became known as the "60/40 Club", but lines had formed and neither sales group would budge. Elected Salesmen's Division President that year had been Peter Mason, who was required to resign upon receiving his Agents' License and was replaced by another elected Director, S.F.W. (Bus) Norman.

The 60/40 Committee dominated the Salesmen's Division's General Meeting on May 14th at the Queen Elizabeth Theatre. Of the 2,300 eligible voters only 1,250 were present and a majority of those passed a motion of non-confidence in the elected Directorate and demanded its resignation. Because of a local Press strike that year, much of real estate's dirty linen didn't get aired in print. The elected Directors refused to resign immediately and because no mid-year election provision existed in the By-Laws, the Board asked a Committee to review the By-laws and make recommendations. Towards the end of the year, however, feelings were running high and the Salesmen's Division Directors resigned, leaving the field open for the Dissident Group to mount an election campaign for the following year.

In an early session the B.C. Government doubled the bonds for real estate agents. Security required increases in progressive steps depending on the number of salesmen the agent employed: $10,000 for an agent with one salesman (up from $5,000) to $100,000 for an agent with 40 or more salesmen (up from $50,000). The Legislature also increased the minimum wage in B.C. by 25-cents an hour to $1.50 and lowered the age of majority from 21 to 19, enabling 19 year olds to vote in municipal elections, purchase liquor, marry without parental consent and enter into contracts-including housing purchases!

In early spring B.C. was very worried about a 7.3% unemployment figure, and also by a metropolitan vacancy rate of only 1.1%. It was at this stage that Vancouver City Council decided to allow non-conforming suites for another 3 years to alleviate the housing shortage. Council agreed the expiry date for these suites in single family and other zoned areas would be renewed on application until December 31, 1972, provided the accommodation was satisfactory but reaffirmed its long-range policy of eventually removing all unauthorized accommodation.

The Provincial budget expanded the Home Acquisition Plan to include either a $500 grant or up to a $2,500 second mortgage loan for the purchase of an older home for at least one year. This programme had previously been limited to new housing. And in consultation with the provincial administrator, the Real Estate Board approved a plan where listings received from the provincial government would be circulated on MLS with no listing broker named, and a commission of 5% would be paid to successful selling agents.

A federal White Paper on Tax reform was studied by the Board, and concern expressed at the potential capital gains tax, which would reduce the use of property as an investment and restrictions suggested on deductibility of capital cost allowances from other income would also slow investment in much needed housing. This was a subject that would be on the Board's agenda for some time.

In Board service it's not ALL work and no play, and in 1970 the "Collapsed Sales", a Barbershop Quartet of Board members was a winner in what was to become a long record of REIBC/BCREA annual conference skit competition successes. The Cariboo Real Estate Board started that annual contest, donating the trophy, a mounted set of Cariboo horns, which came into Vancouver Board possession quite regularly as conventions came and went.

Recognizing that Realtors, as dealers in land, had a prime responsibility for its preservation, a special Committee on Pollution and Environmental Control was established with Ted Henderson as Chairman, required to bring down recommendations on an in-depth program. Through the next two decades both enthusiasm and funding waxed and waned, as did the public's interest. In 1991, however, a more environmentally friendly climate had overtaken the populace, so it was re-established, with the first effort a recycling program that is now supported by approximately half the Board's member-offices.

The year ended with another slight MLS transaction increase to $24,200, from the previous year's $23,600 and no volume increase for the first time in years. There were

In May, 1970, the Board made a major apology to members because a blizzard of listings—250 arrived in one day—caused some production problems and delays. Today, when computers speed the process, along with about triple the staff, that figure doesn't appear daunting, but in 1970 it was a record. This was one of the reasons President Russell appointed a special Committee on Computers to advise on action the Board should take towards automation of the real estate system.

8,116 sales which generated a total of $196,725,317 and the percentage of Sales to Listings was 33.6%.

Even though it was a year of "holding its own", 125 members managed to qualify for the Quarter Million Club and 12 more of the group reached "millionaire" status. I.C.I. listings had increased on the service, and this was a good solid sign. Production costs had been increasing so a new policy of charging $5.00 for re-runs other than regular extension of expiry and collapsed sales was imposed.

The West Vancouver Division Tree Planting programme celebrated its third year. The Richmond Delta Division started MLS tours. The North Vancouver Division negotiated a commission structure on leases for City properties and the Burnaby group expanded its scope to become the Burnaby-Coquitlam Division. And nationally, the Canadian Association of Real Estate Boards became the Canadian Real Estate Association, CREA.

British Columbia started its second century in Confederation in 1971, and Board members did so by electing Mel C. Johnston as President, W.T. (Bill) Moore and Gary Hurst as Vice Presidents and M.J. (Huck) Wenaus as Treasurer. Members of the Salesmen's Division elected a slate made up primarily of 60/40 Policy Committee adherents, and set the stage for a somewhat acrimonious year. George Shaw was named the Division's President and Mel Stoney its Vice President.

Economically, things were upbeat—G.N.P., consumer spending, housing starts (and prices), exports and—of course—Government spending, were all up. But around the Directors' table there were more "downers" than uppers. Leaders of the Vancouver Salesmen's Group tried to start a Provincial Association of Real Estate Salesmen, but grass roots licensees were a busy lot in their home territory, so didn't get enthused about taking on more far-flung responsibilities, or involving themselves in these politics and polemics.

A salesman's campaign of innuendo and misinformation was carried out, and because the Board Directors were trying to be fair and equitable, at first most of it was allowed to be published in the monthly Board publication, the VANCOUVER REALTOR. There were imputations of financial wrong-doing on the part of the Board in distribution of the $18.00 annual fee for Salesmen's Division membership, but rebuttal from Directors revealed that only $1.50 went to the Board annually, while $6.00 went to the Salesmen's Divi-

Mel C. Johnston
President, 1971

124

At that time the Lower Mainland housed over half the province's population and roughly 60% of its labour force. Economic pundits were predicting growth in the service industries, and growing employment in finance, insurance, and real estate would result as Greater Vancouver became more of a "head office" city.

sion, $7.50 to CREA, and $3.00 to the Real Estate Institute.

In an effort to solve differences amicably, a joint Broker/ Salesman Committee was set up, composed of the President, two Vice Presidents, Treasurer and one other appointed Director of the Board, together with the President, two Vice Presidents and two other appointed Directors of the Salesmen's Division. This group agreed to meet on a monthly basis.

Finally, by mid-year, the situation had really deteriorated; Salesmen's Division submissions for the REALTOR magazine were refused as unsuitable and the Division filed a Supreme Court action against the Board, charging it had no right to operate the Multiple Listing Service under its Societies Act registration, and demanding membership and constitutional rights as well as financial interest.

Board voting Members, who had themselves encouraged formation of this Division in the mid-fifties to promote cooperation and unity within the industry, soon set about investigating By-law changes. Early the next year the Membership approved changes that defined the Salesmen's Division role as a Committee of the Board with no dues paying requirement, and voluntary membership.

At that time the Lower Mainland housed over half the province's population and roughly 60% of its labour force. Economic pundits were predicting growth in the service industries, and growing employment in finance, insurance, and real estate would result as Greater Vancouver became more of a "head office" city. So there were many subjects other than the power plays of some salespeople to which the Board paid attention.

Proposed October, 1971, testing of a warhead for the Spartan Missile of the Safeguard ABM system sparked a much heralded environmental campaign by the Board's Public Relations Committee. The underground test, with a force of five megatons, 250 times the power of the bomb dropped on Hiroshima, was scheduled for Amchitka, a 42 mile long Aleutian Island just off the coast of Alaska. It had the potential of triggering a large earthquake, a major tidal wave, or leakage of radiation into air and water which could decimate bird, animal and marine life.

Regular radio advertising was augmented with television ads composed of a marine map of Amchitka which shook as if in a quake, while the voice-over urged viewers to write to President Nixon to stop the potentially perilous blast. CBC Television refused to sell the Board air time for this commercial "because it was too political", and that refusal became news. Oddly, the first newsroom to pick up the story of the refusal was the CBC! That same news item appeared around the U.S. on ABC, CBS and NBC television news casts, resulted in editorial content across Canada and the U.S., providing those "environmental Realtors", a term often used, continental visibililty. Further radio ads objected to a proposed oil tanker route from Alaska to Cherry Point in Washington, passing our shore line, way ahead of the tragic spill of the Exxon Valdez years later.

Public education was seriously considered and a special ll-part television series "Owning a Home" was produced on Cable TV. The series was written by Board staff and Committee members and conducted on air by Board Members, professionals in their fields of sales, conveyancing, development, mortgaging and other important aspects of home ownership. It proved so popular it was updated and repeated twice more in later years, with a phone-in component.

That year's CREA President, Harold Dueck, predicted smaller houses would become the style—down from the average 1,250 square feet to 1,000 square feet, with smaller lots as civic governments started dealing with higher density. Since Condominium construction activity was now increasing in British Columbia, 'smaller' was certainly found in that sector, but it didn't catch on in the the detached housing field. Quite the contrary in the next few decades as demands grew and the 'monster' house became a local issue.

Despite a dissident sales group, the general membership continued to show its preference for Multiple Listing, and the year ended with another leap in dollar volume to $262,915,174. Of the 23,373 properties listed, 9,932 sold, a 42.5% sales to listings ratio. The Quarter Million Club saw 10 more qualifiers reach "millionaire" status, and more companies were receiving merit awards for selling volumes.

Besides local and provincial concerns, Board Committees had also studied proposed federal legislation, such as a draft Competition Act, due to replace the Combines Investigation

Further environmental points were made by the publication of a "how-to" booklet called *"What Can One Family Do?"*, a practical guide to how one family unit could reduce/reuse/recycle and stop wasteful household practices with little difficulty. In the first year over 50,000 copies were circulated through schools, libraries, the Boy Scouts, interested groups and members, and demand continued through the next two years for a total distribution of some 100,000 copies.

*Besides local and provincial concerns, Board Committees
had also studied proposed federal legislation, such as a
draft Competition Act, due to replace the Combines
Investigation Act, which would prohibit 'price fixing' by
professional and service industries.*

Act, which would prohibit 'price fixing' by professional and
service industries. This act would eventually end the Board's
right to set a schedule of commissions and fees.

Changes in federal taxation were still being studied, as
well as amendments to the Unemployment Insurance Act
which included in new coverage those real estate salesmen
who were employed and received regular guaranteed non-
refundable salaries.

John P. Roberts, Past President of the Board and charter
President of the I.C. & I. Division, was named an Honorary
Member.

Past President H.P. (Budge) Bell-Irving, who headed the
Board in 1958, was elected President of the Canadian Real
Estate Association at the October, 1971, Conference. At this
time the Board had been in existence for over half a century,
and many of its Charter Members were no longer living. W.C.
Atherton, a West Point Grey Realtor since before the Exchange was formed in 1919, had survived longer than many
but in 1971 he died at the age of 96. He had served as a
Director of the Exchange and its President in 1946.

Multiple Listing sales started briskly in 1972, in some
districts double but in every one higher than the comparable
months the year before. Robert Andras, who was federal
Minister of State for Urban Affairs, predicted that 1971's record
building boom would be broken this year. The subjects of
fast growth and incipient inflation were on everyone's lips.

T.J. (Tom) Boyle, who had been cited in 1963 for listing the
first large commercial property on MLS, was named President of the Board in 1972. He was joined by Vice presidents
John B. Erickson and Ted Henderson, with Past President
Mel Johnston acting as Treasurer.

The Salesmen's Division was now operating as a Committee of the Board, and Directors received Division Committee
Minutes, often tabling motions which were ultre vires to the
power of a Board Committee. The Board did agree to provide
reasonable expenses for the Salesmen's Division Chairman
and Vice Chairmen to attend the CREA Conference, and paid
registrations for Committee members and spouses for the

*Many British Columbians will remember 1972 as
the year the N.D.P. won its first provincial election with
Dave Barrett as Premier. In the next three years there
would be a number of moves by this government
that required research, comment, and often dissent,
from the real estate industry.*

same event. The Salesmen's Benevolent Fund, which had
been underwritten through Salesmen's Membership Fees,
was now under administration of the Board's Finance Committee and continued to give assistance where Trustees
found need existed.

To satisfy the membership desires of salespeople qualified under Regulation 9.15, a special resolution was approved that these licensees be offered Active Associate Membership status, with no direct voting power but qualification
to be an alternate for Active or Financial Members. Soon
these same qualified salespeople were encouraged to become Active voting members. Membership in the Salesmen's
Division was made voluntary, and fees and dues eliminated.

Many British Columbians will remember 1972 as the year
the N.D.P. won its first provincial election with Dave Barrett
as Premier. In the next three years there would be a number
of moves by this government that required research, comment, and often dissent, from the real estate industry.

In the eleven years it had occupied the building at 1101
West Broadway, demands on services and staff at the Board
had grown. By 1972 the need for more space for the growing
Statistical Department eliminated rental of the portion of the
building addressed 1105 West Broadway. When established
in 1959 the Statistical Department only had Vancouver information, but now had limited property information for Vancouver, Burnaby and Coquitlam areas. Four staff members,
including Statistical Supervisor and long-time Board employee, Lorraine McKeen, were there to assist members by
phone or in-person research. Zoning and sectional maps
were available for sale as well.

The suit brought against the Board in the names of Shaw,
Stoney and Harold Woolsey was slowly proceeding through
the courts but appeals had not been heard by year-end, so
resolution was still on hold.

It was this year that negotiations on jurisdictional boundaries with Westminster Country Real Estate Board also began
in earnest. Memberships of both Boards were sent questionnaires and Directors considered all possibilities, including a

T. J. Boyle
President, 1972

potential combined MLS system. Just as the Greater Vancouver Board had absorbed Boards in North and West Vancouver, Wescoreb had expanded its service area across the Fraser River and had absorbed the old Surrey Real Estate Board. New Westminster President Marlin Loeppky and Vancouver's Tom Boyle had many long and sometimes heated meetings but by the year-end no resolution had been accomplished.

The Legislative and Public Affairs Committee worked with the GVRD on its Livable Region concept. In the same vein, the Public Relations Committee joined with the Community Planning Association to study and produce a report on open space and retention of greenbelts in the Lower Mainland. This was to be a project that took some two years to completion.

Business through the Multiple Listing Service outstripped every previous year, and that despite establishment of a new service by one of the Board's larger members, Block Bros. Realty, which introduced its National Real Estate Service-N.R.S., complete with computerization and catalogues. While many Board members thought it might spell the end to MLS it actually seemed to help. The number of MLS listings did fall but the number of sales rose—as did the ratio of sales to listings.

The improvement in sales led to the variable assessment being reduced from .4% to .3% mid-way through the year. What were the reasons NRS—which is still in existence and working well for that company—didn't destroy Multiple Listing? Was it competition resulting in more realistic prices? Listers on Multiple fully motivated instead of just testing the market? More quality properties being placed on the Service? Everyone who experienced those years has a favorite answer, but suffice to say—both services are alive and well and functioning for clients and customers, and Block Bros. salespeople are still faithful MLS listers. In retrospect, it should be noted that pioneer computerization/catalogue production by Henry and Arthur Block can be cited as the technological "information highway" of its day, smoothing out the bumps and curves and identifying the offramps that would help the Board be totally efficient when it finally computerized.

There was great satisfaction in a 10% increase in sales volume in 1972—$289,292,307.00, despite lowered listings. Members appreciated the decrease in the variable assessment as 9,194 of the 18,160 listed properties sold, for a sales to listings ratio of 50.6%. Inflation was alive and well all over

Canada that year, most likely due to generous labour settlements in the heavily populated eastern provinces, and Vancouver home buyers felt the effects with a big house-price increase. Average transactions on MLS went up to $31,465, a 19% increase from the $26,471 just a year earlier.

John B. Erickson was elected President in 1973, with Ted Henderson and W.A. (Bill) Lindsay as Vice Presidents. Tom Boyle, immediate Past President, was named Treasurer.

At the same time the previous year's slate of Salesmen's Division Directors was returned, with Shaw, Stoney and Woolsey, those named on the Supreme Court writ, still in leading positions. Their demands grew and most were tabled or amended by Board Directors

Condominiums were starting to be built under British Columbia's Strata Titles Act (now Condominium Act) so now Board members had to become familiar with both the Act and selling procedures that would be required for this new multiple ownership opportunity. The Education Committee arranged a series of comprehensive seminars on selling Strata Titled properties.

The NDP's Land Commission Act—Bill 42—which outlined the government's plans on conservation of farmland and parkland, raised an immediate public furore. Many landowners saw potential future sales profit erode under new designations of the Agricultural Land Reserve. The Board's Legislative & Public Affairs Committee prepared a report that was delivered to the Government and circulated to the Media. Of the nine principal positions taken by the Board, eventually five were incorporated into amendments to the legislation. The Board suggested up-to-date expropriation legislation be introduced to ensure individual property rights. While this was not done at that time, any mention of expropriation was excluded from the Bill. Other suggestions—the right of appeal, public hearings and that local municipalities and regional districts be given a role in the provisions were finally all incorporated in the final legislation.

In obvious juxtaposition to Bill 42 was the partnership of the Board and Community Planning Association, formed to establish a Green Urban Land Policy, or GULP, as its resulting publication was called. Board member John D'Eath served as Chairman. Committee members included such well known professionals as Dr. Robert Collier of the School of Community and Regional Planning at UBC, Art Cowie, W.T. Lane, who could not continue as he was named Land

John B. Erickson
President, 1973

130

Commissioner when Bill 42 was proclaimed and later became Director of Regional Development for GVRD, J.L. Bysse, Vice President of the Canadian Real Estate Research Corp.; planners Gerhard Sixta and J.F. Caplette, P.R.U. Stratton, and Dr. C.A. Rowles.

At the beginning of the year the Board had instituted a computer programme for processing sales and Quarter Million Club statistics, and soon the monthly sales picture was programmed into basically the same format used today, in which sales and listings are broken down by firms and branch offices. A consulting firm was retained to advise on setting up a real estate data bank for the use of members, utilizing reliable information on Lower Mainland properties to further relieve the calls now made to Land Registry and Municipal offices.

Finally, after discussions/disputes which had literally gone on for 17 years, an historic agreement was reached between WESCOREB and REBGV. Thanks to the no-nonsense stance of two Presidents, Vancouver's John Erickson and New Westminster's Bill Van Meer—bolstered, the story goes, by a fine Scottish liquid export and cigars from Cuba—agreed to jurisdictional boundaries as they exist today, and a combined listing service used by members of both boards for total circulation of available properties.

The Salesmen's Division Committee wrote to the Attorney General asking for a complete moratorium on recruiting new licensees in 1974 and urging a non-refundable draw for new licensees. This request was refused.

The housing problem was reaching drastic proportions all over the country, with deep repercussions locally. By mid-year the "average" MLS transaction had risen to $38,500, 23% higher than at 1972's year-end. The Board prepared a brief entitled "The Present Housing Problem" and submitted it to both federal and provincial governments, citing as one of the problems the land freeze of the NDP's Bill 42, which put inflationary pressure on available developable land prices. The brief included a five-point plan to solve housing price issues: 1-Reinstate the Capital Cost Allowance—tax writeoff for private investors in residential housing. 2-Tax on recapture of capital cost allowance on sale of income producing property be deferred if proceeds are immediately invested in similar property. 3-Federal sales tax on building materials be rebated. 4-Assistance to low-income families be increased to reflect today's housing cost reality. 5-Ceiling on CMHC mort-

At this time the city was considering development of the south side of False Creek, so to encourage public input into the planning concept, the Board provided funding for a shuttle bus that would eventually carry over 4,000 people to view and give input on proposals. The Board also made civic representation on zoning proposals for the West End, downtown region and Kitsilano.

gage amounts be increased to $40,000 for new houses.

The August edition of the monthly REALTOR magazine introduced a word never before heard in Canadian real estate—franchising. Two entrepreneurs in Toronto were introducing this new service under the name Realty World, aiming to establish a national network of Realty World franchises with individual brokers maintaining their own identities but using combined buying power and corporate umbrella to compete with major companies. Because there was so much going on at the Board, and increased need to keep members fully informed, another institution began—the "Blue Sheet", which was delivered to members daily along with the pre-perforated listings. This gave almost immediate turnaround to important news, announcements, educational opportunities, and 21 years later still fills the same role.

Under the NDP government, British Columbia was faced with a new Landlord & Tenant Act, and Rentalsmen's Act revisions, all of which were addressed by the Legislative & Public Affairs Committee.

The year drew to a close and the country was still in the grip of inflation, house prices in Vancouver kept rising, and now the "average" transaction stood at $41,500, 32% higher than the previous year. The Board's sales volume was up, showing an increase of 13.4% to $327,931,667.00. So typical of a rising market, less listings were processed—14,254— and less sales recorded—7,901—but sales to listings ratio rose to 55% and a record dollar volume was enjoyed. A number of members, including the Salesmen's Committee, were urging the Board to consider Listing Catalogues, and the Multiple Listing Committee undertook research into this possibility.

The Royal Bank Newsletter opened 1974 by saying the real estate market "could cool in '74" because the economy would slow and mortgage interest rates would rise commensurate with the rate of inflation. Vancouver was still striving to become the "Executive City" of the West, and with a rising population there seemed little possibility of any housing price declines. The new Knight Street bridge opened with a bang on January 15, as it registered its first traffic accident in its first open hour.

Ted Henderson was named Board President, and Bill Lindsay and Doug Woodley Vice Presidents. Past President Tom Boyle was again elected and named Treasurer.

Few new faces appeared in the Salesmen's Division

Approximately $60 million in foreign equity had flowed into Vancouver area real estate in 1973, bringing total foreign investment to approximately $140 million, 70% of it having been invested in multiple family housing and most of the rest in office buildings.

E. S. (Ted) Henderson
President, 1974

Committee lineup, with George Shaw and Mel Stoney elected Chairman and Vice Chairman for a fourth consecutive year. Division Membership was now over 2,500, but total ballots cast were decreasing. In 1971, height of the dissident group's popularity, 1,143 ballots were counted. In 1972 there were 948; in 1973, 748 but the fourth year only 694 votes were cast. At a February luncheon meeting of the I.C. & I. Division, a young and then hirsute city alderman–Mike Harcourt–was guest speaker. He said he was "interested and pleased by the stands on housing taken by the Real Estate Board." Harcourt said at that time that one of the biggest housing "hangups" of municipalities is that they feel they lose money on housing. Therefore, the provincial government must change its policies of financing for municipalities!

April 1974 signaled the end of an era in the real estate business. The firm Loewen, Harvey and Morfitt, had established its business at 752 Richards Street in 1893. Now, 81 years later, remaining partners, Wilson G. Morfitt and A. Rout Harvey, who had been Exchange President in 1942, 1943 and 1944, closed the office doors for good. To preserve as much history as possible, the Board purchased the company's massive 1912 edition of a Rickets, Taschereau & Co. Atlas of the Areas of the City of Vancouver, and donated it to the Vancouver City Archives, where early minute papers and books up to 1934 had already been lodged.

As prices of housing kept rising that year, a familiar hue and cry arose also–foreign ownership is at the root of the problem. To investigate thoroughly, the Board commissioned P.S. Ross and Partners to study the impact of foreign investment on both commercial and residential real estate in Greater Vancouver.

This impartial study identified approximately $60 million in foreign equity had flowed into Vancouver area real estate in 1973, bringing total foreign investment to approximately $140 million, 70% of it having been invested in multiple family housing and most of the rest in office buildings. Rather than being a detriment to the local economy, it was shown foreign investors were a major factor in stimulating con-

133

Developing Granville Mall.

struction and employment, providing approximately 5,000 immediate jobs along with a "multiplier" effect of an additional 15,000 jobs as materials were purchased, housing occupied, services used and wages spent. In essence, this widely distributed report found foreign investment to have a positive socio-economic impact and if it were cut off without a corresponding replacement from local investment sources, the impact would be negative and lasting.

The Board Committee studying False Creek voiced its opinion on three design options, urging a mix of market and cooperative housing with open park space and public access to the water as well as preservation of views for the Fairview Slopes. Site preparation began in June, 1974, and twenty years later it is obvious many of the Board's suggestions were followed.

Granville Street as a "people place" became the rallying cry of social planners in '74, so construction of Granville Mall was underway. It was then called a "pedestrian transitway", with vehicular access limited to buses and some taxi traffic. Like so many well laid plans, it was not foreseen that retail marketing would go underground, and that those peopling the place so lovingly laid out with plantings and seating areas would be the city's least desirable pedestrians.

The Board started amassing a series of educational video tapes for members to borrow. In a long established programme, a grant of $1,500 helped the Vancouver Public Library add to its collection of real estate related publications. As its activities increased, so did the Board staff. Keith Robertson was employed as an Executive Assistant in 1974, and was well known to many members as he worked with the Education, Program and MLS Committees until his retirement in 1989.

The end of the single family house was the subject of both REIBC and CREA conventions in 1974. Ten years ago in Canada, delegates were told, the land component of the cost of a conventional home was 20%, but in one decade had risen to as much as 50%. At the same conference Professor Stanley Hamilton of UBC told Canadian Realtors that real estate serv-

The advent of metric measurements encouraged the Board to publish a number of information sheets, set up metric seminars, and provide handy metric converters for members. Twenty years later most people are metric-friendly, but it was a sincere fear two decades ago when contemplated by those who had grown up with Imperial measure. They say some of us still convert Centigrade to Fahrenheit figures (Cx2+30) to see how hot or cold we are.

ices are either too expensive or inefficient, or both, and that the industry as it then existed was obsolete. He suggested auctions, public bureaux to facilitate land transactions or do-it–yourself kits for sellers. Some have been tried in the past twenty years but none have been as universally successful as the "obsolete" real estate industry, still thriving and delivering its services at a more efficient level than ever, thanks to technology, at no greater proportionate cost than of yore.

In a study of the Land Development Process a Committee found that at that time the GVRD needed a supply of 25,000 new housing units each year for a minimum of four years just to catch up to the demand backlog. The first need was more efficient land utilization, total cooperation between the housing industry and all levels of government.

In mid–year Mr. Justice MacFarlane brought down his decision on the class action lawsuit brought against the Board by salesmen Messrs Shaw, Stoney and Woolsey. It was a complete vindication of the Board and its actions and policies over previous years, which should have ended Salesmen's Division difficulties, but did not. Because of the Board's efforts, 20% of its voting membership was now composed of Salesmen licensed under Section 9.15, and President Henderson vowed that improved communications between agents and salesmen and the Board and salesmen, would help to resolve some still smoldering differences.

After two years of preparation, GULP was heralded by media, members, schools, libraries and politicians at every level. This Green Urban Land Policy was prepared through the volunteer efforts of many people of diverse fields, including Realtors. Funding for its design, printing and distribution was freely given by Real Estate Board of Greater Vancouver to provide an overview of the importance of preserving fast disappearing green belts within and accessible to the urban area.

Late this year the Board received a letter from the North Fraser Real Estate Board on behalf of licenced agents and salesmen in Maple Ridge, asking to form a Division for the municipalities of Maple Ridge and Pitt Meadows. Directors approved this request with the Division to become a part of the Board in early 1975.

The last of the Quarter Millionaires and Millionaires were feted in 1974. Not only were rising house prices making the qualifications too easily reached, but the public's perception was that the qualification represented total earnings of salespeople, instead of the dollar volume of all properties they had sold. In just more than 10 years existence, the number of qualifiers had risen from five to more than 300. They all approved the change of name to *Medallion Club*, where qualification limits could be calculated on the market conditions of each successive year.

For the first time in many years the Multiple Listing Service registered a decline in 1974, but the price of housing had soared, with the "average" transaction price on the service that year $57,861, a 40% increase over the previous year. The Board's surplus account was seriously affected, and the variable assessment was raised to .35% and membership dues were doubled to maintain the operations required. Active & Financial members now paid $100 annually; Associate Members with MLS, $100; Active Associates, $24.00 and Affiliates, $30.00.

As is usual in inflationary home price eras, the number of sales licensees increased. The Real Estate Council reported 5,603 Sales Licensees in British Columbia by September, 1974, up 1,164 from the same month a year earlier.

As he passed the reins of the Board to his successor in early 1975, Ted Henderson decried the high cost of governments: federal, provincial and local. They had become Canada's biggest industry, at that time employing 1.2 million Canadians, or one worker in every eight in the Labour force. He reminded those who would follow in Board leadership that it is the responsibility of all thinking people and their associations to resist government intrusion into the free-enterprise areas. He urged the Board to continue to participate in all discussions relating to housing and the future of Greater Vancouver.

W.A. (Bill) Lindsay was named President for 1975, along with Vice Presidents Doug Woodley and R.L. (Dick) Richards, who was also named Treasurer.

A not unexpected result in the Salesmen's Division election saw Shaw and Stoney once again Chairman and Vice Chairmen, still determined in their appeal against the MacFarlane judgment. A new member of the Directorate this year, however, was one E.L (Ted) Burnham, who would continue to toil in the association's volunteer force for years to come. Because of rising numbers of licensees, the Committee sent telegrams to Premier Dave Barrett and Attorney General Alex MacDonald, again asking for an immediate moratorium on recruiting of new licensees throughout the province.

W. A. (Bill) Lindsay
President, 1975

Throughout the years since the Competition Act had been introduced, there was on-going scrutiny from CREA and this Board. The original Bill C-2 was given Parliamentary approval in 1975 after some delays as the government reacted to briefs from industry groups, including this Board and CREA.

At the urging of George Shaw, MacDonald commissioned a real estate industry enquiry by economist, Dr. Gideon Rosenbluth of UBC in 1975. Asked to investigate and report on the structure, organization, regulation, functioning and business practices of the real estate brokerage business, he spent many hours in the next year interviewing people within the business. When his study was released it made little news and less impact and was shelved.

The West Vancouver Division never faltered in its annual community beautification project, and in 1975 under President Howard Bachelor embarked upon a unique project. A giant log was floated along Burrard Inlet to the shore of Ambleside Park and lodged in a special shelter. There famed carver Chief Jeffrey, created a magnificent totem, welcoming all visitors to watch during the process. That totem still stands in the Waterfront Park at Horseshoe Bay, appropriately identified as a gift from local Realtors.

Budge Bell-Irving and Harold Chivers were named Honorary Members for their great body of contribution to the real estate industry.

The Board had continued through the years to maintain public service broadcasting on local radio, and expanded it to include both CHQM and CJOR in 1975, with editorial features entitled *"You and your Real Estate"*, voiced by Past President Ted Henderson. The annual statistical publication "Trends" was once again eagerly received and a sell-out.

Vice President Doug Woodley had chaired the Data Bank Committee for several years, cooperating with WESCOREB's (now Fraser Valley Real Estate Board) Committee to encourage availability of necessary statistical information for members. This finally was possible early in 1975 when Teela Market Surveys started supplying full sales information from Land Registry offices on a monthly basis. Sadly, Doug Woodley did not survive that year to taste the fruits of his success. He died suddenly in August and in honour of his warm personal qualities and outstanding public service, Directors established a Memorial Scholarship in his name for a second year undergraduate in the Faculty of Commerce and Business

Administration at UBC. This scholarship still exists. Peter Williamson was appointed to fulfill the remainder of Doug Woodley's term.

Throughout the years since the Competition Act had been introduced, there was on-going scrutiny from CREA and this Board. The original Bill C-2 was given Parliamentary approval in 1975 after some delays as the government reacted to briefs from industry groups, including this Board and CREA. As first approved, the legislation seemed to relieve some of the more onerous provisions of the bill, but all industry representatives were aware that MLServices were not completely protected, as Bill C-2 was only the first of three stages of reform planned by legislators. At this early stage in 1975, Boards could no longer set a minimum scale of commissions and fees and it was a contravention of the Act for groups to use direct or indirect pressures to prevent lowering of commissions.

During this year President Lindsay and Directors had correspondence and several meetings with the Salesmen's Division Committee regarding its many demands. The Committee was offered some representation on the Board's Directorate, but divisive opinions were rising within the Committee. Its Supreme Court actions had proved very expensive and this was a point of contention. The final disposition of the dissident salesmen's actions against the Board and MLS was through the resignation of eight Salesmen Committee Directors, including Messrs Shaw, Stoney & Woolsey, and subsequent election of E.L. (Ted) Burnham as Chairman. This event strengthened the resolve of Board Directors to give full support to the legitimate aspirations of the Salesmen's Division, and to bring all their energies and ideas into the full range of Board activities.

The Board's dollar volume in 1975 showed a healthy increase to $501,000,000, but because of galloping inflation in the year past, Treasurer Dick Richards warned members that the Board's resources had been materially affected. There had been a 42% increase in the Consumer Price Index in the past five years, 13% of that occuring in 1975 alone.

This general inflation had brought MLS "average" transaction prices to a high of $64,471, an 11% increase over the previous year. Home buyers were hugely impacted by these increases, with first-time buyers often cut out of the market because their incomes had not increased as rapidly as the inflation rate. Home sellers were equally piqued by what was perceived as an inordinately high service charge as prices skyrocketed. But the Realtor and his Board were impacted too. In 1975 there were startling increases in prices of paper and other material goods needed to run businesses. To maintain the economic stability of the Board the variable assessment was raised from .35% to .4%.

The population of British Columbia had shown a distinct change of philisophical allegiance by re-electing a Social Credit Government after a four-year NDP sojourn. In his "state of the country" address in early 1976 Prime Minister Pierre Trudeau said Canadians would be "biting the bullet" as his government's anti-inflation programme would reform our habits, values and institutions. He said the recent B.C. election made him feel Canadians were swinging to the right, with belt-tightening individualism. However, in a typical non-belt-tightening move, the government introduced the Home Ownership Assistance Program—AHOP—a give–away buying incentive to one segment of Canadians which was to prove very expensive to all taxpayers in the long run.

One of the best known victims of the inflationary paper and wage costs of 1976 was the Eaton's Catalogue, a Canadian retail icon which had been published in Canada since Timothy Eaton's first edition in 1884. The last issue was the Spring/Summer edition, and when it was cancelled, so were thousands of jobs across Canada.

Dick Richards was named 1976 President, with Peter Williamson and George Yen as Vice Presidents, Art Shannon as Treasurer. There was an up-beat feeling in Vancouver as the year began, because the United Nations Habitat Conference had been scheduled for Vancouver for the first 11 days of June, and preparations were already underway for over 3,000 United Nations delegates expected. Habitat Festival events surrounding the conference, were planned to continue through mid-July, attracting another 10,000 plus people to the city.

The Salesmen's Division had gained observer status at the Real Estate Council meetings the previous year, and Dick Richards reiterated a previous Board suggestion that the Chairman and Vice Chairman sit at the Board's Directors' table. After By-Law changes were enacted, they were again named full Directors., the Division's powers and authority were restored, and salesmen-members served on Board Committees. Directors of the day gave considerable credit for the breakthrough in cooperation and communication to

R. L. (Dick) Richards
President, 1976

then Division President—Ted Burnham—who continued to be a moving force in the industry for many years.

Mr. Norman G. Thompson, whose background was in the business machine world but also included a stint as a real estate licensee and a WESCOREB executive, joined the Board this year. His knowledge of both what office technology could do and what the real estate business required it to do, were distinct advantages in the on–going march toward computerization which continued throughout 1976. Thanks to years of prior consideration, President Dick Richard's complete confidence, and Norm Thompson's knowledge, "Sam", the first Board mini–computer, was installed in August, beginning the Board's march into the future. Sam was a Hewlett Packard 3000–series ll mini-computer, which was being programmed to process the Multiple Listing work load, the membership roll, collection of MLS statistical data, and MLS assessments.

To accommodate this growing phase the public areas of the Board building were renovated, and no more tenants were able to be housed. More staff, augmented services and a growing membership to be accomodated all added to the diminishing space syndrome.

CREA played a major role in the Habitat exercise in 1976 and used facilities and talents of the Vancouver Board for its major briefs, radio and television advertising, and press conferences. A full schedule of events was planned, with locations scattered from the historic CPR station, to the Court House lawn, to a massive number of native style structures that rose in Jericho Beach Park. As one of the countries with the world's best housing, Canada's role was to give voice to those third-world nations with little or no housing for the masses. Realty groups, builders and architects all gave professional advice, but as one observer said, the problem with Habitat was that voting delegates were all government people, and the governments of the most needy nations had the worst housing records in the world. Some even predicted that Habitat would spell the death knell for the United Nations.

No clear consensus has ever been published, but the

At the Habitat Conference, REBGV President, Dick Richards is congratulated by World FIABCI President P. D. P. Holmes for the Board's publication Through Lions Gate. Others in the photo from left to right are: Bev Komoroski, CREA public relations manager; Jack Pontius, U.S. National Association of Realtors executive vice-president, and Blair Jackson, CREA executive vice-president.

Peter M. Williamson
President, 1977

United Nations is still in existence, many people visited Vancouver in its most attractive months, and the Board's book Through Lions Gate went home with thousands of visitors as a reminder of their visit and hoped for return.

Strict advertising guidelines were circulated by CREA to keep all Boards and their members meeting Combines Act requirements and all members reminded that penalties for offenses could be steep. On a summary conviction a fine not exceeding $25,000 was in place and/or imprisonment for up to one year; On conviction or indictment a fine in the discretion of the court and/or imprisonment of up to five years.

REBGV and WESCOREB continued to pursue the question of amalgamation and what would be gained—or lost—by it. Joining into one Board never happened, but cooperation continued. In August of 1976 a very successful jointly sponsored MLS campaign was launched in print, billboard, bus cards and radio. Seaboard Advertising entered the billboards in the 1976 Canadian Outdoor Advertising Contest where they received "favourable mention", or fourth spot nationally, which convinced both Boards their message had been clear, concise, attractive and pleasing.

Following the lead of other Divisions, the Burnaby/ Coquitlam/New Westminster Division became a major gift-giver to Heritage Village Park in Burnaby. The Division agreed to provide a pioneer real estate office to be placed on the simulated 1890s street and found forms, old listings, clippings, contracts and other memorabilia to complete this living museum contribution.

P.D.P. (Pip) Holmes, a past President of the Victoria Real Estate Board, the Canadian Real Estate Association and the International Real Estate Federation, was named an Honourary Member of the Vancouver Board in 1976.

Ian Dennis, who had been President of the I.C. & I. Division and a Board Director in 1971, was elected a Director at Large in 1976, and Chaired the Legislative & Public Affairs Committee. This Committee prepared a housing brief for provincial legislators urging the Provincial Home Purchase Assistance Act set limits above the Federal Government AHOP level. This bore fruit late in the year when the Minister of Housing announced an increase of 20% above the federal limits.

It was a successful year for Multiple, with a modest 6% increase in average transaction price to $68,694, but a 16% increase in dollar volume to $582,000,000. The problem of inflation was still abroad across the country, and the cost of

office renovation and computer installation required careful financial husbandry. There was a 30% increase in listings in 1976, and the direct cost of processing and circulating those listings necessitated spending of a major part of the Board's revenues. But because the many activities of the Board have always been carried out by a vast pool of volunteer labour, the books remained balanced even though more services and events were offered.

Peter Williamson was elected President in 1977 with George Yen and Ronnie Clarkson as Vice Presidents and Nelson Currie as Treasurer. Most of the membership problems had been laid to rest so this Executive Committee, along with other Directors, set about bettering conditions for all member licensees.

Early in the year the Board mourned another of its pioneer members, Harry E. Bond, who died in his 80th year. He had been a Director of the Exchange and served as its President in 1945. The Board named him an Honourary Life Member in 1960.

Another loss was felt that year when Leslie Charles Creery, who had been the Board's President in 1951 and 1952, died at age 78. A member of the Exchange/Board since 1925, Leslie Creery was top administrator at the birth of the Cooperative/Multiple Listing Service, and had been named an Honourary Life Member in 1968.

Unity problems and threats of Quebec separation were abroad in our country and the national economy was still struggling with slow growth. In 1977 the realty business faced extra challenges of high unemployment and labour conflicts preventing home purchase, mounting interest rates, steadily increasing oil and utility costs and property taxes as well as more government regulation.

The Multiple Listing Rules and Regulations had to be amended to conform to the federal Combines Investigation Act and restrictions it imposed on the industry. All contracts from that point had to state complete terms of sale. "Terms to be arranged" or "offers" were no longer acceptable phrases except where clear title or new construction was involved.

All encumbrances, payments, interest charges and penalties became a part of that contract.

The B.C. Minister of Consumer and Corporate Affairs at that time was Rafe Mair, and the Vancouver Board had had many discussions with him and with CREA regarding a warranty scheme to protect buyers of used homes, which would be mandatory on MLS. The Housing and Urban Development Association (HUDAC-now Canadian Home Builders Association) had previously launched a voluntary New Home Warranty Programme, and Mair was hoping to legislate it as mandatory on all new homes at that time.

The Central Mortgage & Housing Corporation (CMHC) and the Board worked out a plan that year whereby homes foreclosed by the Crown Corporation would be listed on Multiple, and a commission paid to selling brokers.

There were many satisfying experiences that year and one major gratification occured at the Nanaimo hosted BCREA conference in May, when the Board's musical extravaganza "Ouch Canada" took the trophy over heavy competition from the Victoria Real Estate Board, triumphant winners at two previous conferences. This win set the scene for nine successive Vancouver Board triumphs, six for musical presentations and three for 'playlets'. This competition has now been discontinued by BCREA.

While many talented Board members contributed to these skits over the years, no history of the Board would be complete without mentioning those most faithful and dependable who took part year after year. The perennial orchestra included the late Merina Harrison (piano); the late Grahame Budge (saxophone/clarinet); Bruce Allan, (trombone); Alan Creer (drums). Perennial singers included Past President Alf Buttress, Allan Jones and the late George Jones along with perennial actors in almost any role, the late Bus Norman, and Marj Norman, the late Rita Dillon and Past Presidents George Yen and Sue Yen, Maurice Butler and Jo Butler.

Board members on Vancouver's East Side formed the Vancouver East Division of the Board in 1977, with Rick Hannay as its first elected President, who then took a seat on the Board. This solidified Divisional voting power for many more individual Board members, an initiative for more member unity. And it was this year that the North Vancouver Division initiated the first "Climb for Crippled Children", a two mile relay-race on Grouse Mountain. This event, while having metamorphasized in sporting effort through the years, is still an annual event providing funding for children in need and now also involves the West Vancouver Division.

In a further move, President Williamson and Vice President George Yen encouraged pursuing Board sponsored tutorials for pre-licensing students. Because some larger member-firms offered tutorial services as a recruiting measure, the Board felt it must give its smaller member-firms an even playing field by providing impartial pre-licensing training at a reasonable cost. The first session was held late that fall under teacher/member W.H. "Bill" Clark. In 1979 Ms. Jean Huish was employed to plan and conduct in-house training, and continues to administer pre-licensing and agent's course tutorials. Her students' average pass rate of 94% is testament to the success of this Board service to members.

During this year the Salesmen's Division conducted a Membership Campaign, making membership a pre-requisite for use of the Multiple Listing Service. At the request of the Division the Board brought salesmen members under the authority of the Discipline, Complaints & Ethics (Now Business Practices) Committee. In an effort to placate an electorate growing weary of and out-priced by inflation, Governments made this a time of home-buying incentives. There was a glut of new multiple and single family homes on the market after a building binge in the middle of the decade. The Provincial Home Purchase Assistance Act would subsidize those using the federal Assisted Home Ownership Program (AHOP) to ensure payments would not exceed 30% of gross family income. Other federal and provincial programs at large at that time were the Assisted Rental Programme, Home Purchase Assistance, Senior Citizen's Housing and the Home Conversion Loan programme. This largesse was to rebound on governments later.

But the Board provided subsidies too—somewhat more realistic ones, however. To increase lock box security the Board subsidized replacement of existing Supra inserts, an event that was to be repeated several times in future.

A bitter-sweet occurence in 1977 was the retirement of George Muir, Associate Secretary, who had made many friends during his 21 years of service. While George and wife Margaret finally had the opportunity to travel and enjoy their retirement property at Watch Lake, the Board was fortunate to replace him with Earle Moreton, who had been long time Secretary of BCREA. Because he was so well known in the industry and amongst Board staff, Earle fitted in quickly and

Canada went metric on January 1, 1978, but it was a slow and painful process. Despite several years of warnings, articles, conversion tables and handy pocket converters, it was a mysterious year to many members as they struggled with the new system.

George Yen
President, 1978

was a great addition to the Board service side.

After twenty six years offering Multiple Listing services, and with a growing number of members, the Board was becoming a substantial business operation. By year-end it was well launched on its computerization, but aware that hardware was changing almost as fast as the demands made on the programming, budget plans had to include future upgrades in equipment. The human element was not forgotten either, as the Board made it a point that year to implement many improvements in the Group Benefit plan for member-agents and their employees to be made available in early 1978.

The Public Relations Committee launched the annual Senior Secondary Essay Contest in 1977 and also cooperated with the Education Committee on another cable television series called "How to Buy and Sell a Home", starring Board members within their various areas of specialization. CREA gave Canadian distinction to the radio series called "You and Your Real Estate", still being written as a staff function and voiced by Past President Ted Henderson, by asking permission to circulate the copy in both written and tape form to all member-Boards across Canada, un-edited except for regional references.

Another modest decrease in volume was registered through Multiple that year, down 10.8% to $518,970,200. It had been a year of buyers' market conditions and under the circumstances, considered a highly successful year. Average house prices as released by the Service actually registered a decrease from the previous year, but this was the first year the price became purely residential. Before the computer was able to identify the difference between residential, commercial and industrial listings, all calculations had been done by hand, and the simplistic calculation was total dollar volume divided by the number of transactions. Therefore, when only the residential dollar volume was divided by the number of residential sales, the 1977 average residential price went down to $64,500 from the previous year's MLS transaction price of $68,700.

It was also the year of the Horse, 4676, in the Oriental Lunar Calendar system, and became the "Year of Yen" for Real Estate Board of Greater Vancouver. Omens for the Year of the Horse were propitious if caution was used in all planning, and if planning was completed well before any action. Yen proved a highly capable driver when he took the reigns during the Year of the Horse.

As the first Chinese Canadian President ever elected in the industry, George Yen was familiar with lunar prediction, and well qualified to live up to it. Actually, this was not George's first brush with real estate. In the mid-fifties, as a teenager, he delivered supplies to the Vancouver Real Estate Board at 883 Howe Street from his father's grocery store at Howe and Robson.

In 1978, when accepting the gavel as President, he said: " 20 years ago I delivered coffee, milk and tea–tonight you get me."

George was assisted by Vice Presidents Ian Dennis and Art Shannon, with Nels Currie once again serving as Treasurer. Ted Burnham was serving a third consecutive term as President of the Salesmen's Division, sitting on the Board's Directorate, as was Brian Calder, elected President of the I.C. & I. Division.

Harold Davies, 1965 President, and E. Tom Cantell, who had been the Superintendent of Insurance and become a good friend of the industry, were both endowed with Honorary Life Memberships this year.

The West side of Vancouver—then, as now, an area with the highest licensee population—finally formed the Westside Division, electing Pam King as its first President. Perhaps that word should be "precedent", because that enlightened Division did continue to elect as many female Presidents as male ones, setting the stage for the Board's first female President, Janet Wainwright. (1986)

A perfect example of government bumbling is seen in the Canadian Home Insulation Program (CHIP) which was introduced to give grants of up to $350 to Canadians for insulating older homes. In the early '80s it was discovered that Urea formaldehyde Foam Insulation-widely used in this program because of its installation ease-was no longer acceptable under health regulations. A new program was then announced by CMHC—a grant of up to $5000 to homeowners for REMOVAL of the insulation it had encouraged with the original CHIP give-away.

In 1978 Prominent Realtor, Past President and Honorary Life Member of both Real Estate Board of Greater Vancouver and the Canadian Association, Henry Pybus (Budge) Bell-Irving, was recognized for his record of service to his country, province and profession with his appointment as Lieutenant Governor of the Province of British Columbia.

Government contemplation of mandatory warranties on

Early this year the first edition of the *"Professional Standards Handbook"* was circulated by the Real Estate Council, a valuable addition to each licensee's briefcase, where any real estate act rule could be researched. This publication has been successfully updated when needed, and is now circulated under the title Licensee Practice Manual.

re–sale homes was endorsed by BCREA, then Chaired by Board Past President Dick Richards. By June of 1978 the association circulated copies of a Disclosure Statement which had been developed with the cooperation of the B.C. Ministry of Consumer and Corporate Affairs. All BCREA Boards agreed to test this purely voluntary vendor–disclosure which consisted of 4 copies—one for the owner, one posted on the property, one to the listing broker and one copy to be sent to BCREA for monitoring the programme. This experiment was not successful as few vendors would sign, and its voluntary nature didn't encourage use. The far more successful Property Condition Disclosure Statement, introduced by BCREA in 1992, rose from the ashes of this early attempt, but bore the fruits of success because of a higher level of consumerism and threat of imminent government regulation to require full disclosure, plus the decision of Real Estate Boards to make a signed statement mandatory with all Multiple Listings.

The Multiple Listing Committee spent many hours in fine-tuning Data Input Forms to make sure information on circulated listings was the very best. But at the same time some Committee members took time with other Board members and staff to rehearse and fine-tune a BCREA Conference skit. To commemorate the bicentennial of Captain James Cook's mapping voyages that took him to Nootka Sound, the skit "Cook's Tour" was another triumphant trophy taker for the Vancouver Board.

Others played on behalf of charity. Four Vancouver Board Divisions entered the Invitational Bed Racing Championship to help raise funds for Variety Club projects for children. Maple Ridge/Pitt Meadows, North and West Vancouver Divisions combined, Westside and Vancouver East all launched teams to race along the Granville Mall, a community effort that was fun for the participants and provided over $4,000 in funding for the charity.

In August the Public Relations Department put a proud new face on its publications. Up to this time and purely for reasons of economy for the great output required, publications had been manually typed, with lettraset printing and graphic art composed into paste-up pages for off-set printing. The August, 1978, issue of the Vancouver REALTOR showed VANDAT had arrived with phototypesetting equipment that relayed words from a typewriter-like keyboard to a disc which, when put through a photographic process, provided camera-ready copy for paste-up onto page proofs. This mini-

The Legislative and Public Affairs Committee studied and reported on Strata Titles, Residential Tenancy Act, Capital Cost Allowances and Capital Gains legislation. A Rapid Transit Committee had already been formed to keep a watching brief on rapid transit, and the Board made a submission to the City Council on central waterfront development.

publishing system also gave more detail, accuracy and readability to the listings, while reducing production time because of its ultra high-speed cathode ray tube capability. Never again did the Board require typesetting/proof reading services from outside services, saving considerable time and money. Since that time the system has been updated and improved, and now the newest Page–Maker technology is being employed.

Another new face for Vancouverites that summer was Robson Square. The $160 million Arthur Erickson designed complex tied together the old Courthouse/Art Gallery and the new Law Courts buildings, with a "people place" between for walking, sitting, eating, talking, shopping, even skating under a covered plexiglass dome.

After a full review of needs within local charitable groups, the Board selected the Multiple Sclerosis Society as the charitable organization to receive support of Board funding projects. It was hoped to encourage all other Canadian Boards towards the same goal, but most had already chosen a charitable objective so this was never accomplished. From 1978 through 1993, the last full year funding programmes for MS were actively promoted, over $1.7 million was donated to the Society.

As a result of decisions at a Salesmen's Division General Meeting, Directors were asked to disolve the Salesmen's Division as presently constituted and absorb the Division membership into general Board membership. From that time onward sales licensees had direct representation to Board affairs through the Directorates of their Geographical Divisions, each of which elected four sales licensees and four Board members annually. Provision for Active Membership for salesmen after three full years of Division membership was offered all sales licensees. In the first two months twenty salespeople registered to become full voting members, applying for this membership with a $25.00 entrance fee and opting for the then $72.00 annual dues. The length of service requirement has been revised through the years and is now a one-year service qualification.

Ian G. Dennis
President, 1979

The Legislative and Public Affairs Committee studied and reported on Strata Titles, Residential Tenancy Act, Capital Cost Allowances and Capital Gains legislation. A Rapid Transit Committee had already been formed to keep a watching brief on rapid transit, and the Board made a submission to the City Council on central waterfront development. The editorial broadcasts continued on radio and the teaching programme, How to Buy a Home, was repeated on both Rogers and Shaw Cable TV.

The Provincial Government had launched the Family First Home Program in August, which offered a choice of $52.50 per month to qualified families to assist purchasers with monthly mortgage payments in their first years of ownership or a $2,500 lump sum to increase a down payment and to be forgiven over a 5-year period at the rate of 20% per year.

The Canadian dollar was in a weak state that year, and mortgage interest rates had increased to 11.25%. Construction companies were urging removal of the federal sales tax on construction materials to kick-start the building industry, but the B.C. government was convinced the drought was over and economic stability and growth would soon return to the province.

The Multiple Listing Service had, indeed, shown strength with the highest recorded dollar volume in its history. A 16% increase over the previous year brought the dollar volume to over $600,000,000, and home buyers had only noted a modest 3% increase in the average residential price, to $66,250.

As 1979 was born, the Employers Council of B.C. was predicting a 4% economic growth rate for the province, just higher than the 3.5% Canadian average. Council President Bill Hamilton also felt unemployment rates might continue at high levels but that inflation would decrease.

The CREA President Lloyd Metcalf was advising the shortest terms possible on mortgage loans, to be able to take advantage of lowered rates when this expected event took place.

Ian G. Dennis was elected President for 1979, another milestone in the Board's history as he was the first non licensed person to be elected. A Financial Member, Dennis had worked in the mortgage field for some 20 years at that time. Ronnie Clarkson and Art Shannon were named Vice Presidents, and Herman Wiebe Treasurer.

The Bonding Act of 1979 changed the existing regulations by tying the bond to the number of licensees employed. Currently it stands at $10,000 in the case of an agent

*At the October Conference Elmer MacKay the federal
minister responsible for CMHC told over 1,000 CREA
delegates in Vancouver that CMHC found itself
in the real estate business through mortgage defaults.
Over 31,000 AHOP funded units across Canada
had accrued to the Crown Corporation, 2,357 in British
Columbia, due to worsening economic conditions
across the nation.*

employing no more than one salesman, $20,000 when more
than one but not more than ten salesmen are employed
and on up to $100,000 lin the case of an agent employing
more than forty salesmen.

By March 1979 the Board was computer literate enough to
be in the position to provide remote terminal service to
member-offices on a lease or outright purchase basis. Initial
menu offered was the last 5 days of sales and collapses, last
5 days of new listings, the ability to search all current listings,
comparables, amortization tables, and two investment analysis programs with some detailed information on Vancouver
only properties. The Data Bank Committee was negotiating
with other municipalities to obtain their property information for the data bank. Connect time charge established was
$3.00 per hour.

Later in that year seminars were launched to acquaint
members with VANDAT and the intricacies of SAM the
computer. By the time these classes started in August, 77
offices had signed up for service which would be connected
in early September, 1979 to get immediate retrieval from the
data base. Seminars were assigned in the order of planned
terminal connection so immediate on-line service could be
enjoyed. By year-end 160 offices had taken advantage of this
technological opportunity.

Peter Watkinson, Executive Assistant of the Board, retired
after 12 years of stellar service, and was replaced by Alex E.
Scoten, who had previously had many years of Association
experience with the Vancouver Board of Trade.

Vancouver Board scored a "hat trick" at the BCREA Conference in Prince George that year, winning the third consecutive skit trophy in a row with a musical extravaganza
called "Cariboo-boo-choo-choo". At that point Committees
were already preparing for the October CREA Conference in
Vancouver, which was being hosted by REBGV.

But while BCREA convention meetings were on, the Board
also lost an old and valued friend. Ben Sperling, Honourary
Board member who had Chaired the Committee which led
directly to the new 1958 Real Estate Act, died in his 79th year.

He had been a valuable contributing member to the Board for 28 years.

In June bed racers took to the mall for the second time, with Burnaby-Coquitlam-New Westminster, Vancouver East and Vancouver West Divisions again competing on behalf of the Variety Club charity.

Name changes this year saw the Richmond-South Delta Division officially registered, and the Vancuver West Division to become Westside Division.

At the October Conference Elmer MacKay the federal minister responsible for CMHC told over 1,000 CREA delegates in Vancouver that CMHC found itself in the real estate business through mortgage defaults. Over 31,000 AHOP funded units across Canada had accrued to the Crown Corporation, 2,357 in British Columbia, due to worsening economic conditions across the nation.

The Minister also discussed a topic that had long been on everyone's agenda—mortgage interest deductibility for income tax purposes, but as all Canadians know, this subject never got beyond the talking stage and was never acted upon.

Pre-licensing tutorials had been offered on an occasional basis since 1977 but became a dependable new Board service in late 1979 when Jean Huish joined the staff as Training Director. She still administers a full program of pre-licensing and Agents Licensing Tutorials for course registrants.

Sales through the Multiple Listing Service continued to mount in 1979 through a relatively stable year. Residential housing average prices rose about 6% to $70,888 per unit at the year-end, but dollar volume registered a 41% increase and rose to $851,591,714.

Because careful management had kept the Board's resources stable, the year ended with a most particular educational salute. Following its own lead from the fifties when this Board pledged funding for the first real estate education at UBC, and in recognition of the untiring efforts towards that end by Colonel Herbert R. Fullerton, the Board provided $100,000 to endow a chair at UBC. Known as the Herbert R. Fullerton Chair in Urban Land Policy, the funding assists the Faculty of Commerce and Business Administration in providing research support to attract and hold distinguished academics in business administration and related fields. Other British Columbia Boards have added to this endowment through the years.

151

CHAPTER TEN

THE EIGHTIES— DECADE OF GROWTH

Predictions were coming thick and fast—the single detached house would be most popular housing style throughout the '80s, higher prices were expected due to increasing customer demand, and an end to the "interest crunch" was near. The gloomiest view was from the Toronto-based national home building industry (HUDAC), which was that Canada's house building industry was heading into "its worst period in 10 years."

But there was no such gloom and pessimism on the part of the 1980 President, Ronnie Clarkson. Known as the eternal optimist, Clarkson had encouraged his sales force to record heights with his inimitable wit and enthusiasm. Serving as Vice Presidents that year were Maurice Butler and Herman Wiebe, with Art Shannon as Treasurer.

R. G. (Ronnie) Clarkson
President, 1980

One of the major projects this year was surveying members on changing from a loose-leaf to a catalogue system for MLS. In its research, the first questionnaire received over 60% of members in favour of the change, but research and study were to continue for some months. Tenders for the production of catalogues went out in May. After careful study and negotiation, R.K. Printing, which leased space in the Board's building basement, was awarded the contract. The first issues of each of the three catalogues planned were delivered free of charge to all member-offices on January 5, 6 and 7th of 1981.

The fifth revision of the popular book *Through Lions Gate*, with 140 updated pictures and a new design, assured its continuing position as an ambassador of good will for both the city and the Real Estate Board. Originally priced at $3.50 when issued in 1966, this year's price had gone up to $9.00 per copy, reflecting paper and printing cost increases, but still kept at cost price for Board members.)

Gas shortages, which had begun around the world in 1979, continued through 1980 which increased the public's demand for better public transportation.

Directors heard from Ray Nelson, President of the I.C. & I. Division, that the Commerce Undergraduate Society at UBC had recognized Board and Division mentoring and educational assistance to Urban Land students for the third consecutive year. Four years before the Division had established annual dinners with those in the Urban Land Option, setting up discussion groups on topics of specific interest to students, and this "real world" education was invaluable. Ray Nelson, a specialist in investment and commercial fields, joined the staff of the Board as an Executive Assistant in 1986 at the time of Alex Scoten's retirement, and his expertise is well used in assistance to both the I.C. & I. Division, Legislative & Public Affairs and other Committees and Task Forces.

The market was booming as the year advanced. In fact, many instances of "sold before circulated" listings were occuring in several metropolitan areas, so the Real Estate Council issued a blanket warning to all licensees that delay in submitting the listing to the Board to allow a sale by the lister could result in severe discipline.

Rental housing was at a premium, rental rates rising, and even commercial space was hard to find. Mortgage rates were creeping up to double-digit figures, and inflation was causing increases in the price of most goods and services. Compared to other parts of the world, however, Vancouver wasn't faring badly. In 1980 a Tokyo housewife was paying $18.00 a pound for sirloin steak, and a "medium priced" hotel room in London, England, was then $140 Canadian a night. In Israel, expecting 120% inflation that year, a television set cost $1,800-three times the world price.

First mention of a B.C. Real Estate Foundation appears in Directors' minutes of May 28, 1980, when, at the urging of Minister of Intergovernmental Relations, Garde Gardom, a B.C. Real Estate Association Committee studied ramifications of a suggested change to interest bearing trust accounts.

The Department of National Revenue had been reviewing the previously non-profit status of Real Estate Boards, so the CREA Tax Committee, headed by Vancouver Board Past President Dick Richards, prepared a proposal to be submitted to the government. The proposal suggested the Tax Department agree not to assess any previous years if Boards took steps to reduce income to produce no more than a reserve amount equal to that Board's gross annual income (or gross expenses which in some cases could be greater) and that accumulation of capital reserves towards purchase of capital assets for the specific use in Board operation be allowed. It took several years of negotiation, but in 1983

First mention of a B.C. Real Estate Foundation appears in Directors' minutes of May 28, 1980, when, at the urging of Minister of Intergovernmental Relations, Garde Gardom, a B.C. Real Estate Association Committee studied ramifications of a suggested change to interest bearing trust accounts.

The busy business climate this year had attracted many new people to the real estate industry, and by year-end the Board's membership stood at 4,805, with 3,696 of those individuals members of the Salesmen's Division.

Richards was able to report complete success as the Revenue Department had agreed the non-profit status of a Real Estate Board would not come into question if its cash reserves did not exceed a sum calculated by using a specific formula. The Board can use one half the previous year's revenue or the year's total expenses, whichever is less. Depreciation must be deducted from the chosen figure as well as the current year's unappropriated equity less fixed assets and long-term debt, to arrive at the allowable cash reserve.

British Columbia salesmen had been observers at Real Estate Council meetings for several years, but in 1980 changes in the Real Estate Act were effected that ensured three salespeople would henceforth be elected to Council; one each from Vancouver County and Vancouver Island County along with one member representing the remainder of the Province. Further amendments in 1981 saw the Real Estate Council drop the Grade 12 completion requirement for real estate license applicants. The Vancouver Board took exception to this change, but was not successful in its objection.

The busy business climate this year had attracted many new people to the real estate industry, and by year-end the Board's membership stood at 4,805, with 3,696 of those individuals members of the Salesmen's Division.

As this burgeoning membership's needs increased, so did the Board's services. The Data Bank Committee produced the first publication of the Quarterly Statistical Report, residential housing stats by area, with median or "middle" prices used as a more realistic market indicator. This report is still produced, and highly satisfactory for both members helping clients and customers and the Board in answering public enquiries. Another result of increasing demands on the Board's facilities was long-range planning consideration of relocation in new quarters. This subject was never far away from the planning agenda, and finally realized with the completion of the new building in 1994 after a two-year construction period.

Statistics Canada announced in September that one thousand people a week were arriving in British Columbia. In the year that ended May 31, 1980, there was a net increase of 49,598 in population, indicating the strength of B.C.'s economy which, at that time, had not shown the deterioration that more eastern provinces were experiencing. Alberta, also showing stable economic conditions, had a net increase of 42,500 that same year.

REALTORS are known to be generous, and when business is good they are even more so. The North Shore Realtors' Grouse Mountain Run provided funding of over $3,000 to their cause that year, and the Multiple Sclerosis fund raised throughout all Board areas soared to above $40,000 in 1980.

Almost every month that year saw increases in average residential prices calculated from MLS figures, so it was not surprising to find that volume for 1980 soared over the billion dollar mark for the first time.

Thanks greatly to the hard work and influence of Westside Division President Janet Wainwright, and Past President Pam King, more participation was noted from this geographical area than at any time in the service's history. I.C. & I participation on the service also increased 28% that year.

Despite the expenses of setting up the first catalogue system, there was still an excess of revenue over expenditure, and two reductions in assessment fees to a low of .25% by year-end. The MLS and Public Relations Committees were jointly planning a campaign to inform the public of the value of the new catalogue system, which was to start at the beginning of the new year.

Total dollar volume was $1,295,689,685, 51% higher than the previous year, and creating a record for that time. House prices had increased to an average $100,000, and in the prophetic words of President Ronnie Clarkson, "There's no way to go but up......"

But pessimists were out in full force around the country as the year began. One business forecast said "the good news is that 1980 is ending and the bad news is that 1981 is beginning." High inflation, recession in most of Canada and continuing energy problems were cited in all forecasts. Some predictions have come true: "a low priced car will cost from $12,000—17,000 by the '90s" and some have not: "a box of cereal will cost $13.30 by the '90s".

Still riding the crest of the economic wave as the new year began, Board members greeted new President, Maurice Butler, with Vice Presidents Herman Wiebe and Frank Kearney and Treasurer S.F.W. (Bus) Norman.

Maurice Butler
President, 1981

*In an ironic twist, 1981 was the year Americans were
streaming north across the border to buy Canadian gas!
A May Vancouver REALTOR news story says that
January, 1981 border crossings had increased by 50%
from 1980 figures, which in turn were 60% higher than
those in 1979.*

The record business experienced around the province in 1980, but particularly in the metropolitan area, created a heavy demand for real estate licenses. Registration for the year's first course saw applicants lined around the block by the Real Estate Council, an extremely negative media event. The Council asked Boards to question members on the matter of recruitment and prepare recommendations.

The Executive Committee met with the B.C. Assessment Authority on several occasions, to reach an undertaking for the Assessment Roll computer tapes, with the mutually beneficial fact that Vandat Inquiry Program access would be granted to the Authority. Also, due to the uncertainty of fluctuating markets and the increase in housing values, an increase in the basic level on which MLS assessments would be leveled was raised to $150,000 from the previous $100,000.

In an ironic twist, 1981 was the year Americans were streaming north across the border to buy Canadian gas! A May Vancouver REALTOR news story says that January, 1981 border crossings had increased by 50% from 1980 figures, which in turn were 60% higher than those in 1979.

At the 1981 BCREA Conference held at Harrison Hot Springs, then Minister of Consumer and Corporate Affairs, Peter Hyndman, cited the real estate industry for its high ethical conduct through the months of rising real estate prices. During the rising market action, the real estate industry was blamed as a rash of "flipping" properties began. Thinking that those "on the inside" were mostly likely to blame, a full Superintendent's investigation of transactions revealed that only .1% of "flips" had been conducted by those in the real estate profession with the majority tied to the ordinary opportunistic investor. Hyndman singled out the Vancouver Board for its radio broadcasts, *"You and Your Real Estate"*, as the highest calibre public education, and also the Council's pamphlet of the same name.

The Real Estate Council introduced the agent sponsorship program in the form of a "certificate of intended employment" for all new licensee applicants in 1981. This requirement was removed in 1992.

Business continued at its previously frenetic pace for the first five months of the year but unparalleled high prices and interest rates that rose over 20% finally took their toll. The activity paused, slowed and almost atrophied; prices stopped their upward spiral but didn't fall as far as many expected.

The UFFI word, Urea Formaldehyde Foam Insulation became a factor in real estate this year. More and more complaints of allergic reactions to fumes from this insulation were heard. The American government quickly banned its use, followed by the Canadian government, the very one which had offered grants for its installation. CMHC announced grants of up to $5,000 for homeowners to reduce or remove the insulation. Real estate practitioners had to inform themselves quickly, disclose fully if UFFI was present, and make sure the proper phrases/disclaimers were included on contracts. These tax-free grants were available until March 30, 1994.

The Board strongly and publicly supported the waterfront Trade and Convention Centre plans, though they seemed doomed to be destroyed by the current economy.

Past Presidents Art Jacobson and Bert Edwards were named to the ranks of Honourary Life Members this year.

To address both recruiting new licensees or "raiding" existing salespeople to increase sales staff, new By-Laws were approved that restricted recruitment advertising to those already licensed, restricted mention of training courses and also mention of earnings unless those were guaranteed.

Business continued at its previously frenetic pace for the first five months of the year but unparalleled high prices and interest rates that rose over 20% finally took their toll. The activity paused, slowed and almost atrophied; prices stopped their upward spiral but didn't fall as far as many expected. Year-end figures still showed the statistical "average" residential unit price an unprecedented $148,800. Despite some difficulties during the past year, members were generous to the Board's MS Fund, providing just over $20,000, which was matched by the Board to provide another $40,000 donation to that Society for 1981.

Inventory of property at the end of January was a scant 1,984 listings, but it increased sharply as sales became harder to negotiate so the wide circulation of MLS suddenly became almost mandatory. By mid-year inventory increased to 8,471 properties, and a total of 30,561 listings were processed during the full year. Total dollar volume was 19% less than the record set on the rapidly rising market of 1980, but still topped the billion mark at $1,041,546,345.

Some members still preferred the loose-leaf system to catalogues but research showed the new way was more economical. Considering an 18% increase in paper prices that year, had loose leaf sheets been printed instead of catalogues, costs would have doubled. To save up to 40% of current expenditure and have a possible increase in printing frequency, plans to change the then five listings per page to ten were being considered.

The year ended with a negative cash flow and a variable assessment set at .4%. It was then that President Butler and his Executive set in motion a plan to shift the Board's revenue dependency from the variable MLS assessment to more stable sources of revenue.

If predictions were glum as 1981 began, they were even more so as the recession became entrenched in early 1982. Herman Wiebe was elected to lead the Board in this year most REALTORS would like to forget. Frank Kearney and Sandy Tompson were elected to Vice Presidential roles and Neil Neumann was named Treasurer. The timing didn't daunt the Executive, whose philosophy, oft quoted, was " when things get tough, the tough get going..."

Herman H. Wiebe
President, 1982

Economic worries in 1981 saw some functions put on hold to economize. The monthly magazine, THE REALTOR, ceased publication in mid-year, but a year later reappeared as a smaller, more economical quarterly publication, The Quarterly REALTOR. It continued in this format until mid-1991, when it was upgraded to bi-monthly circulation to keep members better informed.

The ten-up catalogue page appeared this year for the first time in the same format that still exists today. That year's cost price to members was $2.50 per copy per week. Through the subscription system, printing costs were reduced because only the number of catalogues ordered were printed. Advent of the catalogue changed the size and the name of the "Blue Sheet", which became the DAILY REALTOR in 8 1/2 by 11 inch size, delivered daily with the Hot Sheets, also a new wrinkle. But old habits die hard, and even today, it's called "the blue sheet...."

Another first in 1982 was the first Multiple Sclerosis Mothers Day Carnation weekend, and Board volunteers have continued to form the backbone of the sales force ever since.

Recycling was going on at that time too. Semiahmoo House, a handicapped facility, was picking up catalogues at member offices, separating them and selling to Community Paper with the understanding that 40% of profits would be returned to the Board for the MS Fund, and 60% retained by the society. Volunteer services often don't last, and even commercial recycling efforts through the years have run into difficulties because of flucutating paper prices. That's why the Board, now financially able to support such an activity, has undertaken to pay for a recycling project through partnership with Dan Foss Couriers, which covers all Board member-offices.

As markets declined, governments worried, and incentive programmes were developed. The British Columbia government increased its B.C. Second Mortgage Loan to $10,000, and at a time when interest rates were as high as 21%, capped its rate at 15%.

Variable assessment was reduced first to .375%, later to .35%, and by November that year to .15%. Dues were increased to reflect extra costs, such as Salesmen's BCREA and CREA annual dues. Cost cutting was being felt all around the province, so the annual BCREA conference was downsized to a one-day event at Delta's River Inn in Richmond, where the Vancouver Board's thespians broke a two-year losing streak by again capturing the skit trophy.

CHOSP grants were available to used home buyers to the end of 1982 and then only to buyers of brand new housing for the first 6 months of 1983, with a purchase cap in this area of $150,000. (The "average" price on Multiple in 1981 had been $148,860 at year-end). The federal government also introduced Canada Home Renovation Plan (CHRP) and the Residential Rehabilitation Assistance Programme(RRAP) at that time, and the provincial government introduced the B.C. Home Program, a loan plan to help those with high mortgage interest rates reduce rates to 12%. This initiative involved a pay back, while all others were grants with no payback provision.

As 1982 advanced, prices declined and affordability returned so the Board's President Wiebe and Past President Butler recorded a television commercial campaign to relay this message to the public. The cable educational series, How to Buy and Sell a Home, was once again aired on Rogers and Shaw cable stations, with open line segments to answer viewers's housing questions directly. Both these efforts,

1982 became the "year of the grant". The federal budget, delivered on June 28th, tried to address the harsh housing reality many people faced under the economic situation of the day. A $3,000 "Canadian Home Ownership Stimulation Plan" (CHOSP) grant to eligible first-time home buyers was introduced nationally. In British Columbia, this could be combined with a grant of up to $2,500 for qualified family buyers, as governments tried to stimulate the economy, the building industry and assist citizens into housing.

combined with the newly available grants, were reflected in increased activity through the Board's MLS.

The Board and Greater Vancouver Regional District joined forces to oppose a proposed transit benefit tax, unveiled as the Transit Service Levy, Bill 9, the Land Use Act. Strongly worded briefs from both groups and appropriate media coverage of the Board's contention the bill would kill development around the route the Lower Mainland ALRT system would take, caused then Municipal Affairs Minister Bill Vander Zalm to "take a second look" and abandon his plan. To encourage realistic listing and faster reporting of sales in a difficult 1982 market, the 'R.L.D.' was introduced—the Realistic Lister's Discount—which is still available.

During this tough year the even tougher Board Committees really got going, so despite early economic doom and gloom, it turned into a banner year for MLS sales and Board community visibility. Even after a slow beginning, $38,800 was given to the Multiple Sclerosis Society for the year's funding.

In a marked turn-around sales through Multiple Listing zoomed 89% over the previous year, but the "average" price dropped to $107,800, one of the reasons for buying activity. It should be noted here that the average price in 1979 was $70,800, so the "low" of 1982 never returned to the previous lows, giving long-term homeownership appreciation a new meaning.

The year ended with a total volume of over $1.3 billion, and a new computer installation early in the new year promised to increase the Board's delivery capacity by sixteen times what it had when first introduced. The Management staff of 9 people agreed to forego any salary increases so the rest of the staff could receive small ones, and careful budgeting kept the Board's resources secure for the coming year.

Past Presidents Alf Buttress and Huck Wenaus were elevated to Honorary Membership status in recognition of their many contributions to building and maintaining a strong real estate organization.

As 1983 dawned, Vancouver's rental construction was at a low point and so were vacancy rates. A "new kid on the block" was the first shopping centre condominium, being marketed in Ontario, a concept that soon spread across the country and is still very much a part of the retail market today.

Northern British Columbians were given an extended tax-free buying break this year, as the federal government extended the CHOSP grant deadline from May to December, to compensate for northern winter conditions which delay building.

By February in southern British Columbia, the time for buying with this grant was fast running out when Frank Kearney accepted the Board Presidency. Chuck Mitten and Sandy Tompson were installed as Vice Presidents and Neil Neumann remained Treasurer.

Eight years before, in 1975, the Board was fortunate to employ Sabine (Misera) Carleton, a charming, velvet-voiced receptionist. In January of 1983 members did a double take when TWO Sabines seemed to be ensconsed behind the reception desk. It was identical twin Ulrike, who was in training to share the reception/switchboard duties with Sabine. Still sharing reception duties and many other jobs too, Sabine and Ulrike have collectively contributed their many talents to Board members for some 30 years and, hopefully, for many more.

The Superintendent of Insurance and Real Estate was studying the question of licensing for property managers under the real estate act. His study resulted in licensing for both agents and salesmen restricted to property management, with applications required before September 30, 1983.

Since it had long been a proponent of the development, Board Directors hailed the April commencement of construction on the Canada Harbour Place cruise ship facility on the old Pier B.C. site, central waterfront. Expo '86 had already been confirmed, and while unemployment was still high, so were hopes that a turn-around could be expected soon.

The deadline for applying for UFFI removal grants was June 30, 1983, so Board members were rapidly spreading the word to homeowners who might have reason to apply.

Canadian Boards joined with the national association CREA in 1983 to point out to their local citizens that Property Rights were not enshrined in the Charter of Rights of the new Canadian Constitution. Because the amendment process had an unwieldy three-year time span, and required approval by seven provinces representing 50% of the Canadian population, it has not not yet been successfully entrenched for Canadian property owners.

The MLS Committee perfected the residential, I . C . & I . and Land Only Data Input forms, which were subsequently amended as needed. Installation of the new Hewlett Packard 3000 Series 64 computer had occasioned some teething problems, but when corrected Board members could point at significant computer use and growth in a short six years. As

P. Frank Kearney
President, 1983

The Executive Committee was investigating the Real Estate Oriented Securities Course proposed by BCREA and to be offered through the facilities of UBC. Finally, by late 1983, a Real Estate Oriented Securities Course was available. All persons involved in such sales were required to have taken and passed the course before January l, 1985.

The Education Committee completed a two-year project in 1983 and published the first edition of Recommended Clauses and Phrases, a very important publication which has endured and is now circulated to all B.C. REALTORS through BCREA, with printings funded by the Real Estate Errors and Omissions Insurance Corp. It also expanded the existing annual Scholarship program by offering two awards to BCIT students in the Marketing Management Program, real estate option.

an indication of growing catalogue size and subsequent rising costs, catalogue prices rose to $3.50 each on subscription and $8.00 each over-the-counter. A new graphing machine improved the monthly statistics package to all member-offices, including bar and pie graphs for instant looks at various market situations. By this time there were thirteen enquiry programs offered on VANDAT, including the newest, Mortgage Rates survey, and an Investment Analysis package.

Federal statistics revealed that 12,335 British Columbians received grants under the CHOSP programme in its first six months of existence in 1982, with 8,529 using the $3,000 to purchase existing housing and 3,806 buyers choosing newly constructed housing. After the May 31, 1983 cancellation of this incentive program, only the Registered Home Ownership Plan (RHOSP) remained for hopeful homebuyers.

Provincially, the previously overflowing housing grant cup was also running dry, and the government cancelled further home-buyer grants. Only the mortgage loan program remained, allowing a second mortgage of up to $10,000 with a cap of $85,000 for the applicable house purchase.

In June the Board's Past President and Honorary Member Col. Herbert R. Fullerton died. Remembered by many for his many educational initiatives for the real estate industry, he was a Past President and Honorary Member of both the B.C. and Canadian Real Estate Associations, and Honourary Member of the Victoria, Nanaimo and Fraser Valley Boards.

Throughout the year there were signs of improvement in the economy. Housing sales in all B.C. communities increased, and mortgage lenders were reporting strong activity compared to the 1981-82 recession period.

Perhaps it was this recovery that encouraged many to use a new technology, computerized telephone solicitation! It was a hit with the real estate industry but not with those who received the calls, and was quickly condemned by the public. Because it could not be prohibited, the Board urged members to use the technology with care and consideration and the Council issued a warning that the salesman and his/her company must be identified by name at both beginning and end of the taped message, and that full discipline would be levied against transgressors.

The Board maintained its impetus that year too, with a 28% increase over the previous year's dollar volume, to a record $1.7 billion. The Variable Assessment was .18% most of the year but by year-end had been changed to .2% to ensure a stable financial position. Another record was the number of properties processed—37,480—a testament to the growing popularity of MLS; its growing efficiency effected 14,516 sales, with an average residential price $115,600, up 7% over the low at the end of the 1982 recession period.

The population of Canada was now some 25 million, and Statscan said three quarters of that number lived in cities, with nearly two-thirds living in owner-occupied housing, one of the world's highest rates. Vancouver's population was 415,000 with 38% under 30, 15% over 65 and the large 31—64 year group making up the other 47%. As 1984 dawned, Alberta and British Columbia were the fastest growing provinces in the country.

Chuck Mitten was elected President in 1984, with Neil Neumann and Sandy Tompson as Vice Presidents, Hershey Porte as Treasurer. Under the direction of this Executive, a Policy Manual was developed for the use of Directors, Division and Committee volunteers, and is still updated annually for circulation to newly elected members.

C. I. (Chuck) Mitten
President, 1984

Expo fever was in the air, as building, planning and promotion for the 1986 exposition began. Expo '86 was to commemorate two centenaries—the completion of the Trans Continental railway that linked Canada as a nation and the incorporation of Vancouver as a city in 1886.

It was to be an unforgettable year, with Pope John Paul 11 making the first-ever papal visit to Vancouver in September, the World Esperanto Conference scheduled, and a replacement for the old Cambie Bridge approved by Vancouver ratepayers. Automated Light Rapid Transit—ALRT—became an acronym everyone knew, and so members could better serve their clients and customers, REALTORS started learning about the value of transit corridors, and increasing density around transit stations, the effects of transit noise and impact of its physical intrusion in neighbourhoods.

Because so many security situations had occured a Lock Box Exchange program by Divisional area was conducted in March. All keys then in use were exchanged for replacement keys, and a lease deposit raised to $50.00 from the previous $25.00 required for new keys. SUPRA key lids or replacement inserts for the old McNair boxes were made on a one-for-one basis as well. This newly keyed system stayed in place for the next decade, until 1993 when another change-over introduced a brand new electronic Supra Advantage Express 11 system for better security.

This year the Board took an active role in reviewing the new Expropriation Act, the Corporation Capital Tax and Vancouver City Zoning. It promoted Private Property Week and joined with the Vancouver Island Real Estate Board to plan, introduce and promote a Realty Watch programme, which was later endorsed by the Fraser Valley Board as well.

The B.C.R.E.A. Government Liaison Committee, with Vancouver Board members included, was instrumental in effecting changes in the prospectus requirements. Amendments meant prospectuses were no longer required for the sale of land in a municipality, if all services were installed or a contract let for installation, if subdivided land was sold by one developer to another, or for industrial or commercial land not to be used for residential purposes.

For the purpose of comparison, the Medallion Club qualification level in 1984 was (a) combined sold listings and sales totaling 18 units or (b) combined sold listings or sales totalling a minimum of 9 units with a dollar volume of $1,800,1000. Ten years later, in 1994, the requirements were 25 units together with $2,475,000 in volume, or 13 units together with $5,450,000 in volume.

Things were now beginning to move more quickly, and it soon became evident that information was soon outdated. The 25th annual edition of *Real Estate Trends in Metropolitan Vancouver* had been published the previous year, and now something more current was needed. A quarterly statistical review called *MetroTrends* was born, incorporating more fast-breaking statistical news, and focusing on certain areas each edition. It returned to its original annual publication in 1986.

This year the Board took an active role in reviewing the new Expropriation Act, the Corporation Capital Tax and Vancouver City Zoning. It promoted Private Property Week and joined with the Vancouver Island Real Estate Board to plan, introduce and promote a Realty Watch programme, which was later endorsed by the Fraser Valley Board as well. This security plan was subsequently adopted by CREA and only recently dropped, along with another Home Security Program, in favour of the more popular Neighbourhood Watch and Block Watch patrols that have endured.

Past Presidents John L. Boultbee and J. Ross Ker, along with the Board's long-time Secretary, Alan G. Creer, were elevated to Honourary Life Member status in 1984.

The advanced computerization enjoyed by this Board was also being noticed by other Boards across Canada. The Investment Analysis Program, developed internally, was successfully marketed to other Boards, and a fund for computer upgrading was established. The year ended without economic trauma, and through the user-pay programa established several years before, the portion of gross revenue received from assessments on MLS sales had dropped to 55% from the previous 75%.

Year-end statistics showed some reductions from the year before with 13,359 sales accounting for a dollar volume of $1.6 billion, a 9% decrease from the previous year's volume. The average residential price was $113,722, almost the same as the previous year, so the industry was happy to advance into a new year with a stable market ahead for both buyers and sellers. REBGV members ended this year on another high note—a donation of $40,000 to the MS Society to support the services of a nurse-coordinator who counseled MS patients and their families.

Stability and moderation were 1985's biggest buzz words, and the real estate industry was confident that the economy would improve steadily as we marched toward EXPO '86. Interest rates were slowly coming down, inflation rates had declined to about 4.3% and increasing employment seemed to signify an end to the recession of the past few years. In a bid for consumer confidence, B.C. Central Credit Union used Real Estate Board statistics to show that housing was once more affordable, particularly for the first-time buyer, comparing the family income needed in 1985 at $36,600 to the $75,500 required to purchase in 1981.

It was this upbeat mood in early 1985 that saw C.H. (Neil) Neumann named President, Hershey Porte and Janet Wainwright as Vice Presidents and Gary Brady as Treasurer.

The problem of automatic dialing telephone solicitation was reduced when the Canadian Radio Television and Telecommunications Commission (CRTC) put stringent new rules in place to eliminate sequential dialing, assure identification of speaker and nature of calls which could only occur between 9:30 a.m. and 8 p.m. on weekdays and noon to 5 on weekends. Machines were also required to disconnet from the line within 10 seconds of the answerer hanging up. Several other important changes were implemented this year. Authority for issuing licensing was transferred to the Real Estate Council of British Columbia. Effective in February, 1985, all license applications, fees, surety bond endorsements, license amendments and general enquiries went to the Council. The Superintendent continued to assume responsibility for review of Accountants' reports on the audit of the trust accounts of agents. The Real Estate Act Audit requirement was also changed so no formal audit would be required and a simpler financial reporting system was introduced.

Another important development occured early in the year when Consumer & Corporate Affairs Minister Jim Hewitt

C. H. (Neil) Neumann
President, 1985

It may seem to us now that they've been around forever, but 1985 was the "year of the electronic zip"— introduction of the retail credit card terminal which replaced the long list of invalid cards that kept you waiting while the retailer checked it. Zip went your card, and almost instant verification speeded up the check-out line.

announced his intention to introduce legislation that would amend the Real Estate Act to establish a Real Estate Foundation. After much representation from this industry, it finally came to pass that interest earned on the money in real estate agents' general trust accounts would be used in the public interest and for the betterment of real estate education and information. Since that time millions of dollars have been generated for such research as Affordable Housing, Continuing Professional Education for licensees, A Real Estate and Land Use Information project through the British Columbia Library Association, grants to SFU, BCIT, Vancouver School Board, Capilano College, University of the Cariboo and the Urban Development Institute for studies as diverse as environmental technology and consumer law and land policy planning.

During the first quarter of 1985 the increasing popularity of VANDAT saw the system respond to 10,000 callers, and new hardware to increase response time had to be installed. (In 1994, with an expanded menu of 32 programmes, and a much expanded membership, a total of 634,431 log-ons was recorded in the first quarter, with an average connect time of 4.9 minutes per call, which totaled 3,112,218 minutes of on-line service.) In mid-1985 business was improving and the Board was increasing its member-services. The Statistical Department's broadened range of information was so useful and popular that over a quarter of calls to this department were found to be from non-members, so security was tightened by requiring callers to identify themselves through membership card numbers. At the same time the Land Title offices also initiated new security methods with a "Direct Access Pass" for admittance behind the counter for the growing number of title searchers.

It was this year the Sinclair Centre heritage project began. This $40 million federal rejuvenation plan joined the 1910 R.V. Winch building, 1911 Customs Examining Warehouse, 1915 Post Office building and 1939 Post Office Extension, encompassing the block bounded by Granville, Howe, Hastings and Cordova. While preserving the heritage aspects of the four buildings, a modern office/retail complex was completed in time for Expo 86.

This year also saw a major change in one of the Board's "heritage" firms, as Macaulay, Nicolls Maitland and Co. joined with Leaseco of Toronto, changed to commercial and industrial brokerage only and joined the Colliers Alliance, an international group based in Sydney, Australia. As Colliers Macaulay Nicolls Inc., the company's stature and service remain unbroken since its beginnings in 1898.

The Board arranged block purchases of Expo 86 passes for the convenience of its members, with a small surcharge on each purchase, which went into the MS Fund, now in its 8th year as the Board's major charity. But Board members were quite aware that other societal issues in the area required attention. A contribution of $15,000 was made to the various Food Banks located throughout the Board's jurisdiction. Employing a pro-rata formula based on population, this donation was divided between the Vancouver, Pocomo, St. Alban's/Richmond, Deltasist, Ridge/Meadows and New Westminster Food Banks.

Board Committees remained busy this year, and kept up with all local issues. The private property rights issue was continued, and various municipal by-laws studied, including suites in residential zones and the Vancouver Plan. On the lighter side, the Cariboo Horns came back to Vancouver when Board thespians were again successful in the BCREA Skit contest in Penticton.

Alan Creer, longtime Vancouver Board Secretary, received Honorary Life Membership in BCREA at that spring conference and the same honour from the Canadian Real Estate Association in the fall. He had been previously so invested by his own Board and a year later by the Real Estate Institute of British Columbia, The Fraser Valley and Victoria Real Estate Boards. Such recognition is a good indication of the collective high regard for his ability, loyalty and contibutions to the real estate industry.

The Board set up a booth at the Edmonton CREA Conference in October, 1985, promoting both EXPO '86 and VANDAT. By this time 13 other British Columbia and Canadian Boards were using VANDAT through this Board's generous sharing of software, and many more were to join. Norm Thompson, the Board's Data Base Administrator, was present to explain the system to Canadian colleagues, and also to hear that CREA recommended VANDAT as the best system for Boards not already utilizing computerization. Indeed, CREA set up a fund to assist smaller Boards in adapting the VANDAT software systems to their needs, and also to translate it into the French language.

This recognition of his system was particularly pleasing to Thompson, and timely in a way none could foresee. Just two

1984 Board President Chuck Mitten successfully urged Vancouver Mayor Mike Harcourt to sign a proclamation for Private Property Rights to be established.

weeks after that Edmonton conference, Norm Thompson died suddenly at the age of 57, leaving much of his planned VANDAT improvement in the hands of his junior staff. A scholarship was established in his memory for assistance to computer students at B.C.I.T.

Vigour was returning to the real estate market, and with that activity comes another—the "buy real estate with nothing down" lecturers. The Real Estate Council issued a sternly worded public warning to property owners and a caution to B.C. real estate licensees that if requested to submit a purchase offer in which the buyer would have no equity interest, REALTORS have a duty to warn owners of the danger involved. Without this warning, the licensee could be liable to discipline for negligence, misconduct or both.

Board 1969 President Hugh Clee was Council Chairman at that time, and he also cautioned purchasers that this method of buying could put themselves in great personal financial jeopardy.

In a well publicized court case in 1985 the Supreme Court ruled the Lord's Day Act of Canada to be of no force or effect because it infringed upon the guarantee of freedom of conscience and religion in Section 2(a) of the Canadian Charter of Rights and Freedoms. The Board's solicitors agreed it seemed there were no more barriers to the signing of Interim Agreements for the sale of real estate on Sundays. The Board's internal Discipline & Complaints Committee instituted a system of fines along with other disciplinary actions, and eliminated the appeal procedure.

When analysing the year end production figures it was found that the strength in the market brought about a substantial increase in sales, breaking the $2 billion barrier for the first time in the Board's history. This remarkable feat also occured in a completely realistic market, free from the false "incentives" of government grants, which had given 1983 a record performance. Affordability was the cornerstone of the market. The average residential price was $112,700, and some 11,000 were sold under that mark, with 7,000 of them purchased for less than $85,000, thus able to qualify for the B.C. Government Second Mortgage.

When 1985 began the Board's variable assessment was .25%, but in successive months had been brought down as low as .1%. The year ended with a minor increase to .12% for 1986 sales, and a satisfactory financial status for the Board for the coming year. In typical REALTOR generosity, $45,000

*Vancouver was one hundred years old in 1986 and had
invited the world to celebrate its birthday at EXPO.
The Real Estate Board prepared to have a place at Expo
and make its mark internationally too, so negotiated
a booth in the World Business Showcase held throughout
the Fair at Canada Place.*

had been raised through individual and Divisional efforts
for the Multiple Sclerosis Fund.

Vancouver was one hundred years old in 1986 and had
invited the world to celebrate its birthday at EXPO. The Real
Estate Board prepared to have a place at Expo and make its
mark internationally too, so negotiated a booth in the World
Business Showcase held throughout the Fair at Canada
Place. Arrangements were made with the Fraser Valley,
Okanagan and Vancouver Island (Nanaimo) Boards who,
along with Vancouver, provided computer accessed property
information to visitors, together with copies of Real Estate
Weeklies and brochures on various real estate subjects. A
consortium of Interior Boards and the Canadian Real Estate
Association also chose to have representation. This booth
generated not only international business, but achieved
international respect for this Board and its efficient delivery
systems. Members enjoyed considerable business activity
between May and October as a result of hundreds of visitor-
requests published on the Daily Realtor during the months
this booth was in operation.

This epic year of celebration had begun with another first—
Janet Wainwright was named President of the Board, the first
woman so named. Hershey Porte and Marline Kolterhoff were
Vice Presidents, and Ted Burnham Treasurer.

Janet (Wainwright) Salmond
President, 1986

Special negotiations helped members go cellular economically by establishing a first lease-purchase programme
with B.C. Cellular. Staff had been preparing a new and final
edition of Through Lions Gate, updated in honour of Expo
year, published on the 20th anniversary of its first appear-
ance. This edition was sold out several years later and never
replaced. The real estate text Home Ownership a Basic
Guide was again rewritten to reflect the current market-
place, government assistance, taxes and interest rates.

Besides being EXPO year, 1986 was "mini-census" year,
the five-year count undertaken after each full survey, the last
of which had been in 1981. but another kind of count was also
being taken by the Board-counting those who were still
members after 25 years of continuous licensing. That first

year 180 "Quarter Century Club" members were identified and the list still waxes and wanes as new members qualify and losses occur through retirement or mortality.

At the suggestion of some members, the Board began offering member-services on Saturdays on a trial basis. Statistical Department phone lines, processing listing extensions and price changes and the sale of supplies was offered. During the three month trial there was so little call for this service that it was discontinued.

A joint BCREA/Canadian Bar Association Committee had been working for three years to prepare a new Contract of Purchase and Sale for use around the Province. In 1986 Board Directors approved the form subject to a continuing amendment procedure for review and possible changes.

The federal government's new Competition Act came into force in mid-year, replacing the Combines Investigation Act. At that time Board rules prohibited solicitation of employees of other member-companies, and denied the advertisment of incentives or gifts to either clients, customers or colleagues. It was to evolve sometime later how the new Act would impact on these existing rules.

One new provincial action was heralded. The Superintendent of Real Estate delegated disciplinary authority to the Real Estate Council. Previously, following a hearing, the Council reported its findings and and recommendations to the Superintendent for a decision and action. Following the change, British Columbia was the first jurisdiction in Canada where the conduct of licensees was judged by other licensees. Not long after, the Board approved Council's request to publish disciplinary decisions relating to its Board members, and this is still done.

It has always been a function of the Board to provide new and improved services and updated information for every facet of the industry. To effect this mandate a library of audio and video educational material was established, and as current members know, it is a very extensive free service offered by the Board. Also, a Committee was established to deal with on-going complaints from Municipal Officials regarding member-advertising of illegal accommodation in residential properties. In mid-1987, after many meetings with these officials, two acceptable phrases were developed for external advertising: "Fully Finished Basement" or "Partially Finished Basement". These two phrases are still the acceptable ones, while the contract submitted to the Multiple Listing Service must disclose the presence of unauthorized accommodation.

Two retirements of senior staff were observed in 1986. Long time Association and Board employee, Earle Moreton, retired as Associate Secretary in 1986, and Larry Buttress, who joined the Board in 1982 as Manager of the MLS Department, was named his replacement. Alex Scoten, Executive Assistant, also retired, and was replaced by Ray A. Nelson.

The success of this Centennial year invigorated the self indulgent Yuppie era, increasing business activity and price rises in almost every retail commodity. The confidence of the period even rubbed off on Board thespians, as they enjoyed another skit trophy win at the spring BCREA conference. Public generosity and REALTOR flower power saw $90,000, the record sales total for MS Carnation days, and by year-end members had donated another $48,000 to the MS Fund. Another record appeared in year-end totals, which rose to $2.4 billion for 19,049 sales, a 13% increase over the previous year. Average residential prices rose to $120,000, a 7% increase over the previous $112,700.

Expo was over, but the memory lingered on. People all over the world remembered the "beautiful, safe, clean, green" city of Vancouver, and many of the wealthiest speculated on a vast area of land on the north side of False Creek that was left behind after the Expo pavilions were removed. Serious and pie-in-the-sky proposals were to titilate the citizenry for over a year as the provincial government sought the most beneficial Development proposals for B.C. Place. In the spring of 1988 the government announced it had sold the Expo site to Concord Pacific Developments, and the Board publicly supported the world class proposals for this newly named "Pacific Place".

E. L. (Ted) Burnham
President, 1987

Fourteen years after leaving the medical supplies business to get his real estate license, and thirteen years after his first volunteer activity in the Salesmen's Division, E.L. (Ted) Burnham was elected 1987 President of the Board, assisted by Vice Presidents Gary Brady and Fred Warkentin, and Treasurer Marline Kolterhoff.

The "I" word was again entering the vocabulary. Inflation was spelled out as a 2-cent per stamp postal increase (to 36-cents in 1987), higher grocery and entertainment costs, local average house prices up almost $4,000 in the first two months of the year. In addition, the housing registration fee was enormously increased by the provincial government in its spring budget. The Social Credit government imposed the

172

The Social Credit government imposed the Property Purchase Tax—now called Property Transfer Tax— which then, as now, started at 1% of the first $200,000 of value and 2% on any remaining balance. Prior to imposition of this virtual capital tax on real estate purchased by British Columbians, the schedule of registration fees was approximately 1/10 of 1% of the property value.

Property Purchase Tax—now called Property Transfer Tax— which then, as now, started at 1% of the first $200,000 of value and 2% on any remaining balance. Prior to imposition of this virtual capital tax on real estate purchased by British Columbians, the schedule of registration fees was approximately 1/10 of 1% of the property value. So the legislation increased the registration fee to a buyer of a $200,000 home ten-fold, from the previous $200 to $2000.

Burnham and his Directorate took the lead in opposing this new tax measure, with radio and newspaper advertising, media interviews, petitions and pre-printed post cards of protest for members, clients and customers to mail to Victoria. Copies of all material developed by this Board were freely given to other British Columbia Boards and BCREA, who all joined the provincial protest. As all licensees even today know, no relief was achieved for the first two years, but in 1989 a paliative in the form of small PPT rebate for purchasers using high ratio financing was introduced, but this ended in June, 1994. In 1994's spring budget Burnham's urgent 1987 request was finally honored by the current NDP government, when it forgave the PTT for first time buyers of properties worth $250,000 or less.

Members in long-distance areas of Sunshine Coast, Squamish, Whistler and the Gulf Islands were now able to access VANDAT without long distance charges through the INET 2000 Network, a national directory of computer databases operated through Telecom Canada. The Board opened an INET 2000 account and paid user costs until late 1991, by which time the company had steadily increased rates to such a level that Board costs were far higher than any long-distance charges that would have accrued to the users, so the service was discontinued.

An ad-hoc Committee was established to review the function and role of the existing Standing Committees, and Vancouver's Education Committee, working with BCREA, finally saw approval of the new Contract of Purchase and Sale form still in use throughout the province.

Vice President Gary Brady had spent several years work-

173

ing with BCREA's Real Estate Self Assurance Fund Committee, proposing mandatory errors and omissions insurance. In 1987 the Legislature approved amendments to the Real Estate Act to accommodate the proposals effective in 1988. Provisions implemented were to increase maximum per occurrence coverage from $100,000 to $200,000 where two or more companies were involved in a claim. When established, start-up premiums were tied to licence renewal dates, with 1/24 of $200 for each month prior to June and the $200 full premium due on June 1/1988.

Making a tangible commitment to the enhanced education of its members, the Board approved an Education Committee recommendation to rebate $250 to any member or salesman completing a course year of the Urban Land Economics Program at UBC. This subsidy is still in effect

Seniors Golf for REALTORS 55 years or over was started in 1987 by President Ted Burnham who, incidentally, was the low-gross scorer in the first tourney, and winner of the Alan G. Creer Trophy, donated by the long-time Board Secretary.

The federal mint was making change in Canada in 1987, by introducing the "loonie" $1.00 coin and phasing out the paper bill. Another spectacular phase-out saw the disappearance of TV real estate gurus who had dominated the small screen and the lecture circuit just two years before. Markets change and so does the message. Some were now peddling no-smoking products or self-improvement schemes, and some just declared bankruptcy—they either ignored or took their own advice—whichever was the wrong course!

Toronto's real estate market had been heating up for two years, and "average" residential prices were $188,000, but by late summer a cooling down was noted. Meanwhile, a local real estate boom was creating delays in Land Title Offices and average local prices had zoomed 13% in less than a year, to $136,400 by September. These national price rises promoted the sense that housing affordability was being eroded, but Canadians could take some small comfort in the knowledge that Japan had a worse housing problem—a small condominium over an hour's train ride from Tokyo would set that country's buyers back $800,000.

Members shooting for Medallion status needed a combined sold listings and sales of 20 units or a minimum of 10 units and dollar volume of $2,000,000. The President's Club qualification was now up to 55 units or $5,000,000 in volume.

Technologically, the Board was still innovating, with FAX

The world's eyes focused on Vancouver again in October, when the representatives of 49 Commonwealth countries arrived for the Commonwealth Conference at the Trade and Convention Centre. Local motorists, however, focused mainly on the many traffic disruptions as police escorted V.I.P.s, closing streets and blocking intersections on the downtown peninsula.

machines installed and made available for member-use and an up-grade in computer equipment to allow members speedier VANDAT access at up to 19,200 baud.

It was a busy but very successful year, Provincial property tax impositions and federal moves affecting salesmen's income tax notwithstanding. The previous record year of 1980 saw 12,000 sales and a dollar volume of $1.3 billion, but 1987 doubled sales to 24,000 properties and tripled volume to $3.3 billion. Members were pleased to learn the new year would begin with a variable assessment rate of only .1%.

Vancouver REALTORS once again demonstrated their generosity in giving time and money for the MS cause. Over $70,000 was realized from the Carnation Days campaign in May, and some $54,000 was presented to the MS Society at year end as a result of the dedication of individuals and Divisions. Further, a special donation of $50,000 was made to the Society for use in providing mobility equipment for MS patients in need.

The new calendar year started with a full schedule of Income Tax seminars to inform members how both federal and provincial taxation changes might affect them. Also, to encourage new applicants for Salesmen's Division membership to be fully conversant with Board policy, rules and standards, an Orientation exam was introduced. This exam was administered by the company manager, and when completed sent to the Board with the Salesmen's Division entrance fee. A mark of 60% was required for qualification, but the unsuccessful applicant could write it again. This written exam was replaced in 1990 by the introduction of a mandatory in-house Orientation Program which is still conducted for all new members.

The Discipline, Complaints and Ethics Committee was renamed "Business Practices", to better describe its function.

Gary Brady assumed the Presidency at the February, 1988, Annual Meeting, along with Vice Presidents Brian Calder and John Eastwood, and Treasurer, Immediate Past President Ted Burnham.

The new Competition Act, proclaimed in 1986, became a matter of deep study and cautions to the real estate industry. Some years before under the Combines Investigation Act the Vancouver Board had removed all reference to any standard commission rates from its by-laws, but now the federal government increased the maximum fine for transgressions from $1 million to $10 million and the maximum liability for

Gary L. Brady
President, 1988

Thanks to strong representation from the Vancouver Board, along with its unassailable reputation, and the cooperation of other strong Boards in Toronto and Ottawa-Carleton, no actual charges were laid but many amendments were achieved in the Prohibition Order. As a result, CREA and its member-boards signed the Competition Law Agreement that is still in force today.

imprisonment to five years. Price setting or commission fixing between any individuals, groups or companies would be punished severely, and the Board made every effort to educate its members, and to maintain compliance with the new legislation.

President Brady and his Executive Committee had a busy year negotiating a three-way agreement by local Boards, Provincial Associations and CREA to bind the parties to the requirements of the Competition Act and provide a monitoring system to ensure Board By-Laws also complied with those requirements. While the Vancouver Board had always been in compliance, not all Boards were as careful, which resulted in allegations of violations made against nine Boards. Thanks to strong representation from the Vancouver Board, along with its unassailable reputation, and the cooperation of other strong Boards in Toronto and Ottawa-Carleton, no actual charges were laid but many amendments were achieved in the Prohibition Order. As a result, CREA and its member-boards signed the Competition Law Agreement that is still in force today. Special recognition must be given to Directors Gary Brady, Brian Calder, John Eastwood, and staff members Alan Creer and Larry Buttress, whose collective wisdom and negotiating skills brought to an end an issue that could have divided the industry and bankrupted real estate boards across the country.

Early in 1988 some seven special Committees were launched to plan, promote and execute the myriad details of a national convention planned for Vancouver that October. Despite the long meetings and constant travel surrounding the serious Competition Act negotiations, Vancouver Board Directors felt their conference hosting role was important, and their hard work paid off. It was to that date the largest CREA Conference on record, with over 1,500 delegates and additional 600 guests attending at Vancouver's stunning new Trade and Convention Centre. It was here, with the famous sails of Canada Place flying proudly overhead, that the Competition Act negotiators' efforts received the unanimous support of real estate boards across Canada, and it was fitting

In September of this year, Stanley Park marked 100 years since its opening in the two-year old frontier city of Vancouver. At the same time the Board could also claim 69 years of service and celebrate the fact that some of its charter members had actually witnessed the original Stanley park opening.

that this agreement be signed in Vancouver and the home Board of so many of the successful participants.

The Prohibition Order defined the acceptable standards of practice by real estate boards and their members under federal Competition Law, and under the agreement, all Canadian Boards circulated it to members and in addition, published it annually for the five years covered from 1989 through 1993.

In early 1988 an additional service for clients and customers and Board members too was introduced in a basic title search program covering all properties listed on MLS. Also, the Canadian Real Estate Research Bureau was born at UBC, thanks to a $500,000 grant from the Real Estate Foundation, $79,500 grant from the Vancouver Board, and $30,000 and $15,000 from the Fraser Valley and Vancouver Island Boards respectively. Part of the Urban Land Division at UBC's Faculty of Commerce and Business Administration, it provides support for graduate students, and publishes reports on various real estate research endeavours.

While its members recognized the Board's role in their business, Directors needed to know how the public viewed both the Board and its members. The Public Relations Committee undertook a survey to learn the public's perception of those who toiled in the real estate profession, and its knowledge of the Real Estate Board's function. It was found that while the individual practitioner got fairly good marks from the public, the Board's recognition factor was as low as 3%, so planning began to educate the public through a communications program.

House prices across Canada were creeping up, with Toronto's average residential unit at $233,000 and Vancouver's rising to $156,500. Regina was the place to be at that time, with average home prices at $71,500.

Because off-shore business was increasing, the Board started accepting FAX copies of contracts AUTHORIZED by FAX, subject to early receipt of signed original documents. As this technology became more and more accepted, and to give members the benefits of its ease and speed, by early 1993 all documents by FAX were accepted by the Multiple Listing Service.

In September, 1988, at Hotel Vancouver, over 300 people rose en masse in a standing ovation to Alan and Marian Creer. They were Past Presidents of the Board, Directors and volunteers who had known Alan and Marian throughout 38

Again, Board members proved charitable, with over $70,000 raised for Multiple Sclerosis in the spring Carnation Campaign and an additional $50,000 through the annual MS fund.

years of devoted service, which was coming to an end with Alan's retirement in December, 1988. Not only his members and staff honored Alan. In October the Faculty of Commerce and Business Administration recognized his leadership in real estate by establishing a "Alan G. Creer Graduate Fellowship" for a student in Urban Land Economics at the Faculty. Later the same month, the man who was already an Honorary Life Member of his own Board, CREA, R.I.(B.C.), BCREA, the Fraser Valley and Victoria Real Estate Boards, was the first annual recipient of the Frank Johns Award from the Executive Officers' Counsel, for his consistent contribution to professionalism, education, and upgrading of the real estate profession.

Larry Buttress, Associate Secretary at that time, was named to take Alan Creer's place on January 1, 1989. Former Maple Ridge/Pitt Meadows Division licensee, Harvey Exner, was appointed Associate Secretary in his stead. Brad Scott, who had started working in the Board's Data department with Norm Thompson in 1978, was named an Executive Assistant with responsibility for Data Processing administration at the same time.

Canadian inflation was alive and well as the year ended— postage was rising to 39—cents per letter on January 1; I.C.B.C. had promised increases averaging $60—$100 per applicant, and housing prices ended the year at $160,400. Membership totals in the Board also reflected the previous active years, as the Salesmen's Division increased to 4,788 members, and with other categories listed, the Board was serving 6,138 individuals working in 533 corporate offices.

But record-breaking year-end figures pleased everyone- 30,865 unit sales meant many satisfied sellers and buyers, and a dollar volume of $5.1 billion was a financial bonus to all those involved. Nine hundred and twenty seven licensees qualified for Medallion status that year, and sales success kept the variable assessment to .1% all through the year.

Again, Board members proved charitable, with over $70,000 raised for Multiple Sclerosis in the spring Carnation Campaign and an additional $50,000 through the annual MS fund.

Brian K. Calder
President, 1989

To comply with Competition Act requirements, the Real Estate Council announced early in 1989 that an annual quota of enrollees in the Pre-Licensing course for British Columbia would be abolished, making room for many more entrants into the real estate industry.

Vancouver taxpayers were invited to Taxation Review Commission hearings in January as a result of assessment increases flowing through the market as housing prices rose. City Council was trying to address this problem for the sake of both residential and commercial property owners. This problem is still with us today, with little hope for a solution short of a complete change in the funding for civic services.

Because of the economy and rising property values, the WOOPIES were leading marketing plans early that year. Those "Well Off Older Persons" had significant economic clout whether they sold their unmortgaged properties or not, and every industry from construction to retailing began courting this new grey power group.

Into this vigorous market activity came President Brian Calder, himself somewhat of a whirling dervish of activity, assisted by Vice Presidents John Eastwood and Rosemary Barnes, with Gary Brady named as Treasurer. This Executive Committee proved more than capable of coping with the spirited year ahead.

Expo, the World Trade Centre and International Financial Centre had all had a part in focusing the world's attention on British Columbia's Pacific Rim position. A new technology called Electronic Funds Transfer—bank debit cards—was just being introduced, and the Chinese calendar ushered in the year 4687, the Year of the Snake, a sign of economic prosperity.

That prosperity manifested itself soon as immigration figures began to burgeon, and home sales soared. In the first quarter, a total of 10,223 residential units sold—55% more than the comparable quarter the year before and more than one-third of total sales for 1988. Vancouver City sales outpaced all other areas, followed by Richmond and Burnaby respectively.

The activity was not only in the market, however, as Directors set heavy volunteer schedules for themselves. Gary Brady was negotiating with CREA and other large Canadian Boards to have an automatic "Large Board" appointment to the Canadian Association Directorate to ensure full representation. The Publicity and Public Relations

179

*As most know, the GST became a most frustrating fact
on January 1, 1991, and the 5% down through Canada
Mortgage and Housing Corporation in 1992. A Task
Force was appointed to study G.S.T. proposals
and to report to the Blenkarn Commission which was
on a Cross-Canada fact-finding tour.*

Committee had worked long and hard to produce a massive internal/external print and radio ad campaign and to effect a complete modern update of Board logo and image. The logo, incorporating a stylized Vancouver skyline and the Convention Centre sails, was registered and made available for identification use by Board members.

In June the social lounge on the second floor of the Board building was re-dedicated and named the Alan G. Creer Lounge, in recognition of how much this Board owes to the individual so honored and to keep alive the knowledge of his contribution. The location changed upon the move into a new Board building in 1994, but the name stayed the same.

Bending to the inroads of technology, the paper-based Statistical Department was finally to be phased out. Faster and more complete information was available through the Board's Menu # 1—Municipal Statistics Program, and long-time statistical manager, Lorraine McKeen was retiring. The area was brought up to date, however, as a Member Services area, with telephones, VANDAT terminals and listing and sales catalogues for personal research.

A number of federal proposals were causing concern to Directors in 1989; one was a proposed federal Goods and Services Tax, and another was a suggestion that Canadians be allowed to buy with as little as only 5% down. The first was considered inflationary, the second as an unrealistic debt assumption. REALTORS across Canada vividly remembered the Assisted Home Ownership Plan (AHOP), a mid-1970s government buying "incentive" which had cost the Canadian taxpayer over $500 million due to mortgage defaults in the early '80s.

As most know, the GST became a most frustrating fact on January 1, 1991, and the 5% down through Canada Mortgage and Housing Corporation in 1992. A Task Force was appointed to study G.S.T. proposals and to report to the Blenkarn Commission which was on a Cross-Canada fact-finding tour.

In due course seminars were arranged to give members an opportunity to know how the proposed G.S.T. would impact on real estate.

Always seeking to offer more convenience to members, by August of 1989 the Board provided the opportunity to pay by Visa or Mastercard for purchase of tickets to social or educational functions and for supplies. Another innovation was the "Lobby Gallery", offering a rotating art show of 6 to 8-week duration so members could enjoy or buy the work of Vancouver's emerging artists.

This year became known as the year of the "Asian Invasion" and rising prices gave the public a negative focus on this industry, despite or possibly because of its very visible advertising campaign. Media from every Canadian province, American state and even overseas focused on Vancouver's real estate market, and President Calder found himself more besieged than most spokesmen before him. He proved capable, however, of being the right man at that time for both the Board and for Vancouver, which was promoted internationally because of the housing market.

Current business activity didn't extinguish thoughts of past contributions, however, so four Past Presidents were named to Honourary Membership Status in 1989: John B. Erickson, E.S. Henderson, R.L. Richards and C.I. Mitten . At the national conference, the Board received the coveted M.I.C.C. trophy for Community Service, and this choice was validated again that year through the largest ever MS contributions—$80,000 raised in May during MS Carnation Days and another $92,000 collected through various member-events. With those 1989 donations, the Board passed the million dollar mark in funding, having donated a total of $1,033,809.22 to the Multiple Sclerosis Society since members of the Board adopted this charity in 1978.

The highly elevated levels of business through the Board were assisted by purchase of a second Series 70 Hewlett Packard Computer and a total of 22 extra telephone lines to provide better access to members.

Still, by year-end, it was an amazed Board of Directors which contemplated the sheer volume created through its 6,000-plus members. Over 36,400 unit sales produced a staggering dollar volume of $7.9 billion, 53% higher than the previous year. Home prices "averaged" $209,670 by year-end, but a review of those sales could still point to over 61% of all residential units being sold below that simplistic average. Housing prices were on the move, but economists said the numbers might not sustain, so the Board moved into the nineties facing mixed possibilities.

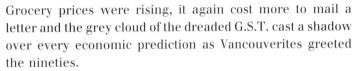

CHAPTER ELEVEN

THE NINETIES

Grocery prices were rising, it again cost more to mail a letter and the grey cloud of the dreaded G.S.T. cast a shadow over every economic prediction as Vancouverites greeted the nineties.

The Chinese Lunar New Year ushered in the Year of the Horse, which promised a spirited year to come, hectic, adventurous, with action the key word for business and projects in the year ahead.

The inescapable spell of Greater Vancouver had lured many new citizens, with the population of the Lower Mainland rising so fast the problems of density, transportation, green space and view corridors became paramount.

The Western provinces were taking the economic lead from Central Canada in gross domestic product growth, but also inheriting the inflation headache. Growing inter-provincial migration into B.C. was added to the rush of off-shore immigration, fueling employment growth in the service and construction industries.

The market stayed active and as prices escalated, some purchasers following the "Horse" philosophy were tempted to be adventurous and "flip" properties on Contracts of Purchase and Sale prior to completion by way of a second contract or assignment of the existing one. The Board issued a very firm caution to its members to avoid participating in such a transaction if she/he had been involved in the original sale.

John Eastwood was named President for 1990, with Rosemary Barnes and Satnam Sidhu serving as Vice Presidents, and Brian Calder remaining on the Executive as Treasurer.

One of Eastwood's first actions was a meeting with then federal Minister of Finance Michael Wilson, on the proposed G.S.T., the security of Immigration Investment Funds and the problems of social housing. Wilson was told the flaws noted in many immigration investment fund programs showed they were being operated by unscrupulous, unbonded individuals and there was no on-going fiscal control over hastily contrived schemes that might return nothing to the immigrant investor. The government of that day didn't act imme-

John D. Eastwood
President, 1990

diately so the problem of faulted funds is still with us and still being investigated by another government.

Business had become so brisk in Multiple that a direct-dial number was established so members would not have to wait through reception transfers. And by the end of the first quarter, rising paper costs meant a slight increase in catalogue prices, but the variable assessment was lowered to .09%.

In 1990 the Board launched its first International Dragon Boat Festival team, so 1994's entry was the fifth consecutive race that included a Board team. The Board now also sponsors a special REALTORS' cup for a race of five or six real estate company paddling teams. This fun-filled and exotic community event was introduced to Greater Vancouver during Expo 86.

But 1990 started as a year for Canadians to anticipate, fear, loathe and learn about the Goods and Services Tax slated to start January 1, 1991. It was especially necessary for REALTORS to understand how this would affect their clients and customers, as well as themselves as individuals and their Corporate identities. The Board published explanatory bulletins from the Department of Finance, launched special seminars and "town-hall" meetings with Revenue Canada staff present to answer questions. A CREA Committee produced and circulated a GST manual to every Canadian Board's member-offices. It provided guidelines on GST use in the many kinds of real estate transactions that could be anticipated. The real estate industry in Canada was possibly one of the best prepared to cope with this new tax, and rightly so because of its responsibility to fully explain its complexities to a woefully uninformed user-public.

A major revision was made that year in the MLS and Exclusive Listing contracts and Lease contracts to accommodate the coming Goods and Services Tax, and during one period old forms were exchanged one for one at the Board.

At the national conference a Vancouver Board recommendation that the three largest Canadian Boards—Toronto, Montreal and Vancouver—be given representation on the CREA Directorate through appointment, was finally approved.

The Bank of Canada was fighting inflation with a high interest rate policy and home sales were falling everywhere in Canada, including Greater Vancouver. As often happens, when price rises affect activity they also multiply consumer complaints, and the Errors and Omissions Insurance Corp

Early this year a plan to allow home-buyers a tax-free withdrawal from existing RRSPs towards home purchase was developed and suggested by the Vancouver Board. This plan was enthusiastically endorsed by CREA and other Canadian Boards and advanced to the Minister of Housing, the Honourable Alan Redway. Strong lobbying on the part of the Canadian real estate industry was successful in 1992, when the plan was introduced as a one-year window of opportunity in the Federal Budget. Extended for one year in 1993, it became a permanent first-time buyers' plan in 1994's budget.

In 1989 Past President Gary Brady had been asked to Chair a Board Premises Committee to establish future space requirements in view of increasing services and expanded staff work load. This Committee also researched costs of relocating, leasing or purchase of an existing property or construction of a new building. By September, 1991, the Board Premises Committee, now Chaired by Firoz Lakhani, proposed to Directors a new building to rise on the ground-level parking area behind the existing building. After their approval, an Extraordinary General Meeting of the members was held in early December where the Directors received an enthusiastic 83% approval from the membership.

was becoming concerned with the number of claims based on misrepresentation.

The Vancouver Board established a Presidential Task Force to prepare a Vendors' disclosure statement for use by its members. BCREA had tried a voluntary disclosure document in the seventies, which failed for the same reason this new initiative seemed doomed—most legal counsel was opposed to the vendor signing such a form. The E.& O. Insurance Corp drafted a proposed Property Condition Disclosure Statement form, and both the Board Task Force and BCREA made various amendment recommendations until agreement on the form was reached.

Copies of the approved Property Condition Disclosure Statement and an explanatory brochure were sent to member-links and sub-member links of the Vancouver Board in late 1991. Early the next year Divisional Annual Meetings proved a good platform for the President to discuss use of this voluntary vendor statement. It was designed to assist the licensee to review relevant aspects of the property at the time of listing, so all the correct information is provided for both parties to any potential transaction. Volunteer use of the form was encouraged in Vancouver, but some B.C. Boards made it mandatory immediately upon submission of any Multiple Listing. REBGV allowed its members time to become thoroughly familiar with it, then made it mandatory with all Multiple listings after September 1, 1993.

At this time the Board was offering 22 menu items on VANDAT and 30 other Canadian Boards and 2 Provincial Associations were using this system on a licensing program which allowed them use of the VANDAT software. The Board was already studying electronic photo transmission, which finally became a fact in early 1994.

A heavy work-load undertaken by the Board Premises Committee to solve financing, construction and design questions continued through the years preceeding 1994 completion of the new headquarters building with entry at 2433 Spruce Street.

Members of the Board Premises Committee known to have done exemplary service included the charter Chairman, Gary Brady, followed by Firoz Lakhani, whose task lasted over three years. Members included Rosemary Barnes, John Eastwood, Ron Downey, Boswell Malcolm, Dick Richards, Ian Dennis and Satnam Sidhu. Thanks to the expertise and professional talents volunteered by this group, the Board's new building became reality in July, 1994.

The Board expressed support for the TRIUMF-KAON project at UBC, urging its members to write to Ottawa for financial support of this facility which could bring much employment and technological achievement to Greater Vancouver. The then Conservative government did announce its intention to provide financial support, but in 1994 the current government took it away in a wave of budgetary restraints.

In 1990 the industry in B.C. was strongly urged to include the Norfolk & Aikens Addendum to reduce a licensee's liability against claims s/he did not prepare a binding Contract of Purchase and Sale. This was particularly important under circumstances where vendors might be relying on all or part of purchase monies to pay out existing financial charges against the property or where a purchaser may require financing to complete. Special Contract of Purchase and Sale Addendum forms were printed and are still available for purchase in the Board's new REALTOR Store.

The Order of British Columbia was bestowed upon H.P. (Budge) Bell-Irving in 1990. A Past President and Honorary Member of both the Vancouver Board (1958) and Canadian Real Estate Association (1975), Budge had been named Lieutenant Governor of the Province of British Columbia in 1978, serving until 1985 as the Queen's representative in his native province.

According to economists, B.C. was showing strong regional growth, with consistent population increases and employment growth. At year-end, the Board looked back at a remarkable 12-month period: busy, productive, frustrating, yet with declining sales and dollar volumes.

But rising interest rates had cut almost half the potential buying public out of the real estate market because they were no longer able to qualify for mortgaging. At the same time housing values continued to creep ahead. At year-end a 36% decline in dollar volume compared to 1989 saw sales total $5.1 billion, but average residential values ended the year at $226,400, an 8% increase over the previous year. While the drop in the numbers concerned the real estate industry as the year ended, it was the complexities of the GST and how it would impact on those first 1991 transactions that was the topic of conversation at most New Years Eve celebrations.

As 1991 arrived, new contract and data input forms were available to reflect the federal taxation and all Board charges for supplies, seminars, fees and dues had to reflect the new

REALTORS were able to look back with pride at a stellar performance on the charitable front. MS Carnation Day sales generated by Board volunteers reached $77,440 and a whopping $97,975 was realized through annual funding events held at all Divisional and Board functionss, making the 1990 total donation to the Multiple Sclerosis Society $175,415, a record annual sum despite the decrease in business for the year.

tax as well. Canadian business struggled to accommodate the extra accounting required to comply with GST regulations.

The Conference Board of Canada was predicting a summer time recovery from the country's economic doldrums, based on the asumption that interest rates would come down and bolster consumer confidence. Vancouver was expected to be the major growth centre throughout the next ten years, and that proved to be true as continuing net in-migration spelled a quick end to the real estate downturn.

Board Committee members contributed to public meetings on the Vancouver Tree Replacement Program, Development Cost levies, the Airport runway expansion and the Vancouver-Richmond Rapid Transit project. In early February the Legislative & Public Affairs Committee was gratified to be informed its recommendation to the federal Government that Investor Immigration programs be allowed to invest in rental housing had been approved. Subsequently a B.C. $35,000,000 pilot project in the social housing area was agreed between federal and provincial Ministers.

Again proving that Board members are influenced more by ability than gender, Rosemary Barnes was elected the Board's second female President in 1991. Satnam Sidhu and Firoz Lakhani served as Vice Presidents and Allan Corbett was named Treasurer.

Early in the year BCREA struck a Task Force to study proposed wide ranging amendments to the B.C. Real Estate Act. President Barnes and Past Presidents John Eastwood and Gary Brady, along with Board Executive Officer Larry Buttress, were involved in Task Force reviews.

Since the early 1970s, the Board had attempted to provide a recycling system that would collect waste paper and old catalogues from member-offices. Because of the confidentiality of the catalogues, private sector recyclers were carefully scrutinized. The need to pick up waste from such a large route, to cut off spines so the glue didn't ruin the recycling process, and sort paper colours proved too much for many of these small businessmen. The need for staff for the labour intensive hand work and the problem of fluctuating paper prices, resulted in many recycling business failures after only a few months, leading to many delays and disappointments in service to members through the years. The conservation objective was seriously addressed in 1991 by establishment of a Conservation and Environment Task Force, which conducted an Environmental audit of the Board and its

Rosemary Barnes
President, 1991

187

operations. It also participated in providing funds for two North Shore community "Operation Oil Tank" events, where students were employed to seek out potentially polluting unused fuel oil tanks in residential yards.

Within a year a fully funded pilot recycling program for Board generated paper products was started on the North Shore, and expanded Division by Division throughout 1993. Finally in 1994, a full recycling program—including office waste and newsprint—was put in place and is working well. Only white stock for covers and inner pages of catalogues is used now to eliminate the colour-sort needed for the recylcing process. The Board's contract courier Dan Foss has a specially marked truck going from office to office to pick up recyclables for delivery to Paperboard Industries' Surrey plant. The Board budgets some $150,000 annually to maintain this program, but Paperboard's payment to the Board for re-usable paper helps defray these costs by 10-20%. Environmentalists say that one tonne of recycled waste paper spares 17 live trees. In the first six months of 1994 some 107 tonnes of waste was picked up at member-offices, saving more than 1,800 trees.

BCREA and Vancouver Board members were studying another modern issue—toxic real estate—and the implications of proposed Waste Management legislation. An intensive one-day seminar on "Hot Property" was offered to REALTORS throughout the province.

Broker load was introduced in mid-1991, allowing members to enter their own OPENS FOR AGENTS, so they would appear quickly on the hotsheets, saving considerable staff time. This opportunity was soon expanded to include Menu #18, the Events registry, allowing members to include their own company events like office picnics and golf tournaments, so other companies could choose non-conflicting dates.

Listings which were submitted without the mandatory data input items (red boxes) completed, began to be identified with the term "INCOMPLETE" printed directly above the picture in September. This flag was kept in place in each publication until all information had been submitted. And since business had picked up considerably, the variable assessment was reduced to.05%, lowest rate in the history of the Multiple Listing Service. Medallion Club qualifications were adjusted to require 28 units together with $2,100,000 in volume or 14 units with $4,725,000 in volume. Presidents'

By 1991, cross-border shopping trips had increased eight times over what was registered in 1987. High levels of taxation on all Canadian purchases were blamed because Canadian shoppers could bring back goods, pay required duty, calculate the dollar differential and still end up with savings. There was some good news, however, as mortgage rates dropped over a percentage point to about 11% at the end of the first quarter, with the promise of more declines as the year progressed.

The same 1992 federal budget document which introduced the RRSP Home Buyers Plan also removed further Lifetime Capital Gains Exemptions for investment housing.

Satnam T. Sidhu
President, 1992

Club participants required 62 units with $4,650,000 in volume or 31 units together with $10,475.000 in volume.

Harvey Exner decided to reactivate his real estate career, so Brad Scott was named Associate Executive Officer of the Board, and Arnelle Wiebe, who had held assistance positions in these disciplines for several years, was named an Executive Assistant dealing with Arbitrations and Business Practices.

The Board's membership was now 8,260, with 6,621 of those members of the Salesmen's Division. This was an increase of 35% in total membership in just three years. Removal of the quota for enrolling in pre-licensing some years before had encouraged more to try for licensing, and the rising population speedily absorbed the extra service provided.

The efforts of this increased membership helped dollar volume soar for 1991, ending the year 55% higher than the previous disappointing year end, $7.5 billion compared to $5.1 billion. A total of 33,914 residential sales proved the stability in the market with a decline of only 2% in average residential prices to $221,900.

Another epic fund raising year was experienced, with over $79,000 raised during the MS Carnation Weekend in May, and a phenomenal $103,000 raised through the MS Fund during the year. Putting all fund-raising efforts together for the fourteen years since the Board had adopted the Multiple Sclerosis Society, over $1.4 million had been donated.

The new year of 1992 came in with the usual postal increase—it now cost 42-cents to mail a first-class letter in Canada. By mid-January that year Greater Vancouver motorists were able to drive the $110 million Cassiar connector, a tunnel and roadway link for the Trans Canada Highway to the Second Narrows Bridge.

Satnam Sidhu was named President, with Firoz Lakhani and Ronald Downey as Vice Presidents and Allan Corbett as Treasurer. Early in the year the federal government had announced the start of a two-year initiative which allowed buyers to choose their first home with a downpayment as low as 5% under CMHC's First Home Loan Insurance Package, with a required mortgage term of 5 years. While educating

189

members to be sure all customers would understand this purchase plan, this new administration also cautioned the buyer publicly on carrying a 95% debt load.

The same 1992 federal budget document which introduced the RRSP Home Buyers Plan also removed further Lifetime Capital Gains Exemptions for investment housing. It was important that members become familiar with this budgetary legislation so they could communicate its complexities to their clients. Based on a sliding scale relative to when the property had been purchased, a portion of the exemption was still available upon subsequent sale.

Agency Disclosure was becoming a spectre on the horizon, and North Vancouver Division President Paulean MacHale was asked to Chair a Task Force to gather all information and liaise with BCREA and its other member-boards on studying the intricacies of this subject. Even then Paulean, daughter of former West Vancouver REALTOR and Board Director Paul Sowerby, had a great interest in this subject, but it was to become an overwheming obsession. She soon became absorbed in all the technicalities of the various agency relationships, and because of the importance of this coming disclosure, the Board asked Paulean to accept a contract position during the research/educational process, temporarily resigning her elected Directoral position.

Informational brochures to explain Agency obligation and responsibility were circulated, and a seminar program launched, but the necessary planning and preparation for Agency operation was to continue for the next two years. Paulean also contributed to the CREA and BCREA Agency Task Forces which had been struck to deal with national and provincial issues surrounding implementation of Agency disclosure.

As the need for advanced general education became evident, the Board secured the services of Lisa Exley, FRI, CMR, a former member who had been licensed in British Columbia since 1977. An energetic staff member, Lisa is still active in coordinating an expanded educational programme for the Board and its Divisions.

Embracing further technological advances, the Computer and Statistical Committee was monitoring several years' development on PC VANDAT, software written especially for the REALTOR, with imaging innovations to allow pictures on the screen and in the printed format. After several years of preparation, PC VANDAT was introduced in early 1994.

A co-listing policy was established by the Multiple Listing Service, NCR forms introduced for easier recycling, and a special environmental strategy saw hotsheets sorted and delivered to match catalogue orders of individuals, saving tons of paper.

Another software program with a forms disc of all current forms, ZipForm XL, was released to enable users to print forms such as Contract of Purchase and Sale and Listing Contracts, on their own PC with a laser printer. Mapping technology came into study at this time too and the MLS Committee proceeded to research and poll the members on a new electronic lokbox system.

Cost conscious governments at all levels had been cutting back on construction of social housing over the past few years and market prices were steadily rising. To discover the public attitude on affordable housing, a survey was conducted by the Legislative & Public Affairs Committee. The results, released through a media conference and reports to all levels of government, showed 65% of respondents considered affordable housing a "Canadian right", over 80% wanted to own their own home but at least 75% believed a shortage of affordable housing was preventing this dream. Blame was mainly focused on the government, but some respondents blamed the development industry as well, and many felt that secondary accommodation in existing housing would help solve affordability problems.

A co-listing policy was established by the Multiple Listing Service, NCR forms introduced for easier recycling, and a special environmental strategy saw hotsheets sorted and delivered to match catalogue orders of individuals, saving tons of paper. Members who wanted full hotsheet mailings were reminded that these were available quickly on Menu 23 or also on order at $7.49 per month. A full range of faxed documents began to be accepted without original-copy follow up this year.

While the Board introduced more speed and efficiency for its members, the Ministry of the Attorney General introduced more expenses for those same people. A surcharge was added to all B.C. On-line Title Searches, fees for copies of survey plans and Section 288 questions were raised, and fees for amendment, transfer or reinstatement of real estate licenses through the Council were doubled to $100.

Another Budgetary threat that concerned this Board and

191

BCREA in 1992 was the intention of government to make Legal Services subject to the (then) 6% Social Services Tax. Legal services related to housing purchase would invoke this tax, so on top of previously increased transfer fees, buyers were again seeing the cash costs of buying increase. The Law Society and industries such as real estate, immediately protested and the Finance Ministry suggestion was later abandoned.

In addition to launching another paddling crew at the International Dragon Boat Races, the Board contributed a team to the Arts Umbrella Sand Castle Building Contest, was a contributing sponsor to both the "Independence '92 Conference", which focused on accessible housing for the disabled and the CHBA "Georgie Awards" for the best of local Canadian Home Builders.

Earlier this year the Superintendent of Real Estate transferred the responsibility for monitoring disclosure statements to the Real Estate Council of B.C., which had just finished its full mailing of a new Licensee Practice Manual to replace the long-standing Real Estate Licensee's Handbook. The Council also discontinued the sponsorship requirement for potential pre-licensing students late in 1992.

By 1992 year-end the Salesmen's Division had added over a thousand members, standing now at 7,693. With other membership categories, the Board was now serving some 9,300 individuals.

While serving in this healthy and active market, Board members volunteered enough time to earn over $71,000 for Multiple Sclerosis during the spring Carnation Days sales blitz, and another $87,000 was realized for the same charity through the MS Fund.

But the most exciting happening for Board members was ground breaking for the new building. The important decisions made at previous meetings of the voting membership finally seemed real. Board members requiring parking were accommodated at the BCAA parking facility on Oak Street, one block east. As the new building was now becoming a reality, the structure at 1101 West Broadway was offered for sale and all Board members given the opportunity to participate in any forthcoming transaction. A sale became final early in 1994 and a lease-back was negotiated so staff could continue to serve members until the move into the new building on June 30, 1994.

Ron Downey participated in a BCREA Property Manage-

Lower interest rates and government programs had increased affordability for many first-time buyers. In Greater Vancouver previous records were broken, with a dollar volume of $9.5 billion, 20% higher than the 1989 high of $7.9 billion. Average residential price throughout the Board's jurisdictional area rose to $245,000. Residential vacancy rates were declining again despite several years of active construction, and both CMHC and real estate analyst and writer, Frank Clayton, were predicting continuing high immigration, a strong economy and rising property values for British Columbia in 1993.

ment Task Force, and after the deliberations and wise counsel of this Committee, the Superintendent of Real Estate would no longer grant restricted licenses to property managers without completion of the salesman's course and examination. Effective March 1 the Errors and Omissions Insurance Corporation extended coverage to Property Management transactions.

In early 1993 the membership approved a streamlining of the Board's Standing Committees. By deleting the Program Committee, the Membership Committee became the Member Services Committee, combining the promotion of Board membership with the planning of its social programs.

Under this new structure Firoz Lakhani was elected President, with Ronald W. Downey and Bonnie Telep serving as Vice Presidents and Glenn Temes as Treasurer. Since many long-time policies were being tested, and many new matters up for consideration, this became the "Year of the Task Force". Special Presidential Task forces were establishing new Charitable Donations objectives, considering One-Tiered membership, Orientation of new Committee Members, changes to MetroTrends and Honourary Membership criteria, along with the existing Task Forces of Board History, Charitable Works, Agency procedures and Conservation and Environment.

Firoz Lakhani
President, 1993

Early this year Directors' approved a recommendation to render the Property Condition Disclosure Statement mandatory as of September 1, 1993. Most other British Columbia Boards had done this the year before, but Greater Vancouver needed time to educate and inform both members and clients. After considerable explanatory Daily REALTOR information, all members knew that as of September 1 each Multiple Listing Contract must be accompanied by a Property Condition Disclosure Statement completed by the Vendor or, if the Vendor did not wish or was unable to complete the form, a signed acknowledgment by the Vendor of receipt of the form.

A Real Estate Board of Greater Vancouver Charitable Fund, administered by the Vancouver Foundation, was established to generate annual income to be disbursed for future charitable needs. Board members are encouraged to help the capital fund grow by making tax-deductible donations to this fund. Only earnings are disbursed, and as the capital grows so will the size of meaningful charitable donations made in the name of all Board members.

After a distinguished half-century career in real estate, much respect and many honors, Dean Mansell died in his 91st year. He was President of the Vancouver Real Estate Exchange in 1947 and again in 1948 when he organized the name change to Vancouver Real Estate Board. In 1951 he served as President of the Canadian Association he had earlier helped establish, and was an Honorary life Member of both this Board and CREA. He was Chairman of Macaulay Nicolls Maitland & Co., one of Vancouver's oldest real estate firms, when he retired in 1976.

To promote the start of construction activity at the Board's new building, a Charity Hoarding Wall was launched, offering local charities free public display space around the site hoarding. The Golden Hammer Ceremony in April featured Architectural artist Robin Ward, who named the three top charity panels for "gold", "silver" and "bronze" awards. Vancouver Mayor Gordon Campbell helped President Firoz Lakhani secure the winning panels on the hoarding. These three winning entries remained on the wall throughout the next 8-month construction period and 24 other Charitable groups were accommodated in four-month display periods. The Board suggests others use this charity hoarding plan to give promotion to deserving groups, to give viewing interest to neighbours of a construction site and discourage graffiti artists.

A pivotal part of the ceremony was presentation of $250 worth of food for the Food Bank, donated in the name of honoured guest, Mayor Gordon Campbell. This gesture was made even more meaningful when Canada Safeway agreed to assist and generously doubled the amount of non perishable goods later loaded into the colourful Food Bank truck and taken to the distribution centre for those in need.

New members are now required to choose from three suggested dates within approximately 45 days of joining the Board to complete a mandatory Orientation Course. Teachers for this course include long-time members, Past President Rosemary Barnes of Park Georgia Rlty Ltd., Julian "Kim" Spencer, of Legend Real Estate Group, Director Glenn Temes of Sussex Group Westmar Realty Ltd. and Director Bonnie Telep of Tri-Tel Realty Ltd.

A massive logistical exercise was carried out successfully in September, 1993, when members of the Multiple Listing Committee, staff and contract workers conducted the mighty "Lock Box changeover". In this mandatory measure, old

At the end of this last year designated for MS funding members continued their historic generosity, with over $80,000 raised in May during Carnation days and at year-end, a further $48,257. These two sums brought the Board's 16 years of Multiple Sclerosis donations to an astonishing total of $1,667,848.00

Supra and McNair keyboxes were exchanged for the more secure Supra Advantage Express 11 electronic system.

The Board became a sponsor of the B.C. Sports Hall of Fame and Museum in 1993 by funding the 1880s Gallery to recognize the birth of the first Canadian Estate Board, which enjoyed a brief lifetime in Vancouver in 1888. Incidental donations were also made to the Evergreen Foundation, Arts Umbrella, Salvation Army and the Missing Children's Society of Canada. It was also agreed to publish pictures of missing children on the back cover of all catalogues.

After a 16 year term at the Board, and twenty previous years of service at CREA and the Canadian Real Estate Institute, Olga Dueck decided to take a well-earned retirement. She was replaced as Divisional Secretary by Stacey Alm.

A study was undertaken to review the Board's charitable endeavours, with proposals taken from organizations whose mandates met the charitable criteria which had just been developed. Through this process it was decided that 1993 would be the last year of support for the Multiple Sclerosis Society, and a commitment to raise $250,000 over a five-year period to fund a Family Suite in Canuck Place was approved. (At the end of this last year designated for MS funding members continued their historic generosity, with over $80,000 raised in May during Carnation days and at year-end, a further $48,257. These two sums brought the Board's 16 years of Multiple Sclerosis donations to an astonishing total of $1,667,848.00)

This is the year a "get tough" policy for delinquent accounts was established, with immediate suspension for member companies whose accounts were overdue more than 30 days. Incomplete Listings were given a ten day grace period after initial receipt, and if corrections were not submitted a $50.00 assessment imposed, followed by a further $25.00 assessment for each subsequent two-week period the listing remains incomplete.

PC VANDAT was in its testing stages, with some 40 members using the system to identify any "bugs" before final

195

As mainstream real estate in both the U.S. and Canada embraced the buyer agency concept, a coordinated study/test was underway in Greater Vancouver. Full disclosure requirements were to be implemented by the end of 1994, under CREA's new Code of Ethics amendment to include written receipted disclosure of a licensee's Agency relationship.

release. Meanwhile, a substantial library of digitized photographs was being stored on the computer in advance of its release. On August 30 this new technology was released for member-purchase, and those with the required hardware were invited to register for PC VANDAT seminars, where software to provide colour photographs of listings and sales was made available.

BCREA was negotiating with B.C. Telephones for industry-wide savings on long-distance telephone calls. Substantial savings were finally in place in late 1993 through the Real Estate Advantage Plus program, covering all member-firms of all thirteen British Columbia Boards. This initiative, unfortunately, was cancelled by the CRTC within the year, and competitive bids for comparable services are now under review. The Association was also studying the need for mandatory on-going post licensing education throughout the industry, and continues to evaluate the needs of provincial licensees and their acceptance of this plan.

As mainstream real estate in both the U.S. and Canada embraced the buyer agency concept, a coordinated study/test was underway in Greater Vancouver. Full disclosure requirements were to be implemented by the end of 1994, under CREA's new Code of Ethics amendment to include written receipted disclosure of a licensee's Agency relationship. Vancouver's Agency Task Force Coordinator, Paulean MacHale, was active on the CREA Committee and soon ready to share her new Agency knowledge with her own colleagues.

The Agency Task Force arranged to field-test its analysis of the assumed Buyer Agency system with a four-month pilot project in the board's smallest Division, Maple Ridge/Pitt Meadows. New documentation included a modified MLS contract clearly stating the seller assumes all salespeople working with buyers represent those buyers as their agent and owe no fiduciary obligations to the seller. Also, listing agents disclose to and get consent from the seller that they will share compensation with any co-operating agents.

Vancouver Board Directors targeted November 15, 1994,

The city had enjoyed a building bonanza in the past twelve months, dominated by condominium construction, but as the new year approached, CMHC was forecasting declines for the year ahead.

as the date for the new Disclosure system to be operational within its area. Comprehensive communication and a full educational program on Assumed Buyer Agency continued with printed bulletins, Managers' seminars, and individual reviews through the intervening period.

Board members and staff were convenienced in November, 1993, when the parkade in the new building was made available for parking even though the upper structure was still under construction. Two levels of member-parking and one for staff has made room for some 145 vehicles—triple the capacity of the previous ground-level parking.

In summing up 1993, one could say it was a year of building, but referring to more than the bricks and mortar of the new headquarters. It was a year of identifying and integrating initiatives that are designed to strengthen service to the Board's membership and to restructure the association so it continues to be a viable part of every REALTOR's business success.

In response to the anticipated changes in the way this industry does business, a governance study by KPMG was commissioned, with a full review of the responsibilities of senior officers and elected officials and recommendations to improve the efficiency and effectiveness of the association.

The 33,225 units sold in 1993 was a decrease of 15% from the 39,484 sales of the year before, and dollar volume was down 4% to $9.4 billion compared to the record 1992 figure of $9.8 billion. At the outset of the year doom and gloomers had predicted wholesale drops in activity, but that didn't happen. While the record of the previous year wasn't broken, the sales outcome was more than respectable, thanks in great part to a good inventory and affordable mortgage interest rates.

The city had enjoyed a building bonanza in the past twelve months, dominated by condominium construction, but as the new year approached, CMHC was forecasting declines for the year ahead. Financial problems were being faced by some business owners and all taxpayers were facing rising costs with shrinking dollars. But as 1994 began, rumours of rising mortgage interest rates and the end of the RRSP Home Purchase Plan, spurred a home buying spree. That gave January's sales figures a healthy increase, with the majority of the activity at the low end of the housing market.

To reflect its significant position in the Greater Vancouver business community, a completely re-designed Annual Report was released to all members and also sent to local and provincial dignitaries and officials early in 1994. This year would launch celebrations of 75 years of continuous association service to Greater Vancouver, and this was the beginning of anniversary recognition by Board officials.

Ron Downey was elected 1994 President, with Allan Corbett and Horace Chan as Vice Presidents, Glenn Temes as Treasurer. The Annual Meeting at which these and other newly elected officials were inducted was held in February at Hotel Vancouver, the same hotel (but different location) where the first Annual Meeting of the Real Estate Exchange had been held in 1920. Some 600 members greeted the unveiling of the Anniversary logo and banner in preparation for further celebrations throughout the year.

A heavy schedule was set out for Board Directors and Committees to accomplish during this special year, with particular focus on the Management Review and defining long-term goals for improving the Board. Included among these tasks were upgrading current technology capability; the future of MLS and how it can be preserved/enhanced, including investigation of the B.C. Tel HomeLine network; preparation of a history of the Board; on-going reviews of existing by-laws with emphasis on a one-tiered membership concept and the Agency educational program, along with other educational endeavours to continue unabated. At the forefront of experiences in this year would be the move into the new building.

Ronald W. Downey
President, 1994

Future homebuyers got good news in February, as federal revenue officials made the RRSP Home Buyers Plan a permanent fixture for first-time buyers of Canadian residential real estate. Mortgage rates had declined somewhat as the Bank of Canada rate went down in January but started rising again by mid-February, so borrowers were on a roller-coaster of decision making to lock-in or pre-approve the best rate. And many Vancouver home owners heaved a sigh of relief when the provincial budget lifted the ceiling on the home-owner grant phase-out that had been imposed the year before, giving some 20,000 B.C. families the full $450 grant.

By the end of the first quarter, mortgage rates had galloped up two percentage points from the previous month, but residential sales had kept pace with their wild ride-being 17% higher than the previous year. The see-saw fluctuation of rates since the year started saw home sales slip on occasion, but by the end of the third quarter when this is being recorded, sales were virtually even with those in the same period last year.

The spring work-load for the MLS staff—when one day over 500 new contracts were submitted—required apologies and requests for patience while the staff dug itself out of the heavy volume. Menu # 28, the New Listings Broker Entry for VANDAT proved to be a boon for many members at that time.

Vancouver Board members who regularly accessed the FVREB computer system had to go back to school, because on May 31 the Fraser Valley Board switched to a new STELLAR 111 system.

In spite of—or perhaps BECAUSE of—Canada becoming an under-ground economy to beat the GST, a Vancouver financial think tank declared June 23, 1994, as the day Canadians had satisfied all our tax obligations and would begin "working for themselves". "Tax Freedom Day", said the Fraser Institute, means we've paid 48 per cent of our income to various levels of government. Despite other taxing problems, REALTORS continued to contribute their time for good causes—MS Carnation Day sales in May, and the Land-lubber paddling team at the International Dragon Boat Festival in June.

For many months the Provincial Association had been fighting for exemption of REALTORS from coverage under the Workman's Compensation Act. It met with only partial success by mid-year, having WCB determination to declare only those real estate salespeople who received full gross commission as independent and thus exempt. An appeal process is underway to expand the declaration to exempt all licensed real estate salespeople through the use of specific contract wording that would meet exclusion requirements.

A reminder of human mortality came to Board members in this 75th anniversary year with news of the death of Harry A. Roberts at the grand old age of 99. Active in the Real Estate Exchange from the late '20s, Harry Roberts became a Director in 1930, was its President in 1936 and 1937 and named to Honorary Life Membership in 1960. "H.A's" 45 years of involvement helped ensure the Board's strength and survival. Peter Williamson, 1977 President, also succumbed this year.

There are changes affecting the real estate community throughout North America and also in other countries. An interesting 1994 news note in the London (England) Sunday Times outlines the efforts of an estate agent moving toward

From south of the border, another test to the creativity of REALTORS has arisen—political correctness in real estate ads! In Pennsylvania a broker found there were certain "red light" words that could run afoul of this new buzzword. The term "executive home" could be construed as racist because most executives are white; "sports enthusiast" could offend the disabled; "quiet neighbourhood" could be code for "no children"; "Master Bedroom" suggests slavery; "adults only" or "no children" could breach fair housing standards; It may sound far-fetched, but in our increasingly litigious world, even we in Canada are not immune.

199

a form of "lock-out" contract to stop vendors seeking higher offers for at least two weeks after agreeing to a sale. A system called "gazumping", where any vendor can accept a higher price or better all-round deal at any time after a previous offer has been accepted, leaves little security for the buyer, and little compensation for the estate agent.

An obscure and almost unseen section in a proposed Municipal Affairs Statutes Amendment Act, became the subject of Vancouver Board/BCREA response to the Minister, Darlene Marzari. Under the proposed law a city could make an official community plan that designates an existing neighbourhood as the site of a possible future government project such as a school or highway without actually acquiring the property or even having funds set aside to acquire it. This would lower property values and even make selling an impossible hardship for owners. It was announced in early June that the section was "being reconsidered", and has since been rescinded.

There was both joy and angst on the July 1st weekend when staff made the move into the new building. After 34 years at 1101 West Broadway, the new address became 2433 Spruce Street, a location behind the old building which had been sold to provide additional financing for the new premises.

The spacious quarters soon became "home" to some 65 staff members who now found themselves scattered in work areas over 3 floors, with plenty of storage space, parking and a flexible, airy multi-windowed work-area.

Members were offered special building tours to acquaint them with the new building and all gave thumbs up to the member-services main floor, where Reception, Multiple Listing, Membership and Ticketing and the REALTOR Store give a one-stop shopping atmosphere. There is also a four-computer work area, a generous number of phone booths and a special copy room, with space reserved for a future members' library.

As we complete this chronicle there are still many changes and unresolved issues ahead. New contracts have been adapted to Agency Disclosure, and Task Forces are wrestling with such important subjects as changing fee systems and membership structure and voting practices.

But one change that looms large is choice of a new Executive Officer to replace Larry Buttress, who regretfully tendered his resignation after 6 years in the top position during nearly 13 years of service at the Board. Ernst and

A move hailed by all existing licensees throughout the province was made in April, when the Real Estate Council of British Columbia proclaimed an English language proficiency course a mandatory part of the provincial pre-licensing program. There had been many complaints about communications problems, they said, and the 2 1/2 hour LPI would ensure a basic proficiency in all those who wished to join the industry.

A major aim of the Board is: "To promote, encourage and protect the ownership of real property and to endeavour to maintain real estate values in the areas served by the Society and to do all things which may be deemed necessary or advisable to make real estate a sound and a desirable investment."

Young, along with elected officials, are reviewing applications as we go to press. This subject will have been resolved and reported to the membership before printing of this publication is complete.

Throughout these pages we have outlined the many events that have contributed to a constantly evolving Board and its service delivery systems.

Some changes must be considered and adopted for the betterment of the industry, but some things will not change, foremost being the foundation upon which this 75-year old association was built.

A major aim of the Board is: "To promote, encourage and protect the ownership of real property and to endeavour to maintain real estate values in the areas served by the Society and to do all things which may be deemed necessary or advisable to make real estate a sound and a desirable investment."

The new premises of the Board symbolizes the pride and wisdom of ownership inherent in the aims and objectives of the Board.

People involved with buying and selling land nurture the changing face of the community. Even before our cities officially began there were brokers to help in the orderly transfer of property from one owner to another. In 1919 a group of those entrepreneurs formed a society to ensure that dealings would always be ethical and standards of practice acceptable.

That Society still exists as Real Estate Board of Greater Vancouver. Past members rose to the challenge of growth and their accomplishments are writ large on the face of the metropolitan area. Now Greater Vancouver is at a new and exciting cross-roads, with a changing cultural vitality and sophistication that will shape its destiny. There are still many contributions to come from contemporary broker-members who maintain the same faith in the ownership of real property that spawned the growth of this city and set the stage for 75 years of success for this Board.

MISSION STATEMENT

Real Estate Board of Greater Vancouver is an Association of Realtors committed to providing its members with the structure and services to ensure a high standard of business practices and ethics and to effectively serve the real estate needs of the community.

REAL ESTATE BOARD
OF GREATER VANCOUVER

75

ANNIVERSARY

EARLY OFFICERS OF
THE REAL ESTATE EXCHANGE

1919 / 1920 / 1921
First President
Served three years
R. Kerr Houlgate

1922 / 1923
President
Served two years
H.R. Budd

1924
President
A.E. Austin
Vice President
A. McC. Creery

Directors
J.W. Allan
W.E. Bland
Col. R. Cram
G.H. Dorrell
S.R. Margetson
J.P. Nicolls
H.V. Sharples

1925
President
A. McC. Creery
Vice President
J.P. Nicolls

Directors
J.W. Allan
W.E. Bland

G.H. Dorrell
S.R. Margetson
G.L. Schetky
H.V. Sharples
E.C. Taylor

1926
President
J.P. Nicolls
Vice President
G.H. Dorrell

Directors
J.W. Allan
H.R. Budd
Col. R. Cram
G.L. Edwards
S.R. Margetson
G.L. Schetky
E.C. Taylor

1927
President
G.H. Dorrell
Vice President
D.W. Reeve

Directors
J.W. Allan
A.E. Austin
H.R. Budd
G.L. Edwards
N.J. Ker
S. MacGregor
G.L. Schetky

1928
President
D.W. Reeve
Vice President
N.J. Ker

Directors
J.W. Allan
A.E. Austin
H.R. Budd
G.L. Edwards
W.S. MacGregor
G.L. Schetky
E.C. Taylor

1929
President
J.W. Allan
Vice President
G.L. Edwards

Directors
A.E. Austin
H.R. Budd
H.A. Burke
F.A. Cleland
N.J. Ker
J.C. McPherson
J.P. Nicolls

1930
President
J.C. McPherson
Vice President
G.L. Edwards

Directors
G.H. Dorrell
A. Rout Harvey
N.J. Ker
D.C. Lee
W.S. MacGregor
J.P. Nicolls
H.A. Roberts

1931
President
W.S. MacGregor
Vice President
D.C. Lee

Directors
A.E. Austin
G.L. Edwards
A. Rout Harvey
R. Kerr Houlgate
N.J. Ker
J.P. Nicolls
H.A. Roberts

1932
President
W.S. MacGregor
Vice President
D.C. Lee

Directors
G.H. Dorrell
G.L. Edwards
N.J. Ker
G.I. Legate
J.P. Nicolls
D.W. Reeve
H.A. Roberts

1933
President
G.I. Legate
Vice President
G.L. Edwards

Directors
G.H. Dorrell
N.J. Ker
D.C. Lee
J.P. Nicolls
D.W. Reeve
H.A. Roberts
E.C. Taylor

1934
President
G.L. Edwards
Vice President
A.M.J. English

Directors
G.H. Dorrell
N.J. Ker
J.C. McPherson
J.P. Nicolls
D.W. Reeve
H.A. Roberts
E.C. Taylor

1935
President
A.M.J. English
Vice President
H.A. Roberts

Directors
G.H. Dorrell
N.J. Ker
A. Rout Harvey
J.C. McPherson

J.P. Nicolls
D.W. Reeve
E.C. Taylor

1936
President
H.A. Roberts
Vice President
G.H. Dorrell

Directors
F.A. Cleland
A. Rout Harvey
D.C. Lee
N.J. Ker
J.P. Nicolls
D.W. Reeve
E.C. Taylor

1937
President
H.A. Roberts
Vice President
G.H. Dorrell

Directors
E.L. Boultbee
F.A. Cleland
A. Rout Harvey
N.J. Ker
W.H. Mowat
D.W. Reeve
J.P. Nicolls

1938
President
G.H. Dorrell
Vice President
F.A. Cleland

206

Directors
E.L. Boultbee
A. Rout Harvey
N.J. Ker
J.C. McPherson
W.H. Mowat
J.P. Nicolls
D.W. Reeve

1939
President
F.A. Cleland
Vice President
W.H. Mowat

Directors
E.L. Boultbee
A. Rout Harvey
N.J. Ker
J.C. McPherson
W.S. MacGregor
J.P. Nicolls
D.W. Reeve

1940
President
F.A. Cleland
Vice President
E.L. Boultbee

Directors
W.C. Bowie
G.L. Fowler
A. Rout Harvey
J.M. Kirkwood
J.C. McPherson
W.H. Mowat
D.W. Reeve

1941
President
E.L. Boultbee
Vice President
A. Rout Harvey

Directors
W.C. Bowie
G.L. Edwards
G.L. Fowler
J.N. Irvine
W.S. MacGregor
J.C. McPherson
D.W. Reeve

1942
President
A. Rout Harvey
Vice President
H.E. Bond

Directors
W.C. Atherton
G.L. Edwards
A.M.J. English
G.L. Fowler
J.N. Irvine
J.C. McPherson
D.W. Reeve

1943
President
A. Rout Harvey
Vice President
H.E. Bond

Directors
W.C. Atherton
G.L. Edwards
A.M.J. English
G.L. Fowler

G.S. Lennie
J.C. McPherson
D.W. Reeve

1944
President
A. Rout Harvey
Vice President
H.E. Bond

Directors
W.C. Atherton
Gordon Bell
G.L. Edwards
A.M.J. English
G.L. Fowler
J.C. McPherson
D.W. Reeve

1945
President
H.E. Bond
Vice President
W.C. Atherton

Directors
Gordon Bell
G.L. Edwards
A.M.J. English
G.L. Fowler
J.C. McPherson
D.W. Reeve
H.A. Roberts

1946
President
W.C. Atherton
Vice President
Gordon Bell

Directors
G.L. Edwards
G.L. Fowler
D.S. Manell
J.C. McPherson
D.W. Reeve
H.A. Roberts
E.P. Taylor

1947
President
D.S. Mansell
Vice President
J.C. McPherson

Directors
Gordon Bell
F.A. Cleland
L.C. Creery
R.A. Pound
D.W. Reeve
S.V. Smith
E.P. Taylor

1948
President
D.S. Mansell
Vice President
S.V. Smith

Directors
Gordon Bell
F.A. Cleland
L.C. Creery
G.H. Johnston
R.A. Pound
D.W. Reeve
E.P. Taylor

1949
President
S.V. Smith
Vice President
L.C. Creery

Directors
Gordon Bell
E.L. Boultbee
F.A. Cleland
R.A. Pound
D.W. Reeve
J.P. Roberts
E.P. Taylor

1950
President
S.V. Smith
Vice President
L.C. Creery

Directors
E.L. Boultbee
F.A. Cleland
W.E. Fowler
J.F. Kelly
R.A. Pound
J.P. Roberts
E.P. Taylor

1951
President
L.C. Creery
Vice President
J.F. Kelly

Directors
E.L. Boultbee
W.E. Fowler
A.B. Jacobson
W.L. Locke

W.G. Morfitt
R.A. Pound
E.P. Taylor

1952
President
L.C. Creery
Vice President
J.F. Kelly

Directors
H.P. Bell-Irving
W.E. Fowler
A.B. Jacobson
Dudley Meakin
W.G. Morfitt
J.P. Roberts
E.P. Taylor

1953
President
J.F. Kelly
Vice President
J.P. Roberts

Directors
H.P. Bell-Irving
J.H. Davies
B.C. Elliott
A.B. Jacobson
R.W. Meakin
J.L. Tennant
F.B. Urquhart

1954
President
Col. Herbert R.
Fullerton
Vice President
R.A. Pound

208

Directors
J.H. Davies
H.B. Itter
A.B. Jacobson
J.J. McCarthy
H.G. McRae
R.G. Patterson
B.I. Sperling

1955
By-laws called for expanded directorate and appointments were made this year.
President
Col. Herbert R. Fullerton
Vice Presidents
R.A. Pound
A.B. Jacobson — appointed
J.P. Roberts — appointed

Directors
Harry Ablowitz
Charlie Brown — appointed
J.H. Davies
H.B. Itter
J.J. McCarthy
Gordon H. MacKenzie — appointed
H.G. McRae
Howard Martin
R.G. Patterson

1956
President
Arthur B. Jacobson

Vice Presidents
J.F. Kelly
G.H. MacKenzie
R.G. Patterson

Directors
H.P. Bell-Irving
Charlie Brown
Harold Chivers
S. G. Freeze
H.B. Itter
Len Korsch
J.K. Laverick
R.A. Pound
F.B. Urquhart

1957
President
Gordon H. MacKenzie
Vice Presidents
H.P. Bell-Irving
H.B. Itter
J.F. Kelly

Directors
Denys H. Back
E. L. Boultbee
Charlie Brown
Harold Chivers
H.A. Gillespie
J. Ross Ker
Len Korsch
J.K. Laverick
F.B. Urquhart

DIVISIONS
*President -
North Vancouver*
J.D. Barlow
*President -
West Vancouver*
John Hawkins

*President -
Salesmen's*
Walter Kerr

1958
President
H.P. Bell-Irving
Vice Presidents
Charlie Brown
Harold Chivers
J.F. Kelly

Directors
Denys H. Back
W.W. Campbell
E.B. Gibbons
H.A. Gillespie
J. Ross Ker
Harold G. McRae
R.E. Slinger
J.A. Townsend
F.B. Urquhart

DIVISIONS
*President -
Burnaby*
John B. Haddy
*President -
North Vancouver*
E.W. Hunt
*President -
West Vancouver*
A.E. Hoover
*President -
Salesmen's*
Bert Edwards

1959
President
Charlie Brown
Vice Presidents
Harold Chivers

J.Ross Ker
J.P. Roberts

Directors
Harry Ablowitz
Denys H. Back
J.D. Barlow
R.D. Burch
G.S. Olson
B.I. Sperling
J.A. Townsend
S.A. Walmsley
M.J. Wenaus

DIVISIONS
President -
Burnaby
John B. Haddy
President -
North Vancouver
David Nicol
President -
West Vancouver
L.E. Kyle
President -
Salesmen's
Bert Edwards

1960
President
Charlie Brown
Vice Presidents
Harold Chivers
J.Ross Ker
J.P. Roberts

Directors
Denys H. Back
H.J. Block
J.L. Boultbee
G.S. Olson
R.A. Pound
R. Taylor

I.J. Udy
S.A. Walmsley
M.J. Wenaus

DIVISIONS
President -
Burnaby
James V. Owens
President -
North Vancouver
David Nicol
President -
West Vancouver
P.Q.R. Sowerby
President -
Salesmen's
G.S. Marshall

1961
President
Harold Chivers
Vice Presidents
Denys H. Back
J.Ross Ker
J.P. Roberts

Directors
J.D. Barlow
J.L. Boultbee
J.H. Davies
John Hawkins
Len S. Korsch
D.C. McPherson
Harold A. Robinson
George O. Treit
J.S. Wood

DIVISIONS
President -
Burnaby
James V. Owens
President -
North Vancouver
David Nicol

President -
West Vancouver
P.Q.R. Sowerby
President -
Salesmen's
Dennis Shaw

1962
President
J.Ross Ker
Vice Presidents
Denys H. Back
John L. Boultbee
J.P. Roberts

Directors
Henry J. Block
W.A. Brown
J.H. Davies
John B. Haddy
John Hawkins
Len S. Korsch
D.C. McPherson
George O. Treit
J.S. Wood

DIVISIONS
President -
Burnaby
W.T. Phipps
President -
North Vancouver
T.F. Fitz-Gibbon
President -
West Vancouver
F.E. Russell
President -
Salesmen's
Dennis Shaw

1963
President
J.P. Roberts

210

Vice Presidents
John L. Boultbee
J.Harold Davies
(Treasurer)
J.S. Wood
Past President
J.Ross Ker

Directors
Henry J. Block
W.A. Brown
S.E. Clarke
J.S. Fraser
A. Les Irwin
Len S. Korsch
D.W. Meakin
D.C. McPherson
M.J. Wenaus

DIVISIONS
President -
Burnaby
Wm. W. Sinser
President -
North Vancouver
H.L. Waddell
President -
West Vancouver
F.E. Russell
President -
Salesmen's
W.E. Clarke

1964
President
John Boultbee
Vice Presidents
W.A. Brown
J. Harold Davies
(Treasurer)
J.S. Wood
Past President
J.P. Roberts

Directors
Bert Edwards
Alf Buttress
S.E. Clarke
J.S. Fraser
A. Les Irwin
Douglas C. Lee
John B. Pringle
D.C. McPherson
M.J. Wenaus

DIVISIONS
President -
Burnaby
Wm. W. Sinser
President -
North Vancouver
H.L. Waddell
President -
West Vancouver
L.E. Kyle
President -
Salesmen's
W.E. Clarke

1965
President
J. Harold Davies
Vice President
Alf Buttress
J.S. Wood
Treasurer
M.J. Wenaus
Past President
John L. Boultbee

Directors
Hugh A. Clee
Bert Edwards
E.R. Grisdale
John Hawkins
A. Les Irwin
Lloyd Montgomery

John B. Pringle
F.E. Russell

DIVISIONS
President -
Investment Commercial
& Industrial
J.P. Roberts
President -
Burnaby
W.A. Lindsay
President -
North Vancouver
H.L. Waddell
President -
West Vancouver
L.E. Kyle
President -
Salesmen's
John Craig

1966
President
M.J. Wenaus
Vice Presidents
Alf Buttress
Bert Edwards
Treasurer
J. S. Wood
Past President
J. Harold Davies

Directors
Grahame Budge
Hugh A. Clee
E.R. Grisdale
W.H. Harrison
John Hawkins
A. Les Irwin
Lloyd Montgomery
F.E. Russell

DIVISIONS

President -
Investment Commercial
& Industrial

T.J. Boyle

President -
Burnaby

A.G. Toppings

President -
North Vancouver

David Nicol

President -
West Vancouver

D.G. Goode

President -
Salesmen's

W.H. Watts

1967

President

Alf Buttress

Vice Presidents

Hugh A. Clee

Bert Edwards

Past President and
Treasurer

M.J. Wenaus

Directors

H.J. Block

Grahame Budge

Gordon Fox

W.H. Harrison

A. Les Irwin

M.C. Johnston

F.E. Russell

H.L. Waddell

DIVISIONS

President -
Investment Commercial
& Industrial

G.W. Calvert

President -
Burnaby

A.G. Toppings

President -
North Vancouver

P.M. Williamson

President -
West Vancouver

D.G. Goode

President -
Salesmen's

W.H. Watts

1968

President

Bert Edwards

Vice Presidents

H.A. Clee
(and Treasurer)

F.E. Russell

Past President

Alf Buttress

Directors

H.J. Block

Grahame Budge

R.G. Clarkson

Gordon Fox

D.G. Goode

W.H. Harrison

M.C. Johnston

W.T. Moore

H.L. Waddell

DIVISIONS

President -
Investment Commercial
& Industrial

J.E. B. Holdom

President -
Burnaby

W.E. Hall

President -
North Vancouver

P.M. Williamson

President -
West Vancouver

R.G. Hurst

President -
Salesmen's

Roger Baigent

1969

President

Hugh Clee

Vice Presidents

H.J. Block

F.E. Russell

Immediate Past
President and
Treasurer

Bert Edwards

Past President

Alf Buttress

Directors

Grahame Budge

R.G. Clarkson

J. B. Erickson

Gordon Fox

D.G. Goode

W.H. Harrison

M.C. Johnston

W.T. Moore

DIVISIONS

President -
Investment Commercial
& Industrial

Quentin Brown

President -
Burnaby

G.H. Charlton

President -
North Vancouver

C.I. Mitten

President -
West Vancouver

R.G. Hurst

President -
Salesmen's

Roger Baigent

1970

President

F.E. Russell

Vice Presidents

H.J. Block

W.H. Harrison

Treasurer

W.T. Moore

Immediate Past
President

Hugh Clee

Past President

Bert Edwards

Directors

Grahame Budge

J. B. Erickson

Gordon Fox

D.G. Goode

R.G. Hurst

M.C. Johnston

W.J. Wenaus

DIVISIONS

President -
Investment Commercial
& Industrial

C.F. Logan

President -
Burnaby

W.A. Lindsay

President -
North Vancouver

J.W. Parr

President -
Richmond-Delta

Norman MacDonald

President -
West Vancouver

J.B. Charpentier

President -
Salesmen's

S.F. W. Norman

1971

Presidents

M.C. Johnston

Vice Presidents

W.T. Moore

R.G. Hurst

Treasurer

M.J. Wenaus

Past President

F.E. Russell

Directors

T.J. Boyle

Grahame Budge

Alf Buttress

R.G. Clarkson

D.G. Goode

E.S. Henderson

Lloyd Montgomery

J.B. Peat

DIVISIONS

President -
Investment Commercial
& Industrial

I.G. Dennis

President -
Burnaby-Coquitlam

K.C. Beach

President -
North Vancouver

F.G. Walker

President -
Richmond-Delta

J.W. Rogers

President -
West Vancouver

J.B. Charpentier

1972

President

T.J. Boyle

Vice Presidents

J.B. Erickson

E.S. Henderson

Treasurer
and Immediate
Past Presidents

M.C. Johnston

Past President

F.E. Russell

Directors

R.G. Clarkson

D.G. Goode

W.A. Lindsay

P.F. Mason

W.T. Moore

J.B. Peat

R.L. Richards

D.P. Woodley

DIVISIONS

President -
Investment Commercial
& Industrial

R.G. Schuss

President -
Burnaby-Coquitlam

R.R. Hamilton

President -
North Vancouver

F.G. Walker

President -
Richmond-Delta

W. I. Munro

President -
West Vancouver

J.B. Charpentier

1973

President

J. B. Erickson

Vice Presidents

E.S. Henderson

W.A. Lindsay

*Treasurer
and Immediate
Past President*

T.J. Boyle

Past President

M.C. Johnston

Directors

H.M. Ballard

R.G. Clarkson

D.G. Goode

W.T. Moore

S.F. W. Norman

R.L. Richards

P.M. Williamson

D.P. Woodley

DIVISIONS

*President -
Investment Commercial
& Industrial*

G.B. Hobbs

*President -
Burnaby-Coquitlam*

R.R. Hamilton

*President -
North Vancouver*

R.H. Sherwood

*President -
Richmond-Delta*

V.G. Lowe

*President -
West Vancouver*

N.N. Currie

1974

President

E.S. Henderson

Vice Presidents

W.A. Lindsay

D.P. Woodley

Treasurer

T.J. Boyle

Past President

J.B. Erickson

Directors

H.M. Ballard

R.G. Clarkson

P.F. Kearney

W.T. Moore

R.L. Richards

D.H. Shaw

P.M. Williamson

George Yen

DIVISIONS

*President -
Investment Commercial
& Industrial*

O.A. Kuys

*President -
Burnaby-Coquitlam*

R.A. Shannon

*President -
North Vancouver*

R.H. Sherwood

*President -
Richmond-Delta*

Paula Verhoeven

*President -
West Vancouver*

N.N. Currie

1975

President

W.A. Lindsay

Vice Presidents

R.L. Richards
(and Treasurer)

P.M. Williamson

Past President

E.S. Henderson

Directors

H.M. Ballard

R.G. Clarkson

N.N. Currie

P.F. Kearney

W.T. Moore

S.F. W. Norman

R.A. Shannon

D.H. Shaw

George Yen

DIVISIONS

*President -
Investment Commercial
& Industrial*

R.G. Harding

*President -
Burnaby-Coquitlam-
New Westminster*

R.G. Chivers

*President -
Maple Ridge-
Pitt Meadows*

A.W. Johnson

*President -
North Vancouver*

J.H. Norton

*President -
Richmond-Delta*

L. Vern Warner

*President -
West Vancouver*

Howard Bachelor

1976

President

R.L. Richards

Vice Presidents

P.M. Williamson

George Yen

214

Treasurer
R.A. Shannon
Past President
W.A. Lindsay

Directors
H.M. Ballard
Maurice Butler
R.G. Clarkson
N.N. Currie
I.G. Dennis
P.F. Kearney
S.F. W. Norman
D.H. Shaw

DIVISIONS

*President -
Investment Commercial
& Industrial*
C.H. Neumann
*President -
Burnaby-Coquitlam-
New Westminster*
G.N. Wilshire
*President -
Maple Ridge-
Pitt Meadows*
A.W. Johnson
*President -
North Vancouver*
J.H. Norton
*President -
Richmond-Delta*
L. Vern Warner
*President -
West Vancouver*
Howard Bachelor
*President -
Salesmen's*
E.L. Burnham
*Vice President-
salesmen's*
John Edwards

1977

President
P.M. Williamson
Vice Presidents
George Yen
R.G. Clarkson
Treasurer
N.N. Currie
*Immediate Past
President*
R.L. Richards
Past President
W.A. Lindsay

Directors
Maurice Butler
I.G. Dennis
P.F. Kearney
Dean Lapointe
S.F.W. Norman
R.A. Shannon
D.H. Shaw

DIVISIONS

*President -
Investment Commercial
& Industrial*
H.H. Weibe
*President -
Burnaby-Coquitlam-
New Westminster*
J.T. McVeigh
*President -
Maple Ridge-
Pitt Meadows*
Frances McCarthy
*President -
North Vancouver*
A.S. Nicol
*President -
Richmond-Delta*
Margaret L. Fox
*President -
West Vancouver*
D.P. Lees

*President -
Salesmen's*
E.L. Burnham
*Vice President-
Salemen's*
John Edwards

1978

President
George Yen
Vice Presidents
Ian G. Dennis
R.A. Shannon
Treasurer
N.N. Currie
Past President
P.M. Williamson

Directors
Maurice Butler
R.G. Chivers
R.G. Clarkson
P.F. Kearney
Dean Lapointe
C.H. Neumann
S.F. W. Norman
H.H. Wiebe

DIVISIONS

*President -
Investment Commercial
& Industrial*
Brian Calder
*President -
Burnaby-Coquitlam-
New Westminster*
J.T. McVeigh
*President -
Maple Ridge-
Pitt Meadows*
Frances McCarthy
*President -
North Vancouver*
G.M. C. Whyte

President -
Richmond-Delta

Ken Hart

President -
West Vancouver

J.M. Wilton

President -
Vancouver East

J.R. Hannay

President -
Vancouver West

Pam King

President -
Salesmen's

E.L. Burnham

Vice President -
Salemen's

W.C. Turner

1979

President

Ian G. Dennis

Vice Presidents

R.G. Clarkson

R.A. Shannon

Treasurer

H.H. Wiebe

Past President

George Yen

Directors

E.L. Burnham

Maurice Butler

Brian Calder

R.G. Chivers

J.R. Hannay

P.F. Kearney

C.H. Neumann

S.F. W. Norman

S.E. Tompson

W.C. Turner

DIVISIONS

President -
Investment Commercial
& Industrial

Dean Lapointe

President -
Burnaby-Coquitlam-
New Westminster

O.E. Jurock

President -
Maple Ridge-
Pitt Meadows

D.W. Carlson

President -
North Vancouver

G.C. Jones

President -
Richmond-Delta

Hans Ounpuu

President -
Vancouver East

Don Magliocco

President -
Westside

Pam King

President -
West Vancouver

Audrey Sayle

1980

President

R.G. Clarkson

First Vice President

Maurice Butler

Second Vice President

H.H. Wiebe

Treasurer

R.A. Shannon

Past President

Ian G. Dennis

Directors

E.L. Burnham

R.G. Chivers

J.R. Hannay

P.F. Kearney

C.H. Neumann

S.F. W. Norman

D.H. Shaw

S.E. Tompson

DIVISIONS

President -
Investment Commercial
& Industrial

R.A. Nelson

President -
Burnaby-Coquitlam-
New Westminster

Lynne A. Willies

President -
Maple Ridge-
Pitt Meadows

Frances McCarthy

President -
North Vancouver

Harold Dueck

President -
Richmond-South Delta

C. Rejane Brown

President -
Vancouver East

Don Magliocco

President -
Westside

Janet C. Wainwright

President -
West Vancouver

Maxwell R. Finney

1981

President

Maurice Butler

First Vice President

H.H. Wiebe

Second Vice President

P.F. Kearney

Treasurer

S.F.W. Norman

Past President
R.G. Clarkson

Directors
E.L. Burnham
Dean Lapointe
W.A. Lindsay
C.I. Mitten
C.H. Neumann
D.H. Shaw
S.E. Tompson
Janet Wainwright

DIVISIONS

President -
Investment Commercial
& Industrial
Hershey Porte
President -
Burnaby-Coquitlam-
New Westminster
Lynne A. Willies
President -
Maple Ridge-
PittMeadows
Frances McCarthy
President -
North Vancouver
Jordy A. Higgins
President -
Richmond-South Delta
J. Howard McCarthy
President -
Vancouver East
Alex Ning
President -
Westside
John D. Eastwood
President -
West Vancouver
Maxwell R. Finney

1982
President
H.H. Wiebe

First Vice President
P.F. Kearney
Second Vice President
S.E. Tompson
Treasurer
C.H. Neumann
Past President
Maurice Butler

Directors
E.L. Burnham
J.R. Hannay
C.I. Mitten
S.F. W. Norman
Hershey Porte
D.H. Shaw
Janet Wainwright

DIVISIONS

President -
Investment Commercial
& Industrial
Daren P. Tourigny
President -
Burnaby-Coquitlam-
New Westminster
Lynne A. Willies
President -
Maple Ridge-
Pitt Meadows
Rose Green
President -
North Vancouver
Ronald D. Ens
President -
Richmond-South Delta
Roberta Tilbe
President -
Vancouver East
Walter Giesbrecht
President -
Westside
Marline Kolterhoff
President -
West Vancouver
Maxwell R. Finney

1983
President
P.F. Kearney
First Vice President
C.I. Mitten
Second Vice President
S.E. Tompson
Treasurer
C.H. Neumann
Immediate Past
President
H.H. Wiebe
Past President
Maurice Butler

Directors
Trevor S. Bennett
E.L. Burnham
J.R. Hannay
Dean Lapointe
Hershey Porte
D.H. Shaw
Janet Wainwright

DIVISIONS

President -
Investment Commercial
& Industrial
Gary L. Brady
President -
Burnaby-Coquitlam-
New Westminster
W.C. Turner
President -
Maple Ridge-
Pitt Meadows
Rose Green
President -
North Vancouver
Barbara Sawchuk
President -
Richmond-South Delta
W.D. Blackall

President -
Vancouver East
Sandy Reed
President -
Westside
Gary Bailey
President -
West Vancouver
K.W. Parkinson

1984
President
C.I. Mitten
First Vice President
C.H. Neumann
Second Vice President
S.E. Tompson
Treasurer
Hershey Porte
Past President
P.F. Kearney

Directors
Trevor S. Bennett
Gary L. Brady
E.L. Burnham
J.R. Hannay
Marline Kolterhoff
Dean Lapointe
D.H. Shaw
Janet Wainwright

DIVISIONS
President -
Investment Commercial
& Industrial
Mike N. Kalin
President -
Burnaby-Coquitlam-
New Westminster
Marco E. Radunz

President -
Maple Ridge-
Pitt Meadows
Rose Green
President -
North Vancouver
Barbara Sawchuk
President -
Richmond-South Delta
Laraine J. Clenahan
President -
Vancouver East
Allan Corbett
President -
Westside
F.G. Warkentin
President -
West Vancouver
Bill Cords

1985
President
C.H. Neumann
First Vice President
Hershey Porte
Second Vice President
Janet C. Wainwright
Treasurer
Gary L .Brady
Past President
C.I. Mitten

Directors
E.L. Burnham
R.W. Downey
K.H. Gillespie
O.E. Jurock
Marline Kolterhoff
D.H. Shaw
F.G. Warkentin

DIVISIONS
President -
Investment Commercial
& Industrial
J.M. Smith
President -
Burnaby-Coquitlam-
New Westminster
Jean Baird
President -
Maple Ridge-
Pitt Meadows
Bonnie Telep
President -
North Vancouver
Diane Jackson
President -
Richmond-South Delta
Betty-Lou Callahan
President -
Vancouver East
Glen G. Magnus
President -
Westside
Gail L. Howald
President -
West Vancouver
Fred T. Brown

1986
President
Janet C. Wainwright
First Vice President
Hershey Porte
Second Vice President
Marline Kolterhoff
Treasurer
E.L. Burnham
Past President
C.H. Neumann

Directors
Gary L. Brady
Allan Corbett
R.W. Downey

K.H. Gillespie
Jordy A. Higgins
P.F. Kearney
Dean Lapointe
F.G. Warkentin

DIVISIONS

*President -
Investment Commercial
& Industrial*

G.A. Hughes

*President -
Burnaby-Coquitlam-
New Westminster*

Rosemary A. Barnes

*President -
Maple Ridge-
Pitt Meadows*

Bonnie Telep

*President -
North Vancouver*

Lou Ann Thompson

*President -
Richmond-South Delta*

Betty-Lou Callahan

*President -
Vancouver East*

Eileen E. Smith

*President -
Westside*

Gail L. Howald

*President -
West Vancouver*

Fred T. Brown

1987

President

E.L. Burnham

First Vice President

Gary L. Brady

Second Vice President

F. G. Warkentin

Treasurer

Marline Kolterhoff

Past President

C.I. Mitten

Directors

Brian Calder
Allan Corbett
John .D. Eastwood
Jordy A. Higgins
Jerry Jackman
Dean Lapointe
Hershey Porte
Eileen E. Smith

DIVISIONS

*President -
Investment Commercial
& Industrial*

Firoz Lakhani

*President -
Burnaby-Coquitlam-
New Westminster*

Rosemary A. Barnes

*President -
Maple Ridge-
Pitt Meadows*

Warren R. Cleal

*President -
North Vancouver*

Satnam T. Sidhu

*President -
Richmond-South Delta*

John E. Cuzner

*President -
Vancouver East*

Richard J. Coates

*President -
Westside*

Leona Giffin

*President -
West Vancouver*

J. B. Charpentier

1988

President

Gary L. Brady

First Vice President

Brian K. Calder

Second Vice President

John D. Eastwood

Treasurer

E.L. Burnham

Past President

C.I. Mitten

Directors

Rosemary A. Barnes
Allan Corbett
Jerry Jackman
Chris O'Brien
Michael W. Ray
Satnam T. Sidhu
Eileen E. Smith
Frederick G.
  Warkentin

DIVISIONS

*President -
Investment Commercial
& Industrial*

Firoz Lakhani

*President -
Burnaby-Coquitlam-
New Westminster*

Kenneth G. Blake

*President -
Maple Ridge-
Pitt Meadows*

Debbie G. Sheppard

*President -
North Vancouver*

Shirley S. Robb

*President -
Richmond-South Delta*

Michael Heinrich

*President -
Vancouver East*

Doris T. Crawford

*President -
Westside*

E.J. Ronald Boulter

President -
West Vancouver

Maureen Bragg

1989
President

Brian K. Calder
First Vice President

John D. Eastwood
Second Vice President

Rosemary A. Barnes
Treasurer
and Immediate
Past President

Gary L. Brady
Past President

E.L. Burnham

Directors

Allan Corbett
R.W. Downey
Jerry Jackman
Firoz Lakhani
Michael W. Ray
Satnam T. Sidhu
Eileen E. Smith
Bonnie M. Telep

DIVISIONS

President -
Investment Commercial
& Industrial

Boswell M. Malcolm
President -
Burnaby-Coquitlam-
New Westminster

Kenneth G. Blake
President -
Maple Ridge-
Pitt Meadows

Debbie G. Sheppard
President -
North Vancouver

Shirley S. Robb

President -
Richmond-South Delta

Michael Heinrich
President -
Vancouver East

Doris T. Crawford
President -
Westside

Wayne Ryan
President -
West Vancouver

Maureen Bragg

1990
President

John D. Eastwood
First Vice President

Rosemary A. Barnes
Second Vice President

Satnam T. Sidhu
Treasurer
and Immediate
Past President

Brian K. Calder
Past President

Gary L. Brady

Directors

E.J. Ronald Boulter
Allan Corbett
R.W. Downey
Jerry Jackman
Firoz Lakhani
Michael W. Ray
Eileen E. Smith
Bonnie M. Telep

DIVISIONS

President -
Investment Commercial
& Industrial

Boswell M. Malcolm

President -
Burnaby-Coquitlam-
New Westminster

Marshall Cowe
President -
Maple Ridge-
Pitt Meadows

Bob Terepocki
President -
North Vancouver

T. W. Hutchinson
President -
Richmond-South Delta

Glenn M. Temes
President -
Vancouver East

Doris T. Crawford
President -
Westside

Wayne Ryan
President -
West Vancouver

Maureen Bragg

1991
President

Rosemary A. Barnes
First Vice President

Satnam T. Sidhu
Second Vice President

Firoz Lakhani
Treasurer

Allan Corbett
Past President

John D. Eastwood

Directors

E.J. Ronald Boulter
R.W. Downey
T.W. Hutchinson
Jerry Jackman
Boswell M. Malcolm
Michael W. Ray

Jarl Rosenberg
Bonnie M. Telep

DIVISIONS

*President -
Investment Commercial
& Industrial*
Horace M.T. Chan

*President -
Burnaby-Coquitlam-
New Westminster*
Marshall Cowe

*President -
Maple Ridge-
Pitt Meadows*
Bob Terepocki

*President -
North Vancouver*
Paulean MacHale

*President -
Richmond-South Delta*
Glenn M. Temes

*President -
Vancouver East*
Doris T. Crawford

*President -
Westside*
Lee Houghton

*President -
West Vancouver*
Maureen Bragg

1992

President
Satnam T. Sidhu
First Vice President
Firoz Lakhani
Second Vice President
R.W. Downey
Treasurer
Allan Corbett
Past President
Rosemary A. Barnes

Directors
E.J. Ronald Boulter
Maureen Bragg
Marshall Cowe
T.W. Hutchinson
Boswell M. Malcolm
Jarl Rosenberg
Bonnie M. Telep
Glenn M. Temes

DIVISIONS

*President -
Investment Commercial
& Industrial*
Horace M.T. Chan

*President -
Burnaby-Coquitlam-
New Westminster*
Raymond J. Soden

*President -
Maple Ridge-
Pitt Meadows*
Maria E. Raynolds

*President -
North Vancouver*
Paulean MacHale

*President -
Richmond-South Delta*
Robert Phillips

*President -
Vancouver East*
Merrily Van Yerxa

*President -
Westside*
Arlene A. Butler

*President -
West Vancouver*
Calvin A. Lindberg

1993

President
Firoz Lakhani
First Vice President
Ronald W. Downey

Second Vice President
Bonnie M. Telep
Treasurer
Glenn M. Temes
*Immediate Past
President*
Satnam Sidhu
Past President
Rosemary A. Barnes

Directors
E.J. Ronald Boulter
Maureen Bragg
Horace M.T. Chan
Allan Corbett
Marshall Cowe
Boswell M. Malcolm
John C. Spencer-
Nairn

DIVISIONS

*President -
Investment Commercial
& Industrial*
J.A. Jack Marriott

*President -
Burnaby-Coquitlam-
New Westminster*
Richard T. Valouche

*President -
Maple Ridge-
Pitt Meadows*
Maria E. Raynolds

*President -
North Vancouver*
Cherry Bouton

*President -
Richmond-South Delta*
Beryl J. Thomsett

*President -
Vancouver East*
Donald G. MacKay

*President -
Westside*
David Scarr

BIBLIOGRAPHY

Board information for this history was compiled primarily from written minutes of the meetings of the Board, from its beginnings in 1888 to the present time. It would be remiss, however, to neglect the mention of many research facilities and publications read to provide a full picture of the periods covered. We appreciate having had access to the following.

Vancouver City Archives
Exchange documentation from 1919 through 1933 was presented to the city's Archival collections in 1956. *Early Vancouver* and other writings by the city's first archivist, Major J. S. Matthews, were very helpful. *Real Estate Values in Vancouver*, a reminiscence by real estate broker J. P. Nicolls, was published by the City Archives in 1954 and was very informative.

Vancouver Public Library
Northwest History section, the newspaper files and the book *Vancouver: A Visual History*, a comprehensive and informative volume written by Bruce MacDonald.

Vancouver—from Milltown to Metropolis
Alan Morley, published by Mitchell Press, Vancouver 1961.

Vancouver and its Region
Edited by Geographers Graeme Wynn and Timothy Oke and published by UBC Press, 1992.

History of the Victoria Real Estate Board
Published in 1981 on the 60th Anniversary of that Board.

City of Vancouver Archives
Photography Credits

14 March 1888

Know All Men By These Presents, That
We the undersigned have this day voluntarily
associated ourselves together for the purpose of forming
an association to be known as The Vancouver Real
Estate Board

Object of the Board

First To provide a uniform schedule of commission
charges for conveyancing

Second To provide a system by which accurate and p[...]
communication can be had between owners of R[...]
Estate and all members of this Board

Third To provide a suitable [ ] for a central office at w[...]
all business of the board can be conducted

Rules and Regulations

Article I The officers shall consist of a President, Vice Pre[...]
Secretary and Treasurer who shall be elected by [...]
board

Article II An executive committee shall be formed consist[...]
from